Reviews

"*Reclaiming Our Identity* is a work that compels its readers to action, but I deeply appreciate the needed reminder that what we do flows from knowing who we are. This thorough exploration of the Christian's identity is fully rooted in the truth found in Scripture. I believe it will prove to be a helpful resource to guide followers of Christ to remember the power of knowing who we are."

Dan Hyun,
Lead Pastor, Village Church Baltimore (Maryland)

"In *Reclaiming Our Identity*, Pastor Chris Davis does an amazing job of navigating the truths of Scripture in concert with our roles as sojourners in this world. He also does not shy away from engaging with the social and political climate in which we find ourselves. Each chapter of this book is established by its predecessor, and it is obvious that Pastor Chris has taken a substantial amount of time to be saturated in the Word of God. The personal stories and life experiences that are imported into each chapter are gems that are yet to be discovered by the reader. I have had the pleasure of knowing Pastor Chris for several years now. The deep level of respect and admiration for Pastor Chris has only grown as the years have progressed. This book, though it demonstrates his eloquence and deep understanding of theology, is accessible for those beginning their journey with Christ to those who have been walking with Him for decades. Enjoy the odyssey you're about to embark on."

Cecil Ramos (M.Ed.),
Overseas Global Worker to Thailand,
Regional Coach with Multiply,
Master's in Ministry, Leadership & Culture (in progress)

"As followers of Jesus, we have an identity crisis. Instead of finding our identity in Jesus, we falsely look to our politics, success, culture, or feelings. Christopher Davis offers us a better foundation for our identity – who we are in God's kingdom. With biblical depth and practical simplicity, *Reclaiming Our Identity* can help us get out of crisis and back on mission!"

Jason Cusick,
Lead Pastor, Journey of Faith Church (Manhattan Beach, CA)
Author of *"Read Me Like a Book: Using Hermeneutics as a Guide to Pastoral Counseling"*

"This book is best not described as a book at all. Rather, I would describe it as a slow, methodical walk through a jewelry store. One in which you, the reader, are the customer, and the jewelry for sale is each a controversial and inflammatory cultural topic begging for your hard-earned money. In this case, the money is your energy and affections. Davis, in this tome, acts as your personal advisor, slowly and carefully using Scripture to thoughtfully help you analyze the legitimacy of each topic through its lens. He ensures that you see each issue biblically, through a redeemed identity in Christ, and as God would ask us to consider it.

If ever there was a time and place for the believer to need such a guide and helper to expound on Scripture for the benefit of our own "Walk," it is now. Don't be tricked into buying the fake gems of the world; instead, rest upon the perfect Word of God to see rightly. This book should be savored and considered slowly as to ensure you invest your energy wisely."

Daniel Morgan,
Executive Pastor, Resurrection Church (Bakersfield, CA)

"What's the relationship between *who we are* and *what we do* for the believer? I've considered questions surrounding the New Testament's indicatives and imperatives concerning believers many times. Over the years, I've come to the conclusion that this is a subject every Christian must answer well, even more so in our present day. If we do not get right the relationship between the gospel and the good that flows out of all who believe it, we compromise both the Great

Commission and the Great Commandment. This is why Chris Davis' *Reclaiming Our Identity* is a necessary book for disciples of Jesus Christ today. He demonstrates convincingly and winsomely that who you are, or *Whose you are*, and how you live are inseparable."

Steve Ross,
Pastor, Arise Ventura (California)
U.S. Urban & Diversity Strategist, Acts 29 Network

"We're in an age where polarizing ideological stances are lurking around every corner seeking to consume the identity of many. The American Church is in need of gospel-centric prophetic voices that will function as a healing agent to produce tangible reconciliation. In his work, *Reclaiming Our Identity,* Chris Davis takes believers on a biblical excursion in order to remind them of their identity in the Lord Jesus. I encourage you to give this book a read, and then pass it to your neighbor on your right."

Derek Berry,
Senior Pastor, The Chapel at Pasadena (California)

RECLAIMING

OUR

IDENTITY

5 ASPECTS OF OUR IDENTITY IN CHRIST
IMPERATIVE FOR EFFECTIVE LIVING

CHRISTOPHER B. DAVIS

 RELEVANT BOOKS

I wrote this book first to the church I pastor, *Northwest Baptist*, then to the previous churches I've pastored in California, and lastly to the Church in America. I am grateful that God has sovereignly called me to be part of and serve my fellow Christian brethren in the U.S.

> "25 I have become its servant, according to God's commission that was given to me for you, to make the word of God fully known.... 28 We proclaim him, warning and teaching everyone with all wisdom, so that we may present everyone mature in Christ. 29 I labor for this, striving with his strength that works powerfully in me." (Colossians 1:25, 28-29, CSB)

I hope this heartfelt and exhortative work will provide a recalibration for us as we desire to represent and live for our magnificent Christ in our ever-evolving world. May this be a blueprint.

Contents

How did this come to be?

To the best of my recollection, the Ferguson, MO event with Mike Brown and Darrin Wilson in 2014 is when I remember the beginning of what has seemed like non-stop conversations with fellow Christians. We've talked about political, social, cultural, and racial/ethnic issues in the U.S.* As you can imagine and probably have experienced yourself, talking about any of these issues will position you in a broad spectrum of views and feelings from others. Fortunately, and many times, unfortunately, I have traversed from one end of this spectrum to the other.

In 2013-2014, I was pastoring in Los Angeles, CA, having conversations and doing events with Anglo ministry friends and comrades who wanted to listen, understand, and serve their diverse communities more mindfully.

---

*To clarify some terms that I will be using throughout this book: "Ethnicity" means *the people group from which you were born*. For example, I have three different ethnicities in my DNA—African, Anglo, Native American. But I was raised African American. Therefore, I am a multiethnic African American. "Culture" is *the traditions, customs, and ways of a certain group of people*, which means you can be part of the same ethnicity and yet from a different culture, or from different ethnicities and part of the same culture. "Race," when used in place of "ethnicity," is a context constructed in 15th century Europe to distinguish non-Europeans from Europeans—(retrieved in 2021 from Encyclopedia Britannica, www.britannica.com/topic/race-human).

In early 2015, I remember being in Texas with a ministry friend at a conference doing roundtables with brethren from different backgrounds discussing what to do regarding these issues.

By the fall of 2015, I was now a pastor at a church in Bakersfield, CA, made up of mostly Anglo conservative evangelicals. Bakersfield is diverse, segregated, and tribal in its ethnic, cultural, and political makeup. My family was the first African American family in the church. I was, for the majority of the members, the first African American pastor they ever had. Therefore, our presence, our different perspectives, and the pastoral preaching helped surface some tribal thinking in our church. Over time we became more multicultural as a church. Becoming more multicultural brings more diverse viewpoints, which is a constant challenge to any tribal kind of thinking from any group.

In 2018, we merged with an all Anglo conservative evangelical church of equal size. (Here's where I insert the emoji with the raised eyebrows). It was almost like erasing the progress and going back to the drawing board. To illustrate my point for the church we merged with, the church had been around for over fifty years and I was the first African American to ever preach from their pulpit. That's how back to the drawing board we went. And history repeated itself for the following year. There was a surfacing of tribalism. The more we meshed as two congregations becoming one, the further the diverse views clashed, which is a constant challenge to tribal thinking.

A year later, in 2019, I was hired by another church in Reisterstown, MD as their senior pastor. Reisterstown is in northwest Baltimore County. It adjoins two more towns—Glyndon and Owings Mills—and another county called Carroll County. Personally, this region reminds me of Bakersfield, CA. It's ethnically and culturally diverse in Reisterstown and Owings Mills but more segregated in Glyndon and Carroll County. This church, which intersects these locations, is a small reflection of the region. It is majority Anglo, though multifarious in other ways—generationally, ethnically, culturally, and socially. While this new church is more diverse than my previous one, you can't have diversity and segregation in this proximity without tribalism. Of course, this all surfaced over the year as we entered

14

2020, with political, ethnic, and social unrest reaching a peak surpassing recent years.

I shared all of this to paint a picture of my 2014 to the present. If you spent 2020 in the U.S., recall how this all played out online and probably offline in every other church in this country. Almost insistently since 2014, I have found myself having these similar conversations with "Christians" offline and online, both male and female, young to old, democrats and republicans, social progressives and social conservatives, and across ethnic lines:

- How do your cultural, social, and political views align with Scripture in the right context?
- Do your cultural, social, and political views help accomplish the mission of God or distract from the mission?
- Considering your cultural, social, and political views, does your demeanor and attitude when interacting with those who disagree align with Scripture?
- Can you see how what you're defending or promoting has become idolatrous when comparing it to Scripture?
- Can you tell if your cultural, social, and political views are more American than biblical?
- Can you tell if your cultural, social, and political views influence how you read, interpret, and apply Scripture? Or, is properly interpreted Scripture the basis for informing your cultural, social, and political views?

Clearly, these conversations were not binary Q&As. But these are the topics that we explored at some point and in some manner. I have been delighted that many of the believers I have conversed with were willing to reason. And I have spoken with a sizable variety of people. However, these topics do not address the actual matter at hand. Surprisingly, the theme in all of these conversations is that I've spent more time explaining to "Christians" *who* they are and *how* to think and be "Christian" *first*.* These topics proved to be the probe that revealed the hidden problem.

Numerous Christians are unfamiliar with their identity as "Christian"—and by "identity," I mean *how one is known in distinguishing them from another or with another*. But I know, it sounds and seems so rudimentary or incompatible, doesn't it, Christians unfamiliar with being Christian? Yet, I keep finding how foreign it is among professing American Christians. Hence, the motivation for this book. I've been repeating the same theme in conversations, sermons, and studies with all kinds of Christians consistently for almost a decade. So I thought to myself, I need to centralize these ruminations and biblical explanations to offer them as part of the solution for believers to be and live as biblical Christians in this world.

"Reclaiming Our Identity" is intended to address *who* Christians are and *how* Christians can (and should) be living effectively in our current days, facing the way the world is now and its ever-changing complexion. Most believers are familiar with being a "follower"/"disciple" of Jesus—though I doubt many comprehend the depth of what this biblically means. But Scripture uses some other particular identifiers to describe our redeemed personhood and prescribe our way of life as believers. These identifiers typically go unknown or unnoticed. They are too often a forgotten and neglected aspect of being a disciple of Jesus. Yet, these identifiers are masterful in communicating who Christians are and how Christians can effectively situate themselves in this world, in every generation, society, and culture.

Think about what you know of a chameleon. Chameleons don't change who they are, do they? Nope. They are never more or less chameleons. Chameleons don't conform to their surroundings, do they? Nope. They adapt to their surroundings, not fuse into their

---

*There are numerous biblical titles for those born-again in Jesus: Christian, believer, disciple/follower, child of God, saint, redeemed, etc. Throughout this book, I will be using several of these biblical titles interchangeably for those born-again in Jesus.

surroundings. They blend into where they are to either attack their prey or defend themselves from predators. But their blending in is not the same as integrating into their surroundings. The chameleon will make itself look like a tree, but it does not become like the tree. There is always a distinction between the chameleon and its surroundings. The chameleon remains as the chameleon.

These are simply two basics about chameleons. Guess what? Scripture identifies Christians similarly. In the Bible, we find descriptions and prescriptions that identify Christians in the world, like that of chameleons in their surroundings. These identifiers keep us anchored in the reality that we are not *of* this world even though we live *in* this world. These identifiers are meant to remind us that the people of God are their own nation, a nation of different people groups living within the nations of the earth. These identifiers are our passport from our home kingdom, displaying that we're merely using visas in these kingdoms of men. These identifiers keep us untethered to the things of this world so we can come, go, pivot, move, and do more freely for God. We adapt and blend. We are not to fuse nor integrate.

From 2010–2019, Marvel movies took over. One of the Marvel blockbusters was "Black Panther." In "Black Panther," to enter Wakanda, you either had to come in with someone from Wakanda or have a unique Wakandan alpha-numeric code on the inside of your bottom lip. This code proved that you were Wakandan. The antagonist of the movie, Kilmonger, was born in California. His dad was a Wakandan, the brother to the king. Before Kilmonger's dad was killed, he gave his son a Wakandan alpha-numeric code. This way, if he ever made it to Africa, he would be allowed in his home kingdom.

These particular identifiers for Christians are like that Wakandan alpha-numeric code. Though we may live in this world (the U.S. and elsewhere), we're not really from here. We've been born-again from another kingdom. And the moment we forget that we're from another kingdom are the moments we forget we're Christian and begin to live in and treat this world—and the things in and of this world—as if it's our home kingdom.

When we don't know who we are in Christ, we can't live from that identity. When we aren't living who we are in Christ in this world, we stop being chameleon-like, and we start believing and acting like we're the tree that we were simply supposed to adapt and blend into. For my Christian brethren of today, specifically living in America, this is not who we are nor how we should be living.

I've learned over the years that I have three voices in my teaching and writing: pastoral, prophetic (as in bold proclaiming and confronting), and professorial. I tend to vary from one to all three in each of my spoken and written works. In this book, you will hear each of these voices. Therefore, I hope you are challenged, educated, revived, and inspired.

Furthermore, some of you are going to read through this and think to yourself, "I know this already." But this book *is not* merely about what you know. It's about *what you do with what you know*. It's about the influence of what you know in your life. Is there an impact in your life from what you know, or is your knowledge dormant? For the Christian, knowledge without transformation is wasteful, and there can be no transformation without a renewing of our mind. So as you read, don't read solely to learn. Read with the intent of impact, influence, and transformation in your life. This is how you can best maximize your time with this book.

Finally, I invite you to travel these pages with me and demystify who you are and how you should be living in this world with its ever-changing complexion. Learn how to reclaim your spiritual sobriety from this world and return to kingdom living as Christians.*

----

*While I'll primarily address issues that American Christians are dealing with in this book, what will be explored is imperative for every Christian. Merely adapt it to your specific context if you live outside the U.S.

CHAPTER 1

Beloved & Begotten

How many of you use the terms "beloved" or "begotten"? If I asked you to raise your hand if you do, I'm assuming not many of you would have. No worries, I'm not much different. The terms are more antiquated than modern. I only use these terms when I read them in Scripture or cover them in a sermon. Depending on the translation you read, you might not even see these terms in your Bible. When I asked our church plant in 2014 what they thought of when they heard "beloved" or "begotten," their answers ranged from caring and intimacy to people like a spouse. Some said Jesus as their answer for both.

While these are not terms we use much today, they still carry weight in how God sees His children compared to unbelievers and the rest of Creation. No other aspect of what God has created is identified with being "beloved by God" or "begotten of God," except His covenant people.

We are the only ones.

BELOVED BY GOD

"Beloved" is a term of endearment. It's used many times throughout Scripture—again, depending on your translation. In the Old Testament, it's used in Songs of Solomon between Solomon and his love interest. In the New Testament, it's used for Jesus. However, across both testaments, it's predominantly used for God's people to describe how loved they are, either by God or by one another. How loved we are regarding each other is subjective—the better the relationship, the greater the extent of love. How loved we are regarding God is objective. It's not influenced in the positive or negative; there is no addition or attrition.

"Beloved," when used in the New Testament as an adjective in the context of believers in Jesus, it's describing us as *personally and especially loved by God*.[1] "Beloved" could very well be written as *agapéd-ones*—i.e., the people dearly loved by God. That's the extent of God's objective love for us; it's personal, special, and unconditional. Thus, to be called "beloved" is to be branded by how loved we are by God.

To be beloved by God

In the Gospel of John, Apostle John is nicknamed by translators as the "beloved disciple" or "beloved apostle." If your Bible translation does headers before passages or chapters, check John 21:20. Notice how they subtitle that final section of the Gospel of John. In the ESV and NKJV, the header identifies John as "beloved." No other apostle, anywhere in the gospels, is singled out by translators as "beloved."

Bible translators recognize Apostle John indicated enough in his gospel that he had a bromance with his rabbi Jesus. Shucks, if you read John's gospel and letters, you can't help but see how obsessed he is with the love of God. He writes on it more than any other New Testament writer. Hence, it's not hard to believe John intimately understood what it meant to be beloved by God. Where then better to turn and explore being "beloved" than John's writings? Case in point, in John's first epistle, we find a compact profile of what it means to be beloved by God.

> "1 See what kind of love the Father has given to us, that we should be called children of God; and so we are. The reason why the world does not know us is that it did not know him. 2 Beloved, we are God's children now, and what we will be has not yet appeared; but we know that when he appears we shall be like him, because we

shall see him as he is. 3 And everyone who thus hopes in him purifies himself as he is pure." (1John 3:1-3, ESV)

Nestled in these three verses is more than there appears to be. When John says, *"See what kind of love the Father has given to us,"* he's expressing the impact of the Father's love. Some of you might be familiar with the Greek term *agapé.* Typically, when regarding God, it's explained as God's unconditional love. *Agapé* is what John is building from here, but not using exactly. The Father's love John is expressing is *a divine preferential affection and kindness.*[2] I love how the NASB says it's a great love "the Father has *bestowed* on us."

Think of a king who bestows a fortune upon some unsuspecting person in his kingdom. The person didn't ask. Therefore, never in a million guesses would the person have expected anything from the king. Yet the king, being a benevolent ruler, decided to bless them to demonstrate his goodness on one of his people.

That's what's happening here. This divine preferential affection and kindness is the Father's object alone to give away, and the keyword is "preferential" because not everyone receives it. The Father has chosen to give this "love" only to believers in Jesus, whom He calls His children. Hence the impact John is expressing, this "love" is not affection and kindness everyone has nor is privileged to receive, only those the Father chooses to bestow it upon. A.W. Tozer, in "The Knowledge of the Holy," remarks about this very point. He says,

> "The Lord takes peculiar pleasure in His saints.... Christ in His atonement has removed the bar to the divine fellowship. *Now in Christ all believing souls are objects of God's delight.*"[3]

♭ Preferential love.

Since we can become and be called children of God simply by way of our belief in Jesus is evidence of the Father giving us this divine preferential affection and kindness. God's children and God's creatures are different. Every human is God's creation. Only those who believe in Jesus are God's children. Every human experiences'

God's love. Only God's children experience His divine preferential affection and kindness in being His child.

> "But to *all who have received him*—those who believe in his name—*he has given the right* to become God's children—children not born by human parents or by human desire or a husband's decision, *but by God.*" (John 1:12-13, NET; *emphasis added*)

> "In this the love of God was *made manifest among us,* that God *sent* his only Son into the world, *so that we* might live through him. In *this is love, not that we* have loved God *but that he* loved us and *sent* his Son to be the propitiation for our sins.... By this we know that we abide in him and he in us, *because he* has given us of his Spirit. And we have seen and testify that the Father has *sent* his Son to be the Savior of the world. Whoever confesses that Jesus is the Son of God, God abides in him, and he in God." (1John 4:9-10, 13-15, ESV; *emphasis added*)

Can you sense John's emphasis on the impact of God's love in these verses? It's God doing all the loving. To experience God's love in this way—*"that we should be called children of God"*—is a divine preference and privilege given by God.

This shouldn't be too foreign for us to grasp, particularly if you're married or have children. At the time of writing this book, my wife and I celebrated our twentieth year of marriage. Woohoo! To explain what a feat this was for us in our marriage is a book, probably two books, in itself. So, using marriage and children as an example, do you share the special, preferential affection and kindness you have for your spouse or children with any regular person? I'm going to take the wild guess and answer "no" for you. To answer "yes" would abase your spouse whom you made particular vows to before God and would trivialize the parental love for the children you birthed and/or raised that God provided you.

Marriage is being and becoming one flesh with each other. There is no other human relationship that is to reach this dimension of intimacy. Biological children are literally from our bodies. They are from our DNA. To get any more personal than the love and rearing of our biological children seems impossible. Additionally, the degree of love that it takes to adopt and raise your non-biological children can feel like they came from your own body. My point, in marriage and with children, there is a special, preferential affection and kindness exclusive to these relationships. Whether on the giving or receiving end, to experience this is to bear the image of God because God is love and has reserved this *"kind of love"* for those He calls His children.

Maybe you're wondering, "So does this mean God shows partiality since only His children experience this divine preferential affection and kindness?" If you thought this, then you have probably heard or read in Scripture that God does not show partiality (i.e., favoritism). This is both true and untrue. It's true because Scripture says it's true.[4] It becomes untrue when we misapply the context. For example...

- ✓ It's *true* because God is *impartial* in how He judges unbelievers.
    - o All unbelievers are judged the same. And, while this may sound contradictory, there is no partiality with God saying He's going to judge one unbeliever stricter than another unbeliever because all will be judged according to their works and the gospel (e.g., Rom. 2:6-15).
- ✓ It's *true* because God is *impartial* in how He loves His children.
    - o All of God's children are loved the same. He doesn't love one of His children more than another. He loves and accepts us all equally and especially.
- ✓ It's *untrue* because God is *partial* in how He is with unbelievers and His children.
    - o As we've already seen, only those who have believed in Jesus are called children of God and experience His divine preferential affection and kindness. Therefore, God *is* partial in this *"kind of love."* Those who are not born-again in Jesus are still dead in their sins and do not get to share in this aspect of God's love. Apostle Paul

says they are "children of wrath," not children of God (Eph. 2:1-3). Does this mean God does not care for unbelievers and does not cover them in His common grace? Absolutely not! God unquestionably cares for and extends common grace to unbelievers.[5] As it was once candidly declared,

"It is to be ascribed to nothing else, that you did not go to hell last night except for His grace; that you were permitted to awake again in this world, after you closed your eyes to sleep. And there is no other reason to be given why you have not gone to hell since you arose in the morning, but that God's hand has held you up."[6]

God is impartial in that He extends common grace for all of His creatures. However, God is partial in His divine preferential affection and kindness He only bestows upon His children.

Child of God, you are special to God. Please understand that. It is an eternal privilege to be beloved by God.

⚘ The beloved.

You know something else interesting about this term "beloved" (agapḗtoi). It is often used in the plural sense. For instance,

"To all who are in Rome, beloved [agapḗtois] of God, called to be saints: Grace to you and peace from God our Father and the Lord Jesus Christ." (Romans 1:7, NKJV; emphasis & brackets added)

"Therefore, my beloved [agapḗtoi] brethren, be steadfast, immovable, always abounding in the work of the Lord, knowing that your labor is not in vain in the Lord." (1Corinthians 15:58, NKJV, emphasis & brackets added)

This means it is also a privilege to be part of "the beloved" and not only individually "beloved." How brilliant of the Holy Spirit to aptly weave in the New Testament believers identified as be-loved and as a bride.

24

"22 Wives, submit yourselves to your own husbands as you do to the Lord. 23 For the husband is the head of the wife *as Christ is the head of the church, his body,* of which he is the Savior. 24 Now *as the church submits to Christ,* so also wives should submit to their husbands in everything. 25 Husbands, love your wives, *just as Christ loved the church and gave himself up for her* 26 to make her holy, cleansing her by the washing with water through the word, 27 and to present her to himself as a radiant church, without stain or wrinkle or any other blemish, but holy and blameless. 28 In this same way, husbands ought to love their wives as their own bodies. He who loves his wife loves himself. 29 After all, no one ever hated their own body, but they feed and care for their body, just *as Christ does the church*—30 for *we are members of his body.* 31 "For this reason a man will leave his father and mother and be united to his wife, and the two will become one flesh." 32 This is a profound mystery— *but I am talking about Christ and the church."* (Ephesians 5:22-32, NIV; *emphasis added*)

"6 Then I heard something like the voice of a vast multitude, like the sound of cascading waters, and like the rumbling of loud thunder, saying, Hallelujah, because our Lord God, the Almighty, reigns! 7 Let us be glad, rejoice, and give him glory, because the marriage of the Lamb has come, and *his bride* has prepared her-self. 8 She was given fine linen to wear, bright and pure. For the fine linen represents the righteous acts of *the saints.* 9 Then he said to me, "Write: Blessed are those invited to the marriage feast of the Lamb!" He also said to me, "These words of God are true."" (Revelation 19:6-9, CSB; *emphasis added*)

As believers, we are not individual brides of Christ. We collectively—believers past, present, and future; believers locally and worldwide (i.e., the Church, the Body of Christ)—are the Bride of the Lamb. So Christian, don't let the concept of your "personal relationship with Jesus" deceptively lead you into privatism. That is anti-gospel and unbiblical. That "personal" concept is half of a whole truth. Our holistic redeemed relationship with Jesus is both individual and corporate, not either/or. You are simultaneously His child and part of His Bride. Your relationship with Him is intrinsically both; it cannot be separated. When we knowingly or unknowingly attempt to do so, we divide His Body, disregard His truth, and sinfully refashion His holistic redemptive relationship with us. To be the Bride is to be the beloved.

Now pause and think about the two relationships that were used earlier to express being beloved? Spouses and children; ergo, the two most intimate and personal relationships are how we are described individually and collectively as God's beloved—as His children and as Christ's Bride.

To be "beloved" and part of "the beloved" is our identity. We cannot separate the two. To want to follow Christ on your own is rejecting and missing out on your identity, and you will never be complete in that way. That's like trying to remove portions of your DNA and still be you. Not possible. Being "beloved" means you are part of "the beloved." You cannot remove either. We need each other. It's our identity. This is how God especially loves us.

Becoming like the Beloved

God never starts something He doesn't intend to complete (Phil. 1:6). Being beloved by God means He loves believers too much to leave us how He found us. Redemption is not without renewal. Regeneration is not without reconstruction. After John explains just how loved believers are by God, he then encourages us with what's coming *as* God's beloved.

> "2 Beloved, we are God's children now, *what we will be has not yet appeared*; but we know that *when he appears we shall be like him*, because *we shall see him as he is*. 3 And *everyone who thus hopes in him purifies himself as he is pure*." (1John 3:2-3, ESV; *emphasis added*)

Did you hear John? There is a you that you have yet to see and yet to be, but one day you will. Wherever you are right now in your life with Christ is not where you will remain. Oh, how this should get us all excited! Is John talking about looking for completion here on earth? Nope. Is he talking about looking for perfect or close to perfect fulfillment here on earth? Nope. John is saying, because we are now children of God—beloved by God—we can expect ongoing personal transformation until the day we see Jesus and receive our fulfillment of becoming like Him, of becoming like *the Beloved*. Apostle Paul penned something similar but earlier in his second letter to the Corinthian Church.

> "12 Since this new way gives us such confidence, we can be very bold. 13 We are not like Moses, who put a veil over his face so the people of Israel would not see the glory, even though it was destined to fade away. 14 But the people's minds were hardened, and to this day whenever the old covenant is being read, the same veil covers their minds so they cannot understand the truth. And this veil can be removed only by believing in Christ. 15 Yes, even today when they read Moses' writings, their hearts are covered with that veil, and they do not understand. 16 *But whenever someone turns to the Lord, the veil is taken away.* 17 For the Lord is the Spirit, and wherever the Spirit of the Lord is, there is freedom. 18 So *all of us who have had that veil removed can see and reflect the glory of the Lord.* And the Lord—who is the Spirit—makes us more and more like him as we are changed into his glorious image." (2Corinthians 3:12-18, NLT; *emphasis added*)

Did you hear Paul? For everyone who has turned to Christ, the veil is removed. No more impediment between God and us. We are not like the people of Israel. In Christ, we can see and reflect the glory of Christ! Paul says it is in both the seeing and reflecting the glory of the Beloved that we are being transformed by the Beloved more and more into the glorious image of the Beloved.

Growing up in the 1980s, I was a comic book and cartoon kid. Before "Power Rangers," there were "Voltron" and "Transformers." Voltron was my favorite between the two. Watching these five little guys jump into these giant lion machines, become this extraordinary machine, and then whip some alien butt was totally awesome! I even watched the Netflix "Voltron" in the 2010s. Still totally awesome! There was joy, a greater power, and confidence in their transformation.

There was becoming something more remarkable in their transformation that wasn't what they were separate.

This is fairly like what John and Paul are expressing. Not everyone had the privilege of becoming Voltron. Only those five guys were selected for this experience. Likewise, we who have had this great love bestowed on us are the only ones being transformed into the glorious image of the One who is doing the transforming. This transformation happens every day of our life in Christ as God is pressing us through the sanctification process to become more and more like the Beloved. For, *"when he appears we shall be like him, because we shall see him as he is."*[7]

⤳ Hope is powerful.

As if knowing that there is a you that you have yet to see and yet to be but one day you will, wasn't thrilling enough, John makes another fascinating point in verse 3. John says this "hope" in Jesus—hoping in becoming like Him and seeing Him as He is—"purifies" us. Hope makes us clean! The context of the Greek term John uses for "purifies" is speaking of *an active moral cleanliness.*[8] He emphasizes how having an eager expectation for our transformation in Jesus and our culmination with Jesus works to keep us morally conscientious.

John is essentially saying hope in Jesus is like soap to dirt. What is soap to dirt? It's a repellent. Now put the imagery together, and remember John is talking about moral cleanliness. Hoping in Jesus—eagerly expecting and desiring to see Him as He is and become like Him—actively works in your life to morally purify you, to keep you clean from reoccurring impurities. Keeping Jesus on our minds keeps the filth away. Hope does the work because we're hoping in Someone who can and will deliver on our hope. This is why John can declare in verse 3 that *"everyone who thus hopes in him purifies himself as he is pure."*

I wonder, maybe part of the reason some Christians find themselves stuck in spiritual neutral, spiritually troubled, or seeing no transformation in their life is that they have not been hoping to see Jesus as He is and to become like Him. Proverbs 13:12 (NASB) says,

"Hope deferred makes the heart sick. But desire fulfilled is a tree of life." When expectations are prolonged or suspended, they make the whole inner person—mind, will, and emotions—distressed and distraught. But when desire comes to pass, it is a source of well-being and happiness.

Christian, when we put our hope in things that cannot deliver— e.g., relationships, family, careers, politics, social causes, ideologies, activities, sex, alcohol, food, wealth, even church—we then make our whole inner person distressed and troubled. We're hoping in what can never deliver lasting satisfaction for our desire (or even someone else's desires). However, hoping in Christ actively works to purify us as He is pure because He is the One doing the work in us. He is the One transforming us from one degree of His glory to another until He brings us into His presence where we see Him face to face. **"True children of God will bear the family likeness, both now, as our hope lends our lives a focused purity resembling His, and at the end, when "we shall be like him.""**[9]

We are guaranteed that since we are beloved by God, we will look and resemble He who has beloved us. Thus, there is no such thing as deferred hope in Christ. It is an active actuality! And as we see the incremental evidence of us becoming more like the Beloved in our lives, that sight will serve as a tree of life in us.

BEGOTTEN OF GOD

To understand being "begotten of God" comes with first understanding how you are beloved by God. Christians are begotten by the Father because He first bestowed His divine preferential affection and kindness upon us. That led to us genuinely believing in and confessing the only Begotten One the Father sent, Jesus Christ, as our Savior and Lord. This is straightforward from God's perspective, but that's not always the case with us.

Many profess to believe in Jesus Christ but are not truly begotten of God because their belief and confession are passive. This is a commonality in America. People assume because "I go to church," or "I was raised Christian," or "I vote _____ (insert whatever political party or values you think affirms you're a Christian)," or "I said a prayer to believe in Jesus," that means you're Christian. Not everything that appears obvious is correct. I like what Dr. Joshua Straub said, **"When we trust God for heaven but not for our daily lives, we walk around with a pseudo-faith."**[10]

The way Apostle John describes belief and confession in his first letter clarifies genuine from the counterfeit. He writes in 1John 5:1 (ESV), *"Everyone who believes that Jesus is the Christ has been born of God, and everyone who loves the Father loves whoever has been born of him."* In this verse, John is articulating belief as *an active and confident trust.*[11]

For example, if I ask you the question, "Do you believe a parachute will keep you safe jumping out of an airplane?" What would your answer be? Probably, "Yes." Some of you might answer analytically about the percentage of deaths from skydiving and declare, "It depends." Some of you might answer like me, "I can't answer this because I don't plan on ever needing a parachute. I'm not jumping out no plane." For those who humored me and answered "yes," thank you. Your "yes" is an example of passive believing. You believe parachutes will keep you safe, but you answered from wherever you are and not in a plane ready to jump.

An active and confident trust that parachutes will keep you safe is getting on a plane and then jumping out with your parachute on; it's taking that belief and acting upon it. Simply saying, "Yeah, I believe parachutes will keep me safe," but you would never get on a plane to jump out with the parachute you believe will keep you safe is passive believing. Acting upon what you claim to believe is the active and confident trust John conveys here, and it's this kind of belief in Jesus as the Christ that produces a person being "begotten of God."

John also wrote earlier in 4:15 that, *"Whoever confesses that Jesus is the Son of God, God abides in him, and he in God."* This "confesses," like belief, is also not passive. It is not a mere acknowledgment. Imagine I called your name from across the room while you were working. You would do what? You would probably lift your head with a nod or respond with a word to let me know I have your attention. That would be an acknowledgment. That's not this kind of "confess" John means. This "confesses" here in the Greek in context is *an agreeing with and admitting the truth of that reality.*[12]

Let's stick with the image of me calling you from across the room. After you lift your head or respond to my calling your name, I tell you it's raining outside. If you do nothing but nod or speak from me having your attention, and then when you go out, you're shocked by the fact that it's raining, all you did was acknowledge what I told you. But, if you got up to go outside, grabbed a jacket or umbrella in anticipation of the rain, and said "thank you" as you exited, that would be agreeing with and admitting the truth of the reality you heard. That is the "confess" John has in mind here. Like belief, this confess is active, not passive.

So why did I spend the time explaining this? Because there are people all across the U.S. sitting in churches and living their life deceived and believing that they're good with God. It's even possible it could be someone reading this book. They say, "I said the prayer. I believed and confessed." If you ask them what they believe, they'll tell you that Jesus died on the cross and resurrected from the dead. However, their belief and confession are not active. They didn't jump out of the plane like they believe the parachute would keep them safe. They simply acknowledged Jesus. Tozer weighs in on this.

> **"There must be an utter committal of the whole life to Christ in faith. This is what it means to "believe in Christ." It involves a volitional and emotional attachment to Him accompanied by a firm purpose to obey Him in all things."**[13]

Someone who has been genuinely begotten of God actively and confidently trusts in, agrees with, and admits the truth that Jesus is their Savior and Lord—their Master and God. How they live their life will reveal they've jumped out of the plane. And it's only because God first bestowed His love on that person that brings them to this point of active belief and confession to become begotten.

Experiencing this kind of love from God leaves no one unchanged. Christians are begotten of God because we were first beloved by God.

To be begotten of God

We know how we became begotten, but what does it mean to be begotten of God? "Begotten," in a given context, could be conveyed in several different terms throughout Scripture. Again, the word "begotten" itself is more archaic than modern. You'll see terms that can translate as "begotten," but you won't think begotten. Some of these terms are *born, birth, bear, make, conceived, brought forth, regenerated, fathered, procreate, or produce.* And any of these could be by either a man, woman, or God.

Begotten of God can be fleshed out to mean *spiritually reproduced in God's image, fathered by God, and descendants of His royal bloodline*. Yup, that's a mouthful. So I'll break this down into three parts.

✦ 1. *"spiritually reproduced in God's image".*

If you haven't caught it yet, to be begotten of God is re-generation, new birth, being born-again. Jesus tells Nicodemus,

> "5 Truly, truly, I say to you, unless one is born of water and the Spirit, he cannot enter the kingdom of God. 6 That which is born [begotten] of the flesh is flesh, and that which is born [begotten] of the Spirit is spirit." (John 3:5-6, ESV; brackets added)

Jesus asserts that to be begotten of the flesh is to be of an earthly nature, and to be begotten of the Spirit is to be of a spiritual nature. Our earthly nature contains our biology and our sinfulness— i.e., what makes us human and what makes us spiritually dead. We inherited our earthly nature from the father of mankind, Adam. Apostle Paul explains in Romans 5:12-18 and 1Corinthians 15:45-49 that every human born from Adam bears his image (human biology) and bears his consequence (sin, death, and condemnation). This earthly nature—human biology and sinfulness—is then passed from human to human as humans reproduce humans.

Just as humans can only give birth to other humans, only the Spirit can produce spiritual life. Paul, juxtaposing Adam and Jesus in the Romans 5 and 1Corinthians 15 passage, explains that Jesus became a new Adam for us. Jesus is like humans in biology. However, He is not from Adam, so He is without sinfulness. Thus, in becoming this new Adam, everyone born-again in Jesus will bear His image (the spiritual) and bear His consequence (declared innocent, recipients of God's all-sufficient grace, sealed with the Holy Spirit and eternal life). This is what every human who is begotten of God inherits from Jesus. Tozer adds a familial component to this thought in "The Pursuit of God" when he wrote, **"The moment the Spirit has quickened us to life in regeneration our whole being senses its kinship to God and leaps up in joyous recognition."**[14]

Sin has deteriorated the original image of God in us. It cursed our earthly nature to die eventually and caused our spiritual nature to die immediately. Being begotten of God is regeneration in the original image we were created. It's spiritual restoration and kingdom admission. It means to be reborn by God *in His image* (His divine imprint being restored upon us), *in His likeness* (His divine resemblance being restored in us and through us), *and with His name* (Him restoring our identity with the Divine). Notice the details of being begotten of God Paul highlights in Romans 6.

> "4 We were therefore buried *with him* through baptism into death in order that, just as Christ was raised from the dead through the glory of the Father, we too may live *a new life.* 5 For if we have been *united with him* in a death like his, we will certainly also be *united with him* in a resurrection like his. 6 For we know that *our old self was crucified with him* so that the body ruled by sin might be done away with, that we should no longer be slaves to sin— 7 because anyone who has died has been set free from sin. 8 Now if *we died with Christ,* we believe that *we will also live with him....* 11 In the same way, count yourselves dead to sin but *alive to God in Christ Jesus.*" (Romans 6:4-8, 11, NIV; *emphasis added*)

Did you hear that, Christian? Our identity is no longer determined by our earthly nature, which includes all of what humans typically identify themselves by—ancestry, ethnicity, sexuality, traits, and so on. Instead, our identity is now determined by our spiritual nature.

ꙮ 2. *"fathered by God"*.

To properly understand being fathered by God, we have to grasp the history of what "begotten" would mean to a Hebrew. The International Standard Bible Encyclopedia states, "to beget" or to be "begotten of" **"denotes the physical relation of either parent to a child...[but more] generally used of a father [and] more rarely [used] of a mother."**[15] As a Hebrew, "begotten of" meant to be born a descendant from your father's or forefather's lineage.

Recall Jesus' genealogies in Matthew and Luke's gospel accounts (Matt. 1:1-17, Luke 3:23-38). Matthew presents Jesus' legal claim to the throne of David from Joseph's side.[16] While Luke presents Jesus' physical claim to the throne of David from Mary's side.[17] You'll notice if you read Luke's genealogy, Mary is never mentioned, just her father's side. Hence, in this particular case with Jesus, this is a perfect example of the consequential importance of being born descendants from your father's and forefather's lineage because these genealogies are presenting Jesus' claim to the throne of David and claim as the Son of God.

As a Hebrew, your identity was directly linked with your lineage. You were known by your father and forefathers—e.g., Isaac, son of Abraham; Jacob, son of Isaac; Jesus, son of David. This aspect of being begotten was significant for a Hebrew. To be begotten connected their present with their past by rooting their individual identity as part of their corporate identity. Every Jew knew they were part of the covenant people of the God of Abraham, Isaac, and Jacob. The past histories, teachings, declarations, and promises are theirs also.

That's what it meant to be "begotten of" to a Hebrew. Therefore, to be begotten of God is communicating that we are identified by the Triune God who has fathered us and directly linked us to His lineage. Hebrew children were known as "son of" or "daughter of" their father or forefathers. We, too, are identified as children "of God," as being born "of the Spirit," and as followers "of Christ."

⚘ 3. *"descendants of His royal bloodline"*.

Did you know there are around 30 monarchies (or kingdoms) that still exist today?[18] I didn't. Guess what else? A descendant of the royal bloodline is ruling the majority of these monarchies. Unless you are born in one of these countries, it can be difficult conceptually for Christians in the U.S. to truly comprehend what it's like to live under a monarchy. American Christians unknowingly tend to have a democracy layered lens that tints a more global perspective.

Think of a movie you've seen with a king or queen. Try to imagine what that must be like to be born into a royal family ruling your home country. Imagine being the son, daughter, cousin, niece, or nephew of King Abdullah II of Jordan, King Philippe of Belgium, Queen Elizabeth II of England, or Mohammed VI of Morocco. Imagine if you were born into that particular family, that royal bloodline. Imagine what that would be like for the rest of your life. You would never have to worry about anything, nor would your children. Even if you married somebody non-royal, that wouldn't matter because you are royalty—e.g., Prince Harry marrying Megan Markle. Your life and your descendants will be cared for so long as that monarchy exists.

Being begotten of God means we're not simply a citizen in God's kingdom or merely a member of His royal family. Being begotten of God means we are the direct offspring of the Most High King of kings! We have been spiritually reborn and fathered by God Himself, adopted and grafted into the royal bloodline of the only Begotten Son, Jesus. That's how we've gained entrance and ennoblement in the kingdom of God. We have the Son of God's royal blood pumping through our spiritual DNA! This is our identity as begotten of God.

"3 Praise be to the God and Father of our Lord Jesus Christ! *In his great mercy he has given us new birth* [fathered us] <u>into</u> a living hope through the resurrection of Jesus Christ from the dead, 4 <u>and into</u>

an inheritance that can never perish, spoil or fade. This inheritance is kept in heaven for you, 5 who through faith are shielded by God's power until the coming of the salvation that is ready to be revealed in the last time.... 23 For you have been born again [begotten], not of perishable seed, but of imperishable, through the living and enduring word of God." (1Peter 1:3-5, 23, NIV; _emphasis_ & brackets added)

According to Scripture, the King of kings is our God, and His rule and kingdom are everlasting.[19] Thus, unlike every descendant of a human monarch, we as the begotten of God never have to worry about our King being overruled, or abdicating His throne, or passing away. His rule and kingdom are everlasting, which means our inheritance, our salvation, and our identity as children of the King are eternally secure.

I hope you now see, to be begotten of God is not simply about believing and confessing Jesus as Savior and Lord to become born-again. To be begotten of God reaches to the eternal depths of the new creations we are in Christ. To be called "begotten" is to be branded by God's relationship to us and with us, just as being called "beloved" is to be branded by how loved we are by God.

Therefore, Christian, do not let our enemy of old nor our enemy of the day reduce this remarkable identity of ours to something frivolous or insignificant. **"[God's] love disposes Him to desire our everlasting welfare and His sovereignty enables Him to secure it."**[20] You are begotten because you were first beloved. This is a profoundly life-altering reality. If you call yourself a Christian and your life is not changed, then you were not changed and are not Christian.

THE DISTINGUISHABLES OF BELOVED & BEGOTTEN

The Christian's identity as God's beloved and God's begotten clearly distinguishes us from everyone else. Again, Tozer does an excellent job of asserting this point.

> "In [the] Christian experience there is a highly satisfying love content that distinguishes it from all other religions and elevates it to heights far beyond even the purest and noblest philosophy. *This love content is more than a thing; it is God Himself in the midst of His Church singing over His people.*"[21]

Knowing *who* we are is foremost. But then we need to know in *what way* this identity distinguishes us and *why*. Otherwise, we may possess all this information and miss out on a fascinating life because we didn't know how to verify if we are actually God's beloved and begotten.

Once more, marriage and children highlight this well. What distinguishes a spouse from a non-spouse? For a spouse, it's a wedding ring, a marriage certificate, and a monogamous love and commitment to whomever they vowed to in holy matrimony. Non-spouses don't possess these distinguishables, only those who are married do. What distinguishes your child from another child? A birth certificate, shared DNA (twenty-three chromosomes from both biological parents), genetic features, physical features, and behavioral characteristics. While every child has this, your child has this explicitly from you. Without the distinguishables for your spouse and children, there would be no way of knowing their identity as your spouse or child.

The same is true for our identity as beloved by God and begotten of God. As a Christian, you cannot say you have been beloved and begotten and not display the commitment to and the traits from the God who treasured and fathered you.

After Apostle John finished telling us how beloved by God we are at the start of chapter 3, he walks into how we are distinguished as beloved and begotten in the remainder of that chapter.

"4 Everyone who makes a practice of sinning also practices law-lessness; sin is lawlessness. 5 You know that he appeared in order to take away sins, and in him there is no sin. *6 No one who abides in him keeps on sinning; no one who keeps on sinning has either seen him or known him. 7 Little children, let no one deceive you. Whoever practices righteousness is righteous, as he is righteous.* 8 Whoever makes a practice of sinning is of the devil, for the devil has been sinning from the beginning. The reason the Son of God appeared was to destroy the works of the devil. *9 No one born of God makes a practice of sinning, for God's seed abides in him; and he cannot keep on sinning, because he has been born of God. 10 By this it is evident who are the children of God, and who are the children of the devil: whoever does not practice righteous-ness is not of God, nor is the one who does not love his brother.*" (1John 3:4-10, ESV; *emphasis added*)

Our Living Righteous

John declares that we are recognized as beloved and begotten, first, by our living righteous. Recall John's fascinating point in verse 3 on "hope in him"—*hoping in Jesus actively works in your life to morally purify you, keeping you clean from reoccurring impurities.* Is it then illogical to reason because hoping in Christ morally purifies us that clean living will follow? Absolutely not. It would be irrational to think it doesn't.

Picture a water filter. If you put a filter on your faucet, it does what? It catches the impurities from the water so that cleaner water pours out. That's John's logical inference. If being beloved by God and begotten of God produces a hope that actively works in the child of God to purify them morally, then living righteous will naturally follow. John doesn't portray living righteous as mechanical or forced. Rather, he repeats in four verses (vv6-7, 9-10) that living righteous flows organically from our new nature. Notice, it's not that it's easy, but that it's ensuing.

What does living righteous look like? In this passage, we find the answer with the meaning of John's repeated phrase, "practice righteousness." This phrase in context in the Greek means *to perform what is right or approved in God's eyes.*[22] Living righteous is living life in a manner that is God-approved. Our choices, our actions, our speech, our thinking, our beliefs, our attitudes, and our emotions are to be employed in a manner that is God-approved. If God does not approve of it in His Word, don't do it, say it, think it, believe it, or entertain it. Living righteous is living conscious of God's approval in all we think, say, feel, and do.

Remember those yellow "what would Jesus do" wristbands? Did you wear one? I did. No shame either. While that question hints in the right direction, the better question and more suitable life filter is "What does Jesus approve?" To ask ourselves this question would cause us to slow down and think, "What does Jesus approve of *according to* Scripture?" before we speak, act, decide, or believe. Obviously, we won't do this perfectly. Yet, as imperfect as we are, because of the indwelling presence of the Holy Spirit, this kind of conscious living will naturally follow from our new nature of being beloved and begotten.

In "A Little Book on the Christian Life"—an adaptation of the chapter from John Calvin's "Institutes" on the life of a Christian—our brother Calvin has much to say about Christians living righteous.

> **"The goal of God's work in us is to bring our lives into harmony and agreement with His own righteousness, and so to manifest to ourselves and others our identity as His adopted children."[23]**

> **"To prompt us toward righteousness more effectively, Scripture tells us that God the Father, who has reconciled us to Himself in His Anointed One, Jesus Christ, has given us in Christ a model to which we should conform our lives."[24]**

> **"We have been adopted by the Lord as children with this understanding—that in our lives we should mirror Christ who is the bond of our adoption. And truly, unless we are devoted—even addicted—to righteousness, we will faithlessly abandon our Creator and disown Him as our Savior."[25]**

"Right living has a spiritual basis where the inner affection of the soul is sincerely devoted to God for the nurture of holiness and righteousness."[26]

This is what it means to live righteously. It's filtering how we live through the question of what Jesus approves. It's not filtering through what we approve based on our feelings, rationale, family, friends, political party, society, culture, ethnicity, etc. *"Little children, let no one deceive you. Whoever practices righteousness is righteous, as he is righteous."*[27]

Our Love for One Another

Next, John declares that we are recognized as beloved and begotten by our love for one another. In verse 10, he wrote, *"whoever does not practice righteousness is not of God, nor is the one who does not love his brother."* Are we to love our neighbor? Absolutely! It's the second greatest commandment. But our neighbor is any believer and unbeliever. John is not talking about everyone here. He's specifically speaking about the family of the beloved and begotten. He says this multiple times in this first letter.

> "9 The one who says he is in the light but *still hates* his fellow Christian *is still* in the darkness. 10 The one who *loves* his fellow Christian *resides in* the light, and there is no cause for stumbling in him. 11 But the one who *hates* his fellow Christian *is in* the darkness, *walks in* the darkness, and *does not know* where he is going, because the darkness has blinded his eyes." (1John 2:9-11, NET; *emphasis added*)

> "11 For this is the message you have heard from the beginning: *We should love one another*.... 14 We know that we have passed from death to life *because we love* our brothers and sisters. The one who *does not love* remains in death. 15 Everyone who *hates* his brother or sister *is* a murderer, and you know that no murderer has eternal life residing in him." (1John 3:11, 14-15, CSB; *emphasis added*)

"*Beloved, let us love one another, for love is from God, and whoever loves has been born of God and knows God. Anyone who does not love does not know God,* because God is love." (1John 4:7-8, ESV; *emphasis added*)

"Everyone who believes that Jesus is the Christ has been born of God, *and everyone who loves the Father loves whoever has been born of him.*" (1John 5:1, ESV, *emphasis added*)

Our love for God in response to being beloved and begotten by God includes loving those who have also been beloved and begotten by God. God is the model of a loving, protective parent. Through John, the Holy Spirit expresses that we can't rightly love God and not love His kids because God *so loves* His kids. Not loving the children of God is to not love the God who brought forth His children in His love.

What does loving one another look like? This is not a quick answer. There is a myriad of applications to loving one another. Answering this question is a book by itself. Nonetheless, staying with the theme of this section, I'll answer only from some particulars in 1John 3.

The Greek term and context for "love" John uses regarding our love for one another conveys *being full of goodwill and exhibiting this goodwill to other believers.*[28] Goodwill is a smorgasbord. It contains several qualities such as compassion, goodness, kindness, thoughtfulness, and understanding. It's possible, the love for one another John has in mind is operating in the fruit of the Spirit toward other believers. Goodwill would contain what the Spirit produces in the life of a believer submitted to Him, yet it's intentionally directed toward other believers.

How tragic is it that Christians are not universally known for exhibiting goodwill to other family in Christ? We are known by our profession of loving God but less known by our actions of loving God's children—children whom He *so loves* that He has made us brothers and sisters in Christ. Our most remarkable testimony to the world that Jesus is God and Savior and that we are indeed His disciples is our love for one another (John 13:34-35; 17:20-23). However, if our conscious pattern is unloving, disliking, unfriendly, or negatively speaking of other professed believers, then the root of that pattern may be that we don't truly love and trust the One who fathered them.

Our love for one another conveys being full of goodwill and exhibiting this goodwill to other believers whether we want to or not and whether they deserve it or not. Our love for one another is meant to be a reflection of God graciously beloving us.

John gives us three points of what it looks like to love one another practically—i.e., being full of goodwill and exhibiting this goodwill to other believers—in verses 16-18.

> "16 By this we know love, that he laid down his life for us, and we ought to *lay down our lives for the brothers.* 17 But if anyone *has the world's goods and sees his brother in need,* yet closes his heart against him, how does God's love abide in him? 18 Little children, let us not love in word or talk but *in deed and in truth.*" (ESV, *emphasis added*)

⚡ What this looks like: *self-sacrifice.*

John's first point is: *self-sacrifice.* Self-sacrifice is about giving up your life for Christian brethren. That would mean:

- ☑ Give up your space for one another.
- ☑ Give up your time for one another.
- ☑ Give up your resources for one another.
- ☑ Give up your comfort for one another.
- ☑ Give up your preferences for one another.
- ☑ Give up your convenience for one another.
- ☑ Give up your rights for one another.

It wouldn't shock me if reading that small list of self-sacrifice caused your flesh to rise in protest. Mine did. If you're like me, I suppose in your thoughts you might've responded with, "Say what now?" And here's the thing, the Spirit knew this would be the believers' response then and our response today. That's why He had John link this point with Jesus' display of love. Even more, the Spirit had John communicate this as non-optional.

This self-sacrifice is not a gesture, as if John is saying, "Hey guys, why don't you try laying down your life for one another. You know, get around to it when you have time, or when you feel like it." Nope, not even close. John writes "we ought" as an indicative instruction "to lay down our lives for each other" just as Jesus laid down His life for us. Jesus gave us the example of how to love one another via self-sacrifice, so we are to do it as He did it; for *"whoever claims to live in him must live as Jesus did."*[29]

↳ What this looks like: *in need & deed.*

John's second point is: *in need and deed.* If you have the resources to meet the needs of the brethren that you know are in need, then meet their needs. The love "in deed" is actually meeting the needs of one another you can meet, and it's to come from a place of compassion rather than because they earned it or even deserve it. Furthermore, "in deed" is not "intending to" or "saying you are/will," and then no actions follow. Hence why John says in verse 18, *"let us not love in word or talk."*

Christian, if you have the resources, then meet the needs of one another. However, if you have the resources to meet their needs and you choose not to, then you cannot claim that God's love abides in you. Why? Because stinginess and close-fistedness are not characteristics of love or God. That is not how God displayed His love toward us.

God did not declare that He loved the world but then kept the Son from coming to meet the world's greatest need. Instead, He saw our need, even as His enemies, declared that He would rectify the situation and then sent the Son to pay off our eternal sin debt completely. That's what loving another "in deed" looks like.

> "It is of the nature of love that it cannot lie quiescent. It is active, creative, and benign…. So it must be where love is; *love must ever give to its own, whatever the cost.* The apostles rebuked the young churches sharply because a few of their members had forgotten this and had allowed their love to spend itself in personal enjoyment while their brethren were in need."[30]

Allow me also to bring some balance here. John is not instructing us to enable idleness or dependency (e.g., 2Thess. 3:6-12). He's not saying give to the point of codependency, nor is he saying give to provide for one another's wants. "Wants" can be lived without. "Needs" constitute necessities or essentials. Some of us may have heard the maxim, "I can give you fish and feed you once, or I can teach you how to fish so you can feed yourself for a lifetime" (my paraphrase). Thomas á Kempis, in his classic work, "The Imitation of Christ," says it this way, **"For one who is in need, however, a good work may at times be purposely left undone or changed for a better one. This is not the omission of a good deed, but rather its improvement."**[31] Thus, the deed of meeting one another's needs would include teaching them how or providing an opportunity to acquire the skill and/or job to meet their own needs. For example, during the early 2010s, we had some young brothers in our church who hadn't graduated high school. We set up times to help them study to get their GEDs. We also helped them with their entrepreneurial endeavors, either investing monetarily, promoting their business to garner clientele, giving them opportunities at our events, supporting them with our space at the church, or educating them in business principles. We helped teach them how to fish for themselves and provided some tools of the trade for their journey.

As beloved brethren, if we have to give, then we are to meet the need. However, if we realize our brethren are constantly in this position, then the greater need we should likewise meet is the skill and/or job to take care of themselves. God has also done and does this for us. God the Son paid off our eternal sin debt. Then, both the Father and the Son give us the Holy Spirit to be with us, to teach us, and to empower us to live for Him according to His Word while we're here. That's deeds of love meeting needs.

✤ What this looks like: *in truth.*

John's third point is: *in truth.* This "in truth" is exhibiting good-will to one another in actuality, which contrasts falsehood, deception, ulterior motives, gossip, slander, etc. To love "in truth" won't speak in lies to one another. To love "in truth" won't attempt or intend to deceive one another. To love "in truth" won't act with ulterior motives toward one another or scheme to get over on one another. To love "in truth" won't gossip, slander, or intentionally misrepresent one another. To operate in any of these ways is both unloving and untruthful.

Regrettably, church hurt is a prime and painful example of many operating unlovingly and untruthfully to one another. For some, church hurt has honestly caused them PTSD. I know and know of African American Christians who suffer from post-traumatic racial injuries unknowingly caused by fellow Anglo-American Christians' political doggedness and/or cross-ethnic blind spots. I know Christians who refuse to return to their church's celebrate recovery because their trust was betrayed. I know younger Christians who are afraid to share their struggles because the older generation of Christians come off so judgmental and graceless. I know young adult Christians who gossip about their peers because of differing social views and have ruined relationships. In these examples of church hurt, there was an absence of exhibiting goodwill in actuality.

Sometimes church hurt is intentional because "hurt people hurt people." Sometimes it's unknowingly. Think of Job's friends. They were there during the most challenging time in his life. They shared their counsel to try and help him make sense of what was happening to him. Rick Holland explains, while **"most of the counsel these friends offer him is theologically accurate,"** it was still **"insensitively applied."**[32] To love "in truth" means we are to speak factually in love seasoned with grace to win one another to the truth. Likewise, it means we are to pursue this actuality with one another through understanding, kindness, and humility because we could be wrong, and loving "in truth" is worth whatever it takes to get it right. As Proverbs 6:16, 19 says,

> "There are six things the LORD hates, yes, seven are an abomination to Him:" two of which are *"a false witness who speaks lies, and one who sows discord among brethren."* (NKJV, *emphasis added*)

Furthermore, this "in truth" also contains addressing with one another what's wrong and unwholesome according to Scripture. You can't say you're exhibiting goodwill to one another in truth and not provide accountability, admonishment, or constructive criticism when you're aware they are dealing with sin, willful immaturity, or irresponsibility. Exhibiting goodwill to a believer you know is dealing with these things is telling them the truth, in a manner seasoned with grace. For, it is loving to inform another believer that what they're doing or not doing is wrong in God's eyes, according to Scripture. But how we do so can invalidate the love, which is why doing so in the manner of grace matters.

Let me say this to all those who got excited or cringed at reading those last two sentences. We don't do this sometimes difficult and awkward tough love "in truth" for correction sake, but for love sake. We aim to win our brother or sister, not punish one another (Gal. 6:1-2, Jam. 5:19-20). God is the Father; He does the chastising (Heb. 12:5-11). We are siblings. We look out for each other.

As Christians, for anyone who professes to believe, we are to love them enough to exhibit goodwill in actuality, not falsehoods, deception, ulterior motives, gossip, slander, or withholding accountability. Consider what Dr. Tim Clinton said, **"Truth without grace leads to legalism and toxic faith, while grace without truth leads to unlicensed tolerance that allows evil to continue."**[33]

⁋ How this looks like today.

These are John's three points of what it looks like to practically love one another: *self-sacrifice, in need and deed, and in truth.* And not to drag this on, but I must say how pitiful it is that this instruction to love one another practically like this would be deemed radical in today's times. Picture it with me. If Apostle John was to teach these truths in today's Christianity—in books, in guest preaching, at conferences, online, etc:

- He would be scolded as a legalist by the professing Christians and churches that believe and aim to be tolerant of lifestyles and views where the Bible is unambiguously in disagreement.

For them, love "in truth" is a tad too much because account-ability and speaking biblical truths would be offensive to those who disagree, no matter how nice it's presented.

- He would be scolded as a liberalist by more dogmatic and conservative professing Christians and churches for being too broad or compromising. These Christians would spend more time arguing with John over who's genuinely born-again. This way, they wouldn't have to love those who disagree doctrinally (in non-essentials), philosophically, politically, or socially. They would say what John lays out is a tad too much because it doesn't allow for name-calling, disfellowship, or the continual neglect of meeting their needs or operating in self-sacrifice toward them.

- He wouldn't let the professing Christians uncommitted to a local church or those not fellowshipping with other Christians off the hook. The best arena to love one another is in community with each other.

- He would also urge those professing Christians wounded by church hurt not to forget the forgiveness part of healing nor let that hurt fill their heart with resentment, causing them to disobey God in this way.

John's three points of what it looks like to practically love one another will be heckled and hated by Christians when it doesn't lean their way, and then loved and lauded when it does. To all of us today, John would demand and is demanding that if you do not love the brethren like this—*in self-sacrifice, in need and deed, and in truth*—then you do not truly love the Father.

Our Belief in Jesus

To resume how John declares that we are recognized as beloved and begotten, lastly, it's by our belief in Jesus. John says in 3:23 that God's commandment is "*we believe in the name of His Son Jesus Christ.*" This seems clear and obvious. But what did I say earlier? Not everything that appears obvious is correct. In this case, the implications of this "we believe..." aren't fully fleshed out here by John.

Our belief in Jesus is our active and confident trust in Jesus as *the only* Savior and God and *our only* Savior and God. It is not the belief in either-or, but both-and. Jesus is the only Savior and God and also our only Savior and God. Many Christians tend to split this up. Some will profess Jesus as the Savior of the world and God of the universe, but then don't live like He's their personal Savior and God. Then you have others who profess and say, "Jesus is my personal Savior and God," yet they're not confident with Jesus as the only Savior and God because of other religions and beliefs. Christian, our belief in Jesus can never be either-or. It must be both-and.

So what does this belief in Jesus look like? This active and confident trust in Jesus as *the only* Savior and God and *our only* Savior and God consequently rejects several beliefs that tend to plague many Christians.[34]

- ✓ Belief in Jesus rejects *pluralism*. Pluralism is the belief that **"humans may be saved through a number of different religious traditions"** and paths of salvation.[35] Have you ever seen the bumper sticker "coexist"? "Coexist" is an example of pluralism. This idea of a "Progressive Christianity" is also pluralism. For example, Oprah said in an interview, **"For me to live in a world that is not inclusive of other people who are not Christian would be the opposite of Christianity."**[36] That's pluralism. You cannot hold to pluralism and say you have a biblical belief in Jesus Christ.

- ✓ Belief in Jesus rejects *polytheism*. Polytheism is the belief in multiple gods. For example, Mormonism would fall under polytheism because they believe that multiple gods exist. Mormonism is not Christianity. Mormons are not Christians. You cannot hold to polytheism and say you have a biblical belief in Jesus Christ.

- ✓ Belief in Jesus rejects *inclusivism*. Inclusivism is the belief that **"it is not necessary for people to know about Jesus or believe in Jesus to receive the benefits of his redemptive work."**[37] In other words, someone may suppose because people simply believe that "God" exists without knowing or believing in "Jesus" that they will still benefit from the death and resurrection of Jesus. The Bible does not teach this. Therefore, you cannot hold to inclusivism and say you have a biblical belief in Jesus Christ.

✓ Belief in Jesus rejects *universalism*. Universalism is the belief that ultimately no person is lost because in the love of God the atonement of Jesus **"is not limited and therefore extends to everyone."**[38] Hence, God will eventually save every person whether they believe in Jesus or not and whether they're religious or not. You cannot hold to universalism and say you have a biblical belief in Jesus Christ.

✓ Belief in Jesus rejects *agnosticism*. Agnosticism is the belief that apart from experience it is impossible to know for certain the existence of anything.[39] Agnosticism is ultimately a denial of faith and any certainty that ensues from faith. Agnostics say, "I don't know if God exists, but I also can't say He doesn't exist." That's the end of it. They don't pursue the discovery of if God does exist. They merely hold that we can't know. You cannot say you have a biblical belief in Jesus and somehow say you don't know or believe that Jesus is the God that exists.

✓ Belief in Jesus rejects *atheism*. Atheism is the belief that God does not exist. This is a no-brainer for Christians, right? Correct! No Christian can be an atheist, right? Right, and wrong. Anyone who professes to be Christian but denies in their living that Jesus is Lord of their life and denies His Lordship in their submission to His Word would be a form of atheism. We can reduce the atheistic life to doing whatever you want and feel and getting as much as possible because this life is all there is. Sadly, many professing Christians live like this. You cannot say you have a biblical belief in Jesus and then live as if Jesus is not *the* God and *your* God because that would be living as if *no* God exists.

✓ Belief in Jesus rejects *relativism*. Relativism is the belief that knowledge, truth, and morality only exist in relation to culture, society, or historical context and are not absolute. Relativism is a contradictory belief because its premise is an absolute. Knowledge, truth, and morality are absolutely subjective. Therefore, any claim must be acceptable. Hence, relativism is a belief that sounds right and knowledgeable but is contradictory and false. You cannot hold to relativism and have a biblical belief in Jesus because these two beliefs contradict one another.

There are far more beliefs and worldviews that I could've included. This should suffice to make the point. Our belief in Jesus means we have an active and confident trust that Jesus Christ is *the only* Savior and God of the world—there is no other "god" or "ways" to be saved. Our belief in Jesus means we have an active and confident trust that Jesus Christ is *our only* personal Savior and God—we submit to Him and His Word as Lord and Master of our life. As Holland candidly notes, *"True Christians are distinguished from unbelievers not only by their obedience, but by their love for Christ."*[40]

Christian, to be beloved by God and begotten of God is a captivating identity that we possess and a holy reality that accompanies it. In no way does what distinguish us mean we will or we have to be perfect. Perfection is never the aim or goal. Transformation is. Transformational living follows God's beloved and begotten.

A pastor I once saw on Twitter years ago tweeted, **"Just as a plane flies according to how its computer is set, your life will fly according to how your heart is set!"** How true! We as God's beloved and God's begotten can be and will be distinguished by living righteous, loving one another, and our belief in Jesus because God has set our heart so. Apostle John has been crystal clear. If you are not distinguished as God's beloved and begotten in these ways, then, at best, you are a rebellious child of God, or, at worst, you are not His child, are still dead in your sins, and destined for God's wrath in eternity unless you repent and believe.

Reading that may not be easy. There may be a part in you that is resisting or playing down this truth. Don't. Let the Spirit work. If your heart has been convicted in any way, I ask that you don't resist it. Respond to God in salvation or surrender.

NOW WHAT?

We have surveyed 1John to understand this esteemed and precious identity we have as beloved by God and begotten of God. We now know our identity as God's beloved means we are exhaustively loved by God. We now know our identity as God's begotten means we have a magnificently new nature, birthright, and heritage. And we now know that this identity of ours penetrates, saturates, and seeps all through our lives. It is distinguishable. It cannot be hidden, nor should we want to hide it. Those of us who now understand this identity should want to proudly declare with our lives and our mouths that we are beloved by God and begotten of God. And, further, we should want to proudly invite others to experience this remarkable reality with God. Listen to this heartfelt expression by Thomas á Kempis on the wonderful effect of divine love.

> "If a man loves, he will know the sound of this voice. For this warm affection of [the] soul is a loud voice crying in the ears of God, and it says: "My God, my love, You are all mine and I am all Yours. Give me an increase of love, that I may learn to taste with the inward lips of my heart how sweet it is to love, how sweet to be dissolved in love and bathe in it. Let me be rapt in love. Let me rise above self in great fervor and wonder. Let me sing the hymn of love, and let me follow You, my Love, to the heights. Let my soul exhaust itself in praising You, rejoicing out of love. Let me love You more than myself, and let me not love myself except for Your sake. In You let me love all those who truly love You, as the law of love, which shines forth from You, commands.""[41]

As excited as you should be about being beloved and begotten, this will be met with constant resistance because it is sin (internally and externally) that wants to rob you of God's identity. Christian, everything in our day is inputting and pulling at you. Think about what you see and hear daily. It's a tug of war for your reasoning, affections, allegiance, and way of life. Fight against pursuing and settling on the love from this world and for the things in this world. Fight against becoming too invested in these temporal things that you misplace your hope in what's here.

My prayer is through understanding your identity as beloved and begotten that the Holy Spirit has begun a healing in you. My prayer is that He deals with any bouts or distresses you may have with insecurities, feelings of insignificance, or struggles with your perseverance, contentment, ungodly desires, misplaced expectations, etc. Let these truths of God work in your soul like medicine. Hold tightly to this identity and reality. Take God at His word. God says...

- ✓ you are His beloved,
- ✓ you are recipients of His divine preferential affection and kindness,
- ✓ you are personally and especially loved by Him,
- ✓ you are a part of a specific people especially loved by Him,
- ✓ you are the beneficiaries of looking like and becoming like the One who beloved you,
- ✓ and this great hope in Christ is morally purifying you.

God also says...

- ✓ you are His begotten,
- ✓ you are spiritually reproduced in His image,
- ✓ fathered by Him,
- ✓ and a descendant of His royal bloodline.

No one or thing can trump God and declare you aren't what He says you are.

Do not let the voice of yourself, the culture, society, educators, politicians, a relationship, comments on social media, nor anyone or anything else lie to you about who you are. If you belong to God, then you are only and forever whom God says you are. Therefore, just as belief and confession are active and not passive, you have to actively and confidently trust in, agree with, and admit these truths to yourself. No matter how many times it takes. No matter how long it takes. It's these truths that can cure your soul issues and cancel out the lies told to you by anyone and anything. Trust God, and daily pray the Holy Spirit applies these medicinal truths in you and uses them as compelling motivators for peace and growth in your life against the onslaught of our day.

The identity we possess is rich and unique. There is no other aspect of Creation that gets to be identified by God as His beloved and His begotten. You matter to God. You are very much significant to Him. You are loved, accepted, and pursued by God. No one else will ever love you, embrace you, or come for you like Jesus. Stop looking everywhere else for what God has already given you. All this does is prolong your hope and makes your mind, your will, and your emotions distressed and distraught. Your identity is secure, along with your future and your inheritance. You are of royal blood. The God of the Universe has fathered you, gave up the Beloved and Begotten One for your sake so that you could become His beloved and begotten. You can live confidently. You are whom He created you as. You will be made morally clean.

Hope in Him. Trust Him. Pursue Him. But, Him alone. This is how we as Christians can live and ought to live in our world today as God's beloved and begotten.

> "It is a strange and beautiful eccentricity of the free God that He has allowed His heart to be emotionally identified with men. Self-sufficient as He is, He wants our love and will not be satisfied till He gets it. Free as He is, He has let His heart be bound to us forever. "Herein is love, not that we loved God, but that he loved us, and sent his Son to be the propitiation for our sins." "For our soul is so specially loved of Him that is highest," says Julian of Norwich, "that it overpasseth the knowing of all creatures: that is to say, there is no creature that is made that may know how

much and how sweetly and how tenderly our Maker loveth us. And therefore we may with grace and His help stand in spiritual beholding, with everlasting marvel of this high, overpassing, inestimable Love that Almighty God hath to us of His Goodness.""[42]

Bondservants

In the summer of 2015, after closing our church plant in Los Angeles, a church in Bakersfield, CA, hired me to be the Groups Pastor. In 2016, my role changed to Pastor of Discipleship. During the meeting with my Senior Pastor where he told me this good news, he asked if I had a five-year plan. I told him I desired to be a senior pastor again by my fortieth birthday, which was only four years away. Every year after, he would check in with me. In the summer of 2018, I began talking with my wife about when I would be looking and applying for senior pastor jobs. The 2018-2019 school year was a big transition year for our kids. Our oldest son would be graduating from high school. Our next son would be graduating from junior high. Our daughter, the youngest, would be graduating from elementary school (sixth grade). If we were going to be open to moving, 2019 was the best time because we would all be transitioning together, not interrupting a school tier and inflicting more hurt than what naturally follows a move at their age. The next transition window would be our daughter's high school graduation year six years later. My wife and I prayed for God's will.

Enter the beginning of the kids' school year in 2018. I informed my Senior Pastor that I would be applying for senior pastor positions in 2019 and ready to move in the summer if a church hired me. February, I began looking and applying. March through May, I was interviewing and having conversations with our kids about my search. June, after the second official visit with a church and preaching twice for their vote, we took our kids to dinner. We told them I had been offered the senior pastor position for a church in Maryland. That was indeed a rough night. Our oldest son would be going away to college ninety minutes north of Bakersfield, CA, and we would be moving three thousand miles across the country. Our two youngest would be leaving their family, friends, and community where they were deeply invested. The more we talked, the more questions they asked, the more the reality sank in.

That night and the next day, my kids wanted to know *why*. Why is daddy leaving the church we all love? Why is daddy leaving the community where we all have friends? Why can't daddy just plant a church nearby? Why Maryland? Why now? Why, why, why. My answer was not what my kids wanted to hear but what they needed to learn at their young age. I proceeded to ask my kids a series of questions.

"Who is your Creator?" They answered, "Jesus."

"Who is your Savior?" They answered, "Jesus."

Then I explained, "For those of us who believe Jesus is our Creator and Savior, we follow Him as His disciple because He created us and He saved us. We can't create ourselves, and we can't save ourselves. Therefore, to be a born-again Christian means our whole life—from the thought of us in the mind of God in eternity past to our never-ending eternal life in Christ—all belongs to God."

"If your life belongs to someone, what is that person called?" They replied, "Your God? Your master?" "Yes!" I agreed.

"And if Jesus is our God and Master, then when our Master tells us to go somewhere and do something, what are we to say?" They responded, "Yes."

"Exactly! How can we respond any other way to the God who created us and saved us? He gave us life twice! To be disciples of Jesus means our life is His to lead. Our primary responsibility as His disciple is to trust and follow our Creator, Savior, and Master no matter the cost. It's not as if He created us and saved us to screw us over. However He leads us, it's always for His glory and good purposes.

At some point in your life as Christians, you're going to face a fork in the road; you will be in a position where you have to give up something to say yes and follow Jesus where He is leading. This is where daddy is with this opportunity. I can put our happiness and comfort first by saying no. But daddy loves God more than he loves y'all. I am Jesus' disciple first. I am your dad after. Jesus is my Master. So if I'm going to choose to please anyone first, it's going to be Him over y'all, mommy, and myself. If I don't follow where He is leading me, I'm not showing you how to live as His disciple. I'm not saying it'll be easy, or that it won't hurt, or that you will always like it. But it's better to obey and suffer than to disobey and suffer."

I went on to give my kids the freedom to not be okay, to vent, and to grieve without any time limits. And after 2020, they better understood. They still missed California. But they grew in their understanding of what it meant to be a follower of Christ. What I was teaching and showing my teenage children is how an aspect of being a disciple of Jesus is that we are bondservants of our Master. Jesus is both our Savior and our Lord. To be a born-again Christian is to believe and follow Him as both.

BIBLICAL BONDSERVANTHOOD

"Bondservant" is not a common term for us today. However, it was most certainly a common term and reality during Bible times. Between both Old Testament and New Testament usage, there are close to a thousand total mentions of *servant, bondservant, slave*, and *bond-slave*. These mentions range from person to person, nation to nation, and person or people to God. According to the two predominantly used Hebrew and Greek terms (*ebed* and *doulos*), a "bondservant" is *the status of a person who willingly or involuntarily submits to another as their master and to the master's will over their own; it is a giving up of personal ownership rights.*[1]

By today's standards, bondservanthood is considered offensive, even if it's voluntary. Often when anyone hears the term "slave" (or anything resembling "slave"), they think of something foreign to the Bible. So let's quickly clear up the past misinterpretation and misunderstanding.

First, the Bible affirmatively rejects the heresy of the Roman Catholic Church, the Church of England, and the Protestant Church during the late 15th century through the late 19th century regarding slavery.[2] Biblical slavery and colonial slavery are two completely different forms of slavery. Easton's Bible Dictionary states,

> "Slavery as it existed under the Mosaic law has *no modern parallel*. That law did not originate but only regulated the already existing custom of slavery (Ex. 21:20, 21, 26, 27; Lev. 25:44–46; Josh. 9:6–27)."[3]

Read the Old Testament laws on slavery. You'll find that the Hebrews were commanded to release their slaves every seven years, and if they were fellow Hebrews, they were to restore to them what they no longer had (e.g., Deut. 15:12-18). You'll also find laws against those who abused their slaves. The slavery permitted in the Bible is more of indentured servitude than what became known as chattel slavery during the colonial era. William Edward Raffety explains,

> "The slavery of Judaism was not the cruel system of Greece, Rome, and later nations. The prime thought is service; *the servant* may render free service, *the slave*, obligatory, restricted service."[4]

Biblical slavery and colonial slavery are two very different things. However, that doesn't mean biblical slavery didn't have its share of abuses. It did. Nor does this mean slavery in the 1st century was better than the slavery that came later.[5] Of course, it wasn't. Sinful men act sinfully across every age and in every place. This reality we also see played out in colonial slavery. Colonial slavery is a severe stain on the Church's testimony of Christ because of its involvement in teaching and practice during the 1400s-1800s. A stain still impacting the American Church's testimony even to this day in the 2020s. Nevertheless, the biblical references of slave or bondservant and its identification with the people of God across both testaments cannot be compared to any other form of slavery.

Second, covenantal bondservanthood is unique to Judaism and Christianity. For any Hebrew to have claimed to be part of the covenant people of God and view themselves above being a bondservant of God would've been a too high view of themselves and an unbiblical view of what it means to be God's covenant people.

> "6 *For you are a holy people belonging to the Lord your God. The Lord your God has chosen you to be his own possession out of all the peoples on the face of the earth.* 7 The Lord had his heart set on you and chose you, not because you were more numerous than all peoples, for you were the fewest of all peoples. 8 But because the Lord loved you and kept the oath he swore to your ancestors, he brought you out with a strong hand and redeemed you from the place of slavery, from the power of Pharaoh king of Egypt." (Deuteronomy 7:6-8, CSB; *emphasis added*)

> "14 "Now therefore fear the Lord and serve him in sincerity and in faithfulness. Put away the gods that your fathers served beyond the River and in Egypt, and serve the Lord. 15 And if it is evil in your eyes to serve the Lord, choose this day whom you will serve, whether the gods your fathers served in the region beyond the River, or the gods of the Amorites in whose land you dwell. But as for me and my house, we will serve the Lord." 16 *Then the people answered, "Far be it from us that we should forsake the Lord to serve other gods, 17 for it is the Lord our God who brought us and our fathers up from the land of Egypt, out of the house of slavery, and who did those great signs in our sight and preserved us in all the way that we went, and among all the peoples through whom we passed. 18 And the Lord drove out before us all the peoples, the Amorites who lived in the land. Therefore we also will serve the Lord, for he is our God."* 19 But Joshua said to the people, "You are not able to serve the Lord, for he is a holy God. He is a jealous God; he will not forgive your transgressions or your sins. 20 If you forsake the Lord and serve foreign gods, then he will turn and do you harm and consume you, after having done you good."

21 And the people said to Joshua, "No, but we will serve the Lord." *22 Then Joshua said to the people, "You are witnesses against yourselves that you have chosen the Lord, to serve him." And they said, "We are witnesses."* 23 He said, "Then put away the foreign gods that are among you, and incline your heart to the Lord, the God of Israel." 24 And the people said to Joshua, "The Lord our God we will serve, and his voice we will obey." 25 So Joshua made a covenant with the people that day, and put in place statutes and rules for them at Shechem. 26 And Joshua wrote these words in the Book of the Law of God. And he took a large stone and set it up there under the terebinth that was by the sanctuary of the Lord. 27 And Joshua said to all the people, "Behold, this stone shall be a witness against us, for it has heard all the words of the Lord that he spoke to us. Therefore it shall be a witness against you, lest you deal falsely with your God." 28 So Joshua sent the people away, every man to his inheritance." (Joshua 24:14-28, ESV; *emphasis added*)

Regarding how the covenant people of God would not have viewed themselves above being God's bondservants, Dr. John MacArthur, in his book, "Slave," notes,

"From the standpoint of Israel's history, *to be a slave of God was to identify oneself with* those who stood at Mount Sinai and with noble intentions proclaimed, "All the words which the Lord has spoken we will do!" (Ex. 24:3). Moreover, *it was to be aligned with* notable men of faith, such as Abraham, Moses, David, and the prophets—spiritual leaders who exemplified wholehearted submission to the will and word of God."[6]

While bondservanthood can be willingly entered between humans or required because of outstanding debt or captivity, this is different in the case of God's people with God. Covenantal bondservanthood is *the characterization of a willing and intimate spiritual servanthood to God where one's heart, mind, will, and body is under the authority of God*. The people of God's bondservanthood is a deserved obligation to God because of God graciously choosing His people, God mercifully rescuing them from their enslavement, and then God lovingly entering into a covenant relationship with them (Ezek. 16:1-63). To a Hebrew during Bible times, across both testaments, bondservanthood was the only appropriate response to God for being part of His covenant people.

An Unsung Example

If I asked you to pick someone in the Bible (excluding Jesus) as a model example of being a bondservant of God, who would it be? Probably David, right? Apostle Paul, definitely. Of course, Moses. Perhaps, the prophet Elijah or Daniel or Apostle John. Before 2020, I would've answered with one of these names myself. But now, my choice is Mary, the mother of Jesus. That woman was a rockstar disciple of Yahweh to me. Every time I explore her life, my respect for her grows.

We all know God chose Mary to be Jesus' birth mother. But what some might not know is that she wasn't immediately excited when she received that news (Luke 1:26-30). Mary went through an internal journey in her conversation with the angel Gabriel. First, she was greatly troubled by what she heard and what it would mean. She was a teenage virgin betrothed to a man. If she ended up pregnant before getting married, it would've ruined her. Her betrothment would be off, and she would be known as a prostitute. Hence, why Joseph said he *"did not want to expose her to public disgrace, he had in mind to divorce her quietly."*[7] Next, she went from troubled to doubtful as to how this would happen. *"How can this be, since I have not had sexual relations with a man?"*[8] But then, after hearing how God would do what only God could do, she ended with a response of faith. *"And Mary said, "Behold, I am the servant of the Lord; let it be to me according to your word."*[9]

Once Mary realized what God was inviting her to participate in was extraordinary, she took her fear and doubt and placed it in God's hands. She demonstrated wholehearted trust in God, which led to her joy of the privilege to participate in His plan. Her song in Luke 1:46-55 was a reflection of how great Yahweh is. You hear her awe that this great God would look upon lowly ol' her to demonstrate His faithfulness to His promises of old. But these weren't mere words for Mary. The Hebrews viewed themselves corporately as one people, and Mary understood herself as a member of the covenant people of God. Yet, in this account, she realizes that she is pivotal to the path of God fulfilling His covenant promises. In verse 48, she expresses, *"from now on all generations will call me blessed"* (CSB). Imagine you discovered that you're part of some royal family in another country, and you were the missing link in unlocking all kinds of riches for every member of the family. That's kind of what's happening here. For Mary, realizing her role for her people in God's plan just made her more humble and viewed God as even greater.

This young woman's faith in her God and subsequent submission to Him is remarkable. Please try to put yourself in her shoes to consider the gravity of her situation. She did not know what would happen to her. As a teenager, she risked her whole future by declaring to Gabriel that she is the Lord's bondservant. She didn't say this to another teenager that she could recant after a night's sleep. She told an actual angel of God to let God do with her life as He pleases; whatever comes, comes. And then, in humility, she raves of God's greatness and consideration of including her in His story. What radical trust in Yahweh! How many of us can honestly say we would've responded the same? I'm not sure I can say I would have, had I been in her specific situation.

Between her exchange with Gabriel and her song after the fact, Mary identified herself twice as a bondservant (Luke 1:38, 48). She called herself a *doulé* of Yahweh—a woman bondslave of God. Mary is the first person in the New Testament to be announced as a bondservant of the Lord. Not a man. A teenage girl. And this was before she was pregnant with Jesus. As a matter of fact, it was her humble admission of being a bondservant of God that permitted her to carry Jesus.

We would never have known of Mary had she been reluctant to serve God in this way and said no. It was her faith and submission to God—her high view of God and proper view of herself—that solidified her specific inclusion in God's story. Her whole life was a testimony of someone who benefited from saying *yes* to God's grace and plan, of someone who was sold out in being the Lord's bondservant no matter the costs. What an overlooked but sincere example of being a bondservant of the Lord. May we learn much from our sister Mary.

BONDSERVANTHOOD FOR BELIEVERS

Like our Jewish brethren, covenantal bondservanthood is also the Christian's deserved obligation to God. Our reasons for bondservanthood, however, are incalculable. Read Apostle Paul's words in Ephesians 1:3-14. God graciously chooses us *in Christ*. God mercifully pays off our eternal debt to Him *in Christ*. God lovingly enters into an everlasting covenant relationship with us *in Christ*. God seals us with the Holy Spirit *in Christ*. Then, like a cherry on top, we know this was accomplished by Christ humbling Himself as a bondservant unto the Father for the sake of His people (Phil. 2:5-8). To believers *in Christ*, especially a Hebrew Christian during the New Testament, bondservanthood takes on a superior meaning as the only appropriate response to God for being part of His redeemed covenant people.

Bondservanthood = Joyful Submission

In the days of Greco-Roman slavery, slaves and servants were commonplace. MacArthur remarked that it was so pervasive it wasn't even questioned.[10] As a result, during the New Testament, a "bondservant" was a spot-on picture for the identity of believers in Christ. Today, on the other hand, the negativity of slavery or servanthood is what's commonplace, not its acceptance. While this is a good thing for upholding a standard of humaneness and combating abuses (especially in industries like labor, prison, and trafficking), we must be on guard for reading the Bible with that negativity of slavery or servanthood.

For the believers who hear or read "slave of Christ" or "bondservant of God" or something of the sort and still cringe, don't reject this identity because of your 21st century context. To cringe may mean you have more of a heart issue than a humane issue. **"From** the entrance of sin into the world," as Dr. Ben Gutierrez points out, "the human heart has longed to control its own fate and destiny and has fought against the ultimate direction and authority of the sovereign Lord."[11] When seeing these descriptions of believers in your reading of Scripture, don't forget who the Author of Scripture is and the time and context in which it was written. Know that the believers during the 1st century would not think or hear or feel bondage and exploitation when claiming to be bondservants of the Lord or being identified as such. They would have reasoned, "Being a bondservant of God is what God is entitled to from me for being our covenant God. This is simply my worship of Him." Notice the tone of how the New Testament uses *doulos*.[12]

> "27 For truly in this city there were gathered together against Your holy servant Jesus, whom You anointed, both Herod and Pontius Pilate, along with the Gentiles and the peoples of Israel, 28 to do whatever Your hand and purpose predestined to occur. 29 And now, Lord, look at their threats, and grant it to Your bond-servants [*doulos*] to speak Your word with all confidence, 30 while You extend Your hand to heal, and signs and wonders take place through the name of Your holy servant Jesus." 31 And when they had prayed, the place where they had gathered together was shaken, and they were all filled with the Holy Spirit and began to speak the word of God with boldness." (Acts 4:27-31, NASB; brackets added)

> "16 It happened that as we were going to the place of prayer, a slave woman who had a spirit of divination met us, who was bringing great profit to her masters by fortune-telling. 17 She followed Paul and us and cried out repeatedly, saying, "These men are bond-servants [*doulos*] of the Most High God, who are proclaiming to you a way of salvation."" (Acts 16:16-17, NASB; brackets added)

> "20 Each person should remain in the situation they were in when God called them. 21 Were you a slave [*doulos*] when you were called? Don't let it trouble you—although if you can gain your

freedom, do so. 22 For the one who was a slave [*doulos*] when called to faith in the Lord is the Lord's freed person; similarly, the one who was free when called is Christ's slave [*doulos*]. 23 You were bought at a price; do not become slaves [*doulos*] of human beings." (1Corithians 7:20-23, NIV; brackets added)

"For am I now seeking the approval of man, or of God? Or am I trying to please man? If I were still trying to please man, I would not be a servant [*doulos*] of Christ." (Galatians 1:10, ESV; brackets added)

"5 Slaves [*doulos*], obey your earthly masters with respect and fear, and with sincerity of heart, just as you would obey Christ. 6 Obey them not only to win their favor when their eye is on you, but as slaves [*doulos*] of Christ, doing the will of God from your heart. 7 Serve wholeheartedly, as if you were serving the Lord, not people, 8 because you know that the Lord will reward each one for whatever good they do, whether they are slave [*doulos*] or free. 9 And masters, treat your slaves in the same way. Do not threaten them, since you know that he who is both their Master and yours is in heaven, and there is no favoritism with him." (Ephesians 6:5-9, NIV; brackets added)

"Paul and Timothy, servants [*doulos*] of Christ Jesus: To all the saints in Christ Jesus who are in Philippi, including the overseers and deacons." (Philippians 1:1, CSB; brackets added)

"7 Tychicus, our dearly loved brother, faithful minister, and fellow servant [*doulos*] in the Lord, will tell you all the news about me.... 12 Epaphras, who is one of you, a servant [*doulos*] of Christ Jesus, sends you greetings. He is always wrestling for you in his prayers, so that you can stand mature and fully assured in everything God wills." (Colossians 4:7, 12, CSB; brackets added)

"James, a servant [*doulos*] of God and of the Lord Jesus Christ: To the twelve tribes dispersed abroad. Greetings." (James 1:1, CSB; brackets added)

"15 For this is the will of God, that by doing good you should put to silence the ignorance of foolish people. 16 Live as people who are free, not using your freedom as a cover-up for evil, but living as servants [*doulos*] of God." (1Peter 2:15-16, ESV; brackets added)

"Simeon Peter, a servant [*doulos*] and an apostle of Jesus Christ: To those who have received a faith equal to ours through the righteousness of our God and Savior Jesus Christ." (2Peter 1:1, CSB; brackets added)

"Jude, a servant [*doulos*] of Jesus Christ and a brother of James: To those who are the called, loved by God the Father and kept for Jesus Christ." (Jude 1:1, CSB; brackets added)

"1 The Revelation of Jesus Christ, which God gave Him to show to His bond-servants [*doulos*], the things which must soon take place; and He sent and communicated it by His angel to His bond-servant [*doulos*] John, 2 who testified to the word of God and to the testimony of Jesus Christ, everything that he saw." (Revelation 1:1-2, NASB; brackets added)

Covenantal bondservanthood for our Christian brethren during the 1st century wasn't a badge of shame or compliance with bondage and oppression. Rather, it was a privilege and pride for them to be the Lord's slave because of Who the Lord is. This is not some mutable human lord they're submitting to; it is the Creator Covenant God who came in the flesh fulfilling His promises and prophecies to eternally rescue them. Does that sound like anything shameful or of bondage and oppression? Nope, not even close.

Recall John the Baptist in Luke 1:15-17. He was prophetically foreordained to be a bondservant of God in his life and ministry for the Messiah. John didn't have an option. He didn't get a say. He would be the kind of person God declared him to be—a godly, Spirit-filled man. Similarly, our brethren in the 1st century did not regard their bondservanthood as optional. They understood bondservanthood as their only proper response of worship to God. To be a *doulos* in their life and ministry for the risen Messiah and Master wasn't repressive or inhumane. It was a divine honor and freedom to belong to the Lord of lords, serving Him and with Him in His work in their lives and the world.

↳ Salvation → Lordship → *doulos.*

As new covenant believers living outside of the time of the Bible, we need to know that nothing has changed for us. Not a single thing. Our bondservanthood is inextricably connected to Jesus' Lordship. If you profess Jesus as *your* Lord, He is *your* Master and *you* are His *doulos.* This reality is embedded in our profession of faith because it is indebted to the Author of this faith.

There are two often go-to passages for describing how we are saved. What would you say they are? I'm assuming the majority of us would say one is Ephesians 2:8-9. Some may go elsewhere for the second, but I have no doubt many would say Romans 10:9-10. If these weren't your two, roll with it because these are the two I'm using.

In Ephesians 2:8-9 and Romans 10:9-10, have you ever noticed how lordship and salvation—our *doulos* and our *sótéria/sózó*—are two sides of the same coin?[13]

> "1 Brothers and sisters, my heart's desire and prayer to God on behalf of my fellow Israelites is for their salvation [*sótéria*]. 2 For I can testify that they are zealous for God, but *their zeal is not in line with the truth.* 3 For ignoring the righteousness that comes from God, and seeking instead to establish their own righteousness, *they did not submit* to God's righteousness. *4 For Christ is the end of the law, with the result that there is righteousness for everyone who believes.* 5 For Moses writes about the righteousness that is by the law: "The one who does these things will live by them." 6 But the righteousness that is by faith says: "Do not say in your heart, 'Who will ascend into heaven?'" (that is, to bring Christ down) 7 or "Who will descend into the abyss?" (that is, to bring Christ up from the dead). 8 But what does it say? "The word is near you, in your mouth and in your heart" (that is, the word of faith that we preach), 9 because if you confess with your mouth that Jesus is Lord and believe in your heart that God raised him from the dead, you will

be saved [*sózó*]. 10 For with the heart one believes and thus has righteousness and with the mouth one confesses and thus has salvation [*sótéria*]. 11 For the scripture says, "Everyone who believes in him will not be put to shame." 12 For there is no distinction between the Jew and the Greek, *for the same Lord is Lord of all, who richly blesses all who call on him. 13 For everyone who calls on the name of the Lord will be saved [sózó].*" (Romans 10:1-13, NET; *emphasis* & brackets added)

In Romans 10:1-13, we see from Jews to gentiles we are to *submit* to God's way to receive God's *salvation—doulos* and *sótéria/ sózó*, two sides of the same coin. Christ is both Lord and Savior. You have to admit and submit to both to receive what God promises. Hence, we who have been saved are bondservants. Lordship and salvation are inseparable.

"1 *And you were dead* in your trespasses and sins 2 in which you previously walked according to the ways of this world, according to the ruler of the power of the air, the spirit now working in the disobedient. 3 We too all previously lived among them in our fleshly desires, carrying out the inclinations of our flesh and thoughts, and we were by nature children under wrath as the others were also. 4 *But God,* who is rich in mercy, because of his great love that he had for us, 5 *made us alive with Christ even though we were dead in trespasses.* You are saved [*sózó*] by grace! 6 *He also raised us up with him and seated us with him in the heavens in Christ Jesus,* 7 so that in the coming ages he might display the immeasurable riches of his grace through his kindness to us in Christ Jesus. 8 For you are saved [*sózó*] by grace through faith, and *this is not from yourselves; it is God's gift—* 9 not from works, so that no one can boast. 10 For *we are his workmanship,* created in Christ Jesus for good works, which God prepared ahead of time for us to do." (Ephesians 2:1-10, CSB; *emphasis* & brackets added)

In Ephesians 2:1-10, we see we were once under the owner-ship of sin, the world's ways, and Satan. We were their *doulos'*. However, because of God's grace and our faith in Jesus, those of us who have been redeemed from our former ownership are now under new ownership—God's ownership. Our salvation in Christ (*sózó*) brings us into our new and liberating bondservanthood to God (*doulos*). Thus, in this passage, ownership (which is correlated with lordship) is inextricable from salvation.

Salvation belongs to God alone. Salvation is an act of God alone. Therefore, those whom God saves belong to God. No question. No option. All or nothing. He is Lord *and* Savior. Those of us who believe in Him are His redeemed *doulos'*. Jerry Bridges penned this well when he said, **"Our concept of God and our relationship with Him determine our conduct."**[14]

Our bondservanthood should not make us cringe but rather rejoice! Jesus has taken full responsibility for the ownership of our lives. Think about the significance of this! Between our old ownership and our new ownership, is there any question about the better master? Absolutely not! So then, why do you consciously resist submitting to your new Master and eagerly run back to your cruel old master in certain areas of your life? Is the Egypt we needed rescuing from better than the freedom we now have as Christ's slaves? Only those who do not realize they're enslaved would say yes. But those of us who have been rescued from our former enslavement, our bondservanthood in Christ is liberty, not bondage. Our Heavenly Master died for us so that we can freely live with Him now and for eternity. His ownership of our lives is always with our best interest in mind. The moment we think His ownership and our bondservanthood is oppressive—because sin and self are not encouraged but denied for a better way—we have believed the lie of our old ownership who's irate that we're no longer under its dominion. As a matter of fact, our resistance to submit as bondservants of Christ is self-suppression of our freedom to live for God and with God. *"For freedom, Christ set us free. Stand firm then and don't submit again to a yoke of slavery."*[15]

This shouldn't be too impersonal for us to grasp. In a way, as underaged children, we were bondservants of our parents. Our parents did for us what we couldn't do. Our parents directed us on what to do and where to go. We submitted while we were under their care and authority. Similarly, our identity as a beloved and begotten child of God does not negate our status as His bondservant. Quite the contrary, it helps us to understand the intimate nature of our submission to our Master and His care and authority over us (1Pet. 1:13-2:3).

> "As His enemies, we did not even deserve to be His slaves. Yet, He has made us both His slaves and His children. The incomparable reality of adoption is this: If God is our Master, then He is also our Father."[16]

Remember, Jesus modeled this first. The Son came to earth as a bondservant of the Father. In doing so, He gives us the poster example of the attitude of joyful submission. The Son of God humbly came as a slave of God to die as a slave of sin to make slaves of sin into slaves and sons of God. We are beloved and begotten bondservants of God! We are not either/or, nor one over the other.

Jesus identifies His bondservants as His friends and family, going as far as to reveal and include us in His plans (John 15:9-15, Rom. 12:1-2). This relational identification is elevation, liberation, and intimacy within our bondservanthood, not eradicating it.[17] Our old ownership doesn't treat its slaves as anything but puppets. Human masters treated their slaves as property, even the so-called "nice ones." Jesus, on the other hand, adds the relational dimension to our bondservanthood. He initiates the intimacy between Him as the Master and us as His servants. Recall what covenantal bondservanthood is—*the characterization of a willing and intimate spiritual servanthood to God where one's heart, mind, will, and body is under the authority of God.* Our submission as bondservants of Christ reminds us and displays to others the kind of Master Jesus is.

Bondservanthood = A Life of Godliness

Submission is not without purpose. God does not merely deserve and receive our bondservanthood; He has designed purpose in it. This purpose, for example, is why Paul and Peter could instruct the believers who were servants of human masters (including the cruel ones) to submit to them as unto their heavenly Master because they knew what was built into our bondservanthood to God. Purpose always adds color to enhance the virtue of whatever we're undertaking or suffering.

God doesn't waste worship. Our joyful submission to God is what produces godliness in our lives. And don't freak out reading "godliness" and presume something unattainable or pompous. "Godly" simply means *reflecting God,* which is what God Himself produces in us. In his book, "The Godly Man's Picture," Thomas Watson expounded on the nature of godliness.

> "By nature we inherit nothing but evil. 'When we were in the flesh, the motions of sins did work in our members' (Rom. 7:5). We sucked in sin as naturally as our mother's milk, but godliness is the 'wisdom from above' (Jas. 3:17). It is breathed in from heaven. *God must light up the lamp of grace in the heart. Weeds grow of themselves; flowers are planted. Godliness is a celestial plant that comes from the New Jerusalem*. Therefore it is called a 'fruit of the Spirit' (Gal. 5:22). A man has no more power to change himself than to create himself."[18]

God takes what He's rightfully due—our worshipful submission—and recycles something valuable for His worshippers from it—our godliness. That's why it's foolish of us to withhold from God, giving Him anything less than wholeheartedness. First, He is most worthy of it. Secondly, we shortchange ourselves in return. God's not stingy or like a bill collector. He's not saying or thinking, "You owe me for your salvation, so pay up." Nor is He like, "Mine, mine, mine." God gives first. We receive, then we give back to God. God reciprocates more for our well-being. And on goes the cycle. So don't listen to the lies of the enemy and fear submission. Don't shortchange your bondservanthood. If you want to be godly in your life, your bondservanthood to God is the key.

God's character standard is a fixed target: holiness. We never have to worry about His target moving for any reason. However, that's never the case outside of God. The standard set by everything else is a moving target. It changes with the times and by whoever is pulling the strings in that society or culture. Hence, Christians cannot live according to the standards of the day or the culture because where it goes, so will you (Eph. 4:14). As God's bondservants, we must live according to His unchanging standard in His Word and aim for His target only, which we can now do with confidence because we've been made holy in Christ (Rom. 11:16-18, 1Pet. 1:14-16). This is our duty and honor.

Not that any of this will be easy, but our lives as redeemed bondservants are to be marked by godliness—i.e., *being someone with a consistent conduct that reflects God's character standard of holiness*. Our godliness, in little or much, should excite other believers and spur them toward more godliness. It should also unassumingly annoy unbelievers because our character and conduct look radically different than theirs. But, again, this is not to imply it will be easy. Similarly, the challenge and difficulty of godliness should not detract us. Instead, it should remind us of our Savior and Lord who first submitted and suffered with the same purpose of hitting God's target.

> "8 Even though Jesus was God's Son, *he learned obedience from the things he suffered.* 9 In this way, God qualified him as a perfect High Priest, and he became the source of eternal salvation for all those who obey him." (Hebrews 5:8-9, NLT; *emphasis added*)

> "For the joy set before him he endured the cross, scorning its shame, and sat down at the right hand of the throne of God. Consider him who endured such opposition from sinners, *so that you will not grow weary and lose heart. In your struggle against sin, you have not yet resisted to the point of shedding your blood.*" (Hebrews 12:2-4, NIV; *emphasis added*)

We are not submitting to a Master who does not understand our struggles in godliness. Jesus can empathize and sympathize with us in every way (Heb. 2:9-18; 4:14-16). So we aim for God's target with our Lord's example as the paved path to follow and the Holy Spirit empowering and encouraging us along the way.

Picture a track meet. The Father is the organizer and official of the meet. His grace keeps us from being disqualified and gives us unlimited opportunities to finish once we start.[19] The track is the path paved by Jesus (Heb. 12:1-2). Moreover, our Lord is running the race with us but as the pacesetter. He never leaves the track. It is He our eyes are to be focused on as we run the race. And, last but not least, the Holy Spirit is the coach.[20] He provides the water for when we're thirsty and the internal strength and determination to not quit when our body feels weak or falls at times during the race. Do you see the picture? The meet is rigged for our success, not our failure!

⚘ The power in choice.

Godliness is not beyond us, Christian. It is in us and ahead of us. That's why our bondservanthood to God is key. We submit to the Spirit in us; we grow in godliness. We submit to living according to the paved path of our Lord; we grow in godliness. In Romans chapters 6 and 8, Paul labors this very point.

> *"12 Do not let sin control the way you live; do not give in to sinful desires. 13 Do not let any part of your body become an instrument of evil to serve sin. Instead, give yourselves completely to God, for you were dead, but now you have new life.* So use your whole body as an instrument to do what is right for the glory of God. 14 Sin is no longer your master, for you no longer live under the requirements of the law. Instead, you live under the freedom of God's grace. 15 Well then, since God's grace has set us free from the law, does that mean we can go on sinning? Of course not! *16 Don't you realize that you become the slave of whatever you choose to obey? You can be a slave to sin, which leads to death, or you can choose to obey God, which leads to righteous living.* 17 Thank God! Once you were slaves of sin, but now you whole-heartedly obey this teaching we have given you. 18 Now you are free from your slavery to sin, and you have become slaves to righteous living. 19 Because of the weakness of your human nature, I am using the illustration of slavery to help you understand all this. *Previously, you let yourselves be slaves to impurity and lawlessness, which led ever deeper into sin. Now you must give yourselves to be slaves to*

righteous living so that you will become holy. 20 When you were slaves to sin, you were free from the obligation to do right. 21 And what was the result? You are now ashamed of the things you used to do, things that end in eternal doom. 22 But *now you are free from the power of sin and have become slaves of God.* Now you do those things that lead to holiness and result in eternal life." (Romans 6:12-22, NLT; *emphasis added*)

"5 Those who are dominated by the sinful nature think about sinful things, but those who are controlled by the Holy Spirit think about things that please the Spirit. 6 *So letting your sinful nature control your mind leads to death. But letting the Spirit control your mind leads to life and peace.* 7 For the sinful nature is always hostile to God. It never did obey God's laws, and it never will. 8 That's why those who are still under the control of their sinful nature can never please God. 9 *But you are not controlled by your sinful nature. You are controlled by the Spirit if you have the Spirit of God living in you.* (And remember that those who do not have the Spirit of Christ living in them do not belong to him at all.) 10 And Christ lives within you, so even though your body will die because of sin, the Spirit gives you life because you have been made right with God. 11 The Spirit of God, who raised Jesus from the dead, lives in you. And just as God raised Christ Jesus from the dead, he will give life to your mortal bodies by this same Spirit living within you. 12 Therefore, dear brothers and sisters, *you have no obligation to do what your sinful nature urges you to do.* 13 For if you live by its dictates, you will die. But *if through the power of the Spirit you put to death the deeds of your sinful nature, you will live.* 14 *For all who are led by the Spirit of God are children of God.*" (Romans 8:5-14, NLT; *emphasis added*)

Did you notice the instructions and results of our bond-servanthood? We are not slaves of sin anymore. The liberating power of being a slave of Christ is that we can say *no* to sin and *yes* to godly living. Just because we *can* sin (and *will* sin) no longer means we *have to* give into sin. Before Christ, we didn't have another option instead of sin. We couldn't put up a fight. We were *doulos'* of sin. It was sin or more sin. Even our good deeds and virtues were saran-wrapped in sin. But now, being redeemed bondservants of Jesus, we have the option to choose sin or choose what's right in God's sight. And our

> *slaves of sin*
> *= everything's wrapped in bondage*
>
> *slaves of Christ*
> *= the power of freedom in God*

choice is not within our strength but by submitting to the Spirit or our flesh. Submission enables power: the power to sin or the power to live godly. So be careful, there is freedom or bondage in whatever *we choose* to obey.

I'm sure none of us would argue against this point: no one likes to submit. Am I right? Who likes being under the subjection of another? I can't see anyone eager to raise their hand for this. And that's because we all have this inclination to seek to be free or autonomous. Yet, freedom and autonomy haven't been reality since Adam and Eve disobeyed God and got kicked out of the garden of Eden. Since the fall, all of humanity are born slaves of sin; only those born-again are now slaves of Christ (Rom. 5:12-21). Thus, being slaves of Christ is not solely liberation from slavery to sin but also a boast of God. Recall how God boasted of His power to deliver His people from the hand of Pharaoh (Exod. 3:19-22; 7:1-5, Rom. 9:17). Similarly, our bondservanthood to God is God declaring or boasting of the kind of Christians we are to be—we are His workmanship. Like any artist who signs their work so the world may know who's behind its creation, God is doing the same with us. To God, this intimate spiritual servant-hood is His workspace to produce something with us for His glory—a holy people made up of individual godly persons.

God's finished product is what we long for. The in-between, however, is often underwhelming because our bondservanthood isn't ideal. External things and internal things make being a bondservant a moment-by-moment battle. But the end result is partly produced from the in-between. Have you ever built something with your hands or seen someone build something with their hands? Often the work leading to the finished product isn't appealing. Even with clear instructions, the nails and screws neatly packaged and numbered to make it handy, the creative process leading to the finished product is still messy. Hence, part of the pressure and distilling process we experience in our lives via people, situations, and internal conflicts (between the Spirit and our flesh) is our Master at work refashioning His servants according to His likeness. That's the power of grace in our mess! That's Christ's power being impeccably shown in our weaknesses (1Cor. 12:7-10).

> "Believers are also trained in obedience by means of the cross. For thus they are taught to live according to God's will rather than their own. *If everything went according to their own plans, they would never know what it means to follow God*.... Therefore, we shouldn't run from all the ways in which our heavenly Father shapes us in obedience, for it's right that we prove ourselves obedient to Him in every circumstance."[21]

I know for Christians that are born and raised in the 20th-21st century U.S., we've been reared in a democratic mindset. We presume that we can vote in or vote out what we like or dislike, and we can protest what we like or dislike until we feel heard or something changes. The problem with this mindset is it smuggles into our Christianity at times. While we now have the freedom to choose, godliness is not up for vote or protest. Our bondservanthood is not on the floor for debate. We are God's workmanship! Don't allow the democratic mindset to cause you to protest and resist submission and the discomfort that comes from our Master refashioning His servants according to His likeness.

It is to our benefit to comply with our Master's workmanship in our lives. In the words of the Marvel movie "Doctor Strange," *"You cannot beat a river into submission. You have to surrender to its current and use its power as your own."* I know it's from a movie, but it's so much truth in this. As bondservants, we're to surrender to our Master's work in the life He purchased for us. It's in this process of surrendering that we will find hope and strength, especially in the uncomfortable and messy areas in our lives. For when we are weak, then we are strong; when we submit, we find power.

Being a slave of Christ is a way of God bragging on what He's going to make with our lives now that He has ownership. It's God's "show and tell" to the world around us. Therefore, if the life of a professing Christian is marked more by ungodliness than godliness, one has to wonder if that person is truly under God's ownership. **"A blush of godliness is not enough to distinguish a Christian...godliness must be the temper and complexion of the soul."**[22] It's possible then that a professing Christian is still a slave to sin, deceived by repeating a prayer for salvation with no sincere belief in Jesus, and have been perpetuating as if they've been set free without the power to support it. Hence, they can't live godly because they haven't been made godly by being truly saved and sealed with the Holy Spirit.

> "When godliness has taken root in the soul, it abides to eternity: 'his seed remaineth in him' (1John 3:9). Godliness being engraved in the heart by the Holy Ghost, as with the point of a diamond, can never be erased."[23]

On the other hand, for those of us genuinely regenerated, if we're not careful, idolatry can creep in unchecked and temporarily steal our allegiance to our Master (1Cor. 10:1-14). Some sins we know are no-no's, so those things don't tend to sneak in unchecked. Oftentimes it's the pet sins, the unknowns, and the liberties that entrap us. If we're not willing to give up what's deemed off-limits by God nor give up what's permissible for what's holy, whatever that thing is, is an idol. Anything we are not willing to give up for the sake of becoming more like Jesus in our life has become an idol. So be alert for pet sins, unknown sins, liberties, and anything else becoming your master over Christ (1Cor. 6:12). We do not have to willingly give ourselves over to an idol. Furthermore, we can be honest and repent of any idolatry that has ensnared us. All of this is included in the power of freedom we now have in Christ as His bondservants.

Can you think of any idols that have crept in your life unchecked, poaching your allegiance to Jesus?

♩ Nazirite-like dedication.

Are you familiar with the Nazirite vow in the Old Testament (Num. 6:1-8)? The Nazirite vow was like the Hebrew version of a monk. The main point of the vow was about dedicating one's life as a holy offering to God for a period or indefinitely. One Bible scholar wrote,

> "In the circumstances of an ordinary vow, men consecrated *some material possession*, but the Nazirite *consecrated himself or herself*, and took a vow of separation and self-imposed discipline for the purpose of some special service, and the fact of the vow was indicated by special signs of abstinence."[24]

Being a redeemed bondservant of God is akin to the dedication of a Nazirite vow, but for the duration of our life, not simply a season. Our bondservanthood is a whole life total dedication to our faith in God, our reverence of God, and our service to God. As previously stated, yes, this is not without its difficulties. But part of what makes this harder is we don't fight for it. We're not committed to our bondservanthood like Nazirites or monks are to their vows.

Think of what you have been dedicated to, whether currently or for a period in the past: Your career? Your studies? Your children? Your marriage? Your relationships? Your fun? Your hobbies? Your financial freedom? Your social causes? Your politics? Your health? If it wasn't one of these, what was it? What does that dedication look like for you? Now answer this honestly. Have you ever been dedicated to God like what you've shown to those other things? How long did it last? Why did you stop?

I believe there are two reasons we don't fight to commit to this kind of dedication to God. First, our lack of fight is from not esteeming being a bondservant of Christ as a solemn identity we possess. Our bondservanthood is not some mere product of salvation. It is our deserved obligation to God for all it took to obtain the eternal salvation we didn't deserve from Him in the first place. Our brother Watchman Nee aptly conveys this in his classic work, "The Normal Christian Life." He says,

"Presenting myself to God implies a recognition that I am altogether his.... There must be a day in my life when I pass out of my own hands into his, and from that day forward I belong to him and no longer to myself."[25]

Second, our lack of fight is from justifying and compromising too easily, whether to sin, or self, or something else that has become an idol. I don't think we realize, though, that when we do this, we make it easier to continue and harder to fight. Our submission to our flesh in these recurring moments enables more power to sin, not more power to live godly.

To be a bondservant of the Lord is to be wholly consecrated to God for His purposes. This consecration is **"not to Christian work, but *to the will of God, to be and to do whatever he requires.*"**[26] Hence, this cannot be done flippantly—just like a Nazirite vow was not made lightheartedly (e.g., Eccl. 5:1-6). Therefore, we have to stop sacrificing godliness because we have believed the lie that it's more expendable than the effort and results of actually pursuing it. As Thomas á Kempis articulates,

> **"The religious [man] who concerns himself intently and devoutly with our Lord's most holy life and passion will find there an abundance of all things useful and necessary for him."[27]**

Therefore, be determined for this. Fight for it. Grind for it. Press for it. If our bondservanthood is not worth this kind of effort, essentially, we're declaring Jesus is not worth this kind of effort.

Throughout the New Testament, we see believers who lived like this was worth it and were taught it was worth it. Subsequently, we are too.

- In Paul's first letter to the church of Thessalonica, he was willing to call his life of godliness to the stand before the believers and declare God would be a witness on his behalf (1Thess. 2:10). That's boasting in bondservanthood!
- In Paul's first letter to Timothy, he instructed Timothy to *train in godliness*, said he and other leaders labor the same, and

then told him to command and teach the church to do likewise (1Tim. 4:7-11).

> *"For the training of the body has limited benefit, but godliness is beneficial in every way, since it holds promise for the present life and also for the life to come."* (1Timothy 4:8, CSB; *emphasis added*)

- In Paul's letter to Titus, he explains that the Father sent Jesus—the grace of God in the flesh—*to train us in godliness* so we can live effectively in this world, setting us apart to be His godly people zealous for good works (Tit. 2:11-14).
- Then notice in Romans 12:1-2 how Paul implores every Christian toward this end as our only acceptable response to the mercies of God.

> *"1 Therefore, I urge you, brothers and sisters, in view of God's mercy, to offer your bodies as a living sacrifice, holy and pleasing to God—this is your true and proper worship. 2 Do not conform to the pattern of this world, but be transformed by the renewing of your mind. Then you will be able to test and approve what God's will is—his good, pleasing and perfect will."* (Romans 12:1-2, NIV; *emphasis added*)

Being a bondservant of God is an earnest dedication to all things God, which then produces a life of godliness—that holy and pleasing life to God. This is our true and proper worship of Him, Paul says. Hence, this is what makes godliness godly: *wanting more of God.* The desire for God is hardwired in every beloved and begotten believer in Christ. It's there and will always be there. Jerry Bridges endearingly portrays this like such,

"True godliness engages our affections and awakens within us a desire to enjoy God's presence and fellowship. It produces a longing for God Himself."[28]

Christian, God brags on His holiness through the life of His bondservants. We are refurbished canvases He turns into His masterpieces. For we have died to our former ownership, and our new life under God's ownership is now hidden with Christ in God (Col. 3:1-4).

WHO IS PREEMINENT IN OUR LIFE?

In 2020, my wife's word for the year was "preeminent." She wanted to consciously emphasize that Jesus was preeminent at the beginning of her day and in her focus and worship throughout the day. That's a tall task, but it yielded great rewards in her life.

Preeminent is a rich word. It is not used much in our day, yet its substance is meaty. Preeminent means *superior above or before others*, whether in value, rank, importance, capability, authority, etc.[29] It's a term of classification. There's preeminent and then everything else that's not preeminent. Preeminent is only ever first place.

While the storied theme of the Bible is redemption, I believe the theological theme of the Bible is about preeminence.

- ✓ Creation theologically highlights the preeminence of its Triune Creator.
- ✓ The fall theologically highlights what happens when humanity assumes they are preeminent.
- ✓ The first advent of Christ theologically highlights the pre-eminence of the Son and the only way to an eternally satisfying life is in Him.
- ✓ The coming of the Holy Spirit theologically highlights the preeminence of God's regenerating and sanctifying work, and His indwelling presence, power, and seal for born-again believers.
- ✓ The second advent of Christ theologically highlights how God's preeminence is settled, every knee will bow and every tongue will confess Jesus Christ is Lord.

From the beginning to the first advent, God repeatedly revealed His preeminence and the rewards of worshiping Him as such. From the first advent to the second advent, God continues to reveal His preeminence and the rewards of worshiping Him but *in Christ*. And, from the fall to the second advent, God repeatedly exposes mankind's fixation and consequences of their pursuit of preeminence.

After reading over all of this, did your mind wander to what you know of the Bible? Do you see how it fits in this theological theme? For me, it's kind of hard to unsee it once you've seen it. And that was simply a snapshot of the macro-level. The micro-level, on the other hand, is far more personal.

Who's Sitting on Your Throne?

During Jesus' time on earth, He grounded His discipleship in pre-eminence. Whomever or whatever is preeminent in the life of His disciple is whom or what we are following or will follow. Notice what He explains in Matthew 10.

> "32 Everyone who acknowledges me publicly here on earth, I will also acknowledge before my Father in heaven. 33 But everyone who denies me here on earth, I will also deny before my Father in heaven. 34 Don't imagine that I came to bring peace to the earth! *I came not to bring peace, but a sword.* 35 'I have come to set a man against his father, a daughter against her mother, and a daughter-in-law against her mother-in-law. 36 Your enemies will be right in your own household!' 37 *If* you love your father or mother more than you love me, *you are not* worthy of being mine; or *if* you love your son or daughter more than me, *you are not* worthy of being mine. 38 *If* you refuse to take up your cross and follow me, *you are not* worthy of being mine. 39 *If* you cling to your life, you will lose it; *but if* you give up your life *for me,* you *will* find it." (Matthew 10:32-39, NLT; *emphasis added*)

Talk about drawing a definitive line in the sand. Jesus hit what more typically are the treasures of one's heart. He said parents and children, then in Luke 14:26 He includes siblings and spouses, and ends in Matthew 10:39 with one's self. He challenged the throne. Jesus unambiguously declared that if He is not the prime priority— one through nine—in the life of His disciples, we are not worthy of being His. If He does not sit and reign on the throne of our lives unchallenged, we are not worthy of being His.

What's more, when we fight to have control of the throne of our lives, we're fighting against the One who absorbed the wrath of God we deserved to bring us into an eternal relationship with Himself. Recall in covenantal bondservanthood that our lives are redeemed *for* one—one-way submission, one ownership, and one solitary dedication to one Master (1Cor. 8:6). Yes, that's tough to hear, tougher to follow, and may be frightful to swallow. But that's preeminence. Only One is worthy of our submission. Only One is worthy of our total dedication. Only One is worthy of our worship. Only One is worthy of the throne. When Jesus enters into the picture, things cannot and will not remain the same in the throne room of our lives.

To the one who professes to follow Jesus, to be His bondservant, Jesus didn't mince His words. He set the boundary. He drew the circle of exclusivity. If He is not preeminent in one's life, then that person does not deserve fellowship or friendship with Him nor the spiritual blessings that follow that relationship. Let's be honest here. This disqualifies all of us. No one is making it into that circle. Right? However, Jesus does not intend to condemn. His intent is to expose and challenge what's preeminent. It's sincerity over duplicity. For those who *think* they are His disciples, what's preeminent in their life may rightly expose them as not truly belonging to Jesus. For those who are *actually* born-again, Jesus challenging whatever is preeminent in our life will lead to conviction and repentance.

The stories of Judas and Peter are fitting. Judas followed Jesus but did not belong to Jesus (John 13:18-27, Matt. 26:20-25). What was preeminent in Judas' life was never Jesus; it was money (John 12:1-8, Matt. 26:14-16). Peter, similarly, followed Jesus and also denied Him (Luke 22:14-62). But unlike Judas, Peter actually belonged to Jesus (John 15:16). Thus, he repented and submitted to Jesus as preeminent in his life after being challenged and corrected (John 21:1-19). Peter's faith in Jesus was sincere, and he responded to Him as preeminent. Judas' following of Jesus was duplicitous, and he responded with his own preeminence rather than repentance, which led to suicide from his guilt (Matt. 27:1-5).

Peter is the archetype Christian. He followed and denied. We follow and deny. He was taught the preeminence boundary by Jesus and then was reminded of it before Jesus was crucified and after He resurrected. We also need to be repeatedly reminded of the pre-eminence boundary that Jesus set so we can keep repenting and resubmitting to Jesus as preeminent in our life. We act like Peter all the time, don't we? The greater travesty is when we minimize and justify the preeminence of ourselves or other people and things over Jesus or put far less effort in upholding Jesus as the preeminent One in our life. Kempis hit the nail on the head when he noted,

> "Alas, after very little recollection we falter, not weighing our deed by strict examination. We pay no attention to where our affections lie, nor do we deplore the fact that our actions are impure."[30]

Just as godliness is a marker of being a bondservant, Christ as preeminent is a marker of being a bondservant. If this marker is not present in the life of one who professes Jesus as Savior and Lord— i.e., there is no fruit of Christ's preeminence—then their profession is likely duplicitous (2Cor. 13:5).

✤ The revelation of trust.

Have you ever seen the graphic floating around online of the young child holding a teddy bear and Jesus holding an enormous teddy bear behind His back? In the picture, Jesus has His hand extended as in the gesture for the child to give Him the bear because He has a better gift in return. And, if I recall right, the caption displayed the child reluctant to give up the bear to Jesus, unknowing that what Jesus has to give in return is greater than what is being held on to. That picture perfectly captures what Jesus is explaining about preeminence: *Do you, without exception, trust My rule of your life entirely?* The things we hold as preeminent in our lives—our teddy bears—absolutely fail compared to what comes with upholding the preeminence of Jesus in our lives.

Humor me for a moment. Compare everything you have held as preeminent in your life to Jesus. Has anything ever been better to you than Jesus?

- ◆ The sin you go back to regularly that gives you that temporary fix—is it busyness, indifference, defensiveness, control, pride, lust, addictions, selfishness, so on—has that treated you better than Jesus?
- ◆ How about your spouse, parents, friends, or another relationship, has he or she or they treated you better than Jesus?
- ◆ Money or success, has that treated you better than Jesus?
- ◆ The expectations you have of what God is supposed to do for you, has that treated you better than what Jesus has actually done for you?
- ◆ What about your career or education; has that treated you better than Jesus?
- ◆ For those who champion their political party or rights as citizens, has that treated you better than Jesus?
- ◆ Has the U.S. as a country treated you better than Jesus?
- ◆ Has your ethnic culture or heritage treated you better than Jesus?
- ◆ Any causes you fight for—political, social, personal—has that cause or the beneficiaries of that cause treated you better than Jesus?
- ◆ Let's do the negative. Are the things you *don't* do that you are supposed to be doing as a Christian spouse, parent, child, sibling, friend, employee, neighbor, church member, and so on, has that lack of effort or disobedience to God treated you better than Jesus?

For born-again believers, although we do these very things probably more than we want to admit, the answer to each of these questions is a resounding "no." No one who has indeed tasted and seen the goodness of the Lord can turn around and say anything else is better.[31] However, because we do periodically place these things above Jesus, we must understand the magnitude of what it's broadcasting. Whenever we hold anything preeminent in our life other than Jesus, we declare to ourselves and everyone else that "_____" is a better Savior and Lord to us than Jesus. Ouch. What piercing this should be to all our hearts.

I remember when my mother first read my memoir. She was deeply hurt. My mom didn't realize all the things I had done and experienced. Thus, my experiences felt like an indictment of her parenting. That's not entirely wrong, but it took about a year and several conversations before she could understand it from the child's perspective, not the parent. My wife and I have three children, so I can empathize with my mom. I too would feel like I failed as a parent if I read a memoir like mine from one of my kids.

While there is never a case of failure on Jesus' part as our Savior and Lord, that's the perception being broadcasted. Whenever we hold anything else as preeminent in our lives, our living memoir at that time communicates to ourselves and others that "_____" is a better Savior and Lord to us than Jesus.

I'm not trying to provoke thoughts of an unattainable standard or evoke feelings of condemnation. We are under grace! More precisely, this is meant to arouse humility, repentance, and submission. We settle and compromise too quickly in our Christian life than we do in battling for Christ's preeminence. We often forget that grace empowers us to pursue Christ more; it does not enable us to camp out in the nebulous world of "I'm a work in progress" without actually progressing (Rom. 6:1-14). Dr. Tim Clinton captures it right, **"Grace brings freedom, but in the grand paradox of grace, it also makes us willing slaves of God."**[32] Because of grace, we are sanctified and being sanctified (Heb. 2:9-18; 10:10-25). Because of grace, we are not and will not remain the same as we were before Christ (2Cor. 3:13-18). Therefore, sometimes we need to be vividly awakened out of our spiritual slumber. Sometimes we need to be told the harsh reality that we desire our sins and selfishness more than Jesus. Sometimes we need to be reminded, **"God's grace makes a dramatic claim on our lives. We have been rescued, but we are no longer our own."**[33]

All of this brings us back to what Jesus is essentially teaching about preeminence in several discipleship passages—Matt. 10:16-39; 16:21-28; 19:16-30, Luke 14:25-33, John 12:20-26:

> "If *you do not* give up everything—not some things, but every-thing—for Me, then you will only ever possess that little teddy bear. However, if *you do* radically reprioritize your affections and strive to uphold Me above all in your life, you will gain Me and everything that comes with Me. That's bearing your cross and following after Me: constantly entrusting Me your teddy bears. For then, and only then, is when you will find out what life truly is." (my amplified paraphrase)

The one who continues to hold onto the perishing things of this life over Jesus—that which we do, desire, have, love, and live for—cannot also hold onto Him simultaneously. Hence, why Jesus said that person is not worthy of Him—i.e., is not deserving of fellow-ship or friendship with Him and the spiritual blessings that follow that relationship.[34] Again, I know that may sound harsh and/or unattainable. But that's not the sound our hearts should hear.

If this sounds harsh to you, that's because you're looking at it from a human's perspective, which is often selfish and entitled. From the Creator and Savior's point of view, it's not harsh; it's appropriate. He created us when He didn't have to. He went to extreme measures to save us when He didn't have to. Is He not then worthy of every-thing from us? Is it not then disrespectful for us to hold onto the perishing things of this life over Him?

If this sounds unattainable to you, that's because deep down inside you don't *want* to give Jesus everything. Thomas Watson puts an introspective spin on this.

> **"If we are the prizers of Christ, we cannot live without him;** *things which we value we know not how to be without.* **A man may live without music, but not without food. A child of God can**

lack health and friends, but he cannot lack Christ.... Let us test by this – *do they prize Christ who can manage well enough to be without him?*"[35]

To hold our teddy bear means we cannot hold Jesus' teddy bear. Our hands and hearts are preoccupied. We have to let go of one to receive the other. Those who trust Jesus with their teddy bears—who they are and will be, what they have and will have—in return lose nothing and rather gain the greatest treasure ever, more of Him. A.W. Tozer calls this *"the sweet theology of the heart which can be learned only in the school of renunciation."*[36] And this is not a one-time interaction, is it? Nope. We somehow manage to get them little teddy bears right back in our hands. However, because of grace, this is a recurring interaction between Jesus and us: failing and growing in our trust of Him to re-hand Him our teddy bears when we place them in His seat of preeminence in our lives.

John Calvin summarizes all of this ever so pointedly when he writes,

> "God's kindness should cause us to reflect on and delight in His goodness. But our perverse ingratitude is such that we make His kindness a means of growing ever more spoiled. Thus, we must be restrained by some discipline so that we don't break forth in obstinacy—acting wickedly because of our great wealth, becoming puffed up with pride because of honors, or growing arrogant because we possess other goods in ourselves or our circumstances. *The Lord Himself providentially opposes, conquers, and restrains the ferocity of our flesh by the medicine of the cross. He does this in ways that uniquely serve each believer's well-being."*[37]

In abandoning ourselves like instructed by Jesus, in relinquishing our entitlements and attitudes of "what's ours" or "what we deserve," in displaying our trust of Him as preeminent, we are then primed to delight in a sweet and closer companionship with our

Savior and Lord. Jesus truly becomes our everything *when* we trust Him with our everything.

> *"The man who has God for his treasure has all things in One.* Many ordinary treasures may be denied him, or if he is allowed to have them, the enjoyment of them will be so tempered that they will never be necessary to his happiness. Or if he must see them go, one after one, he will scarcely feel a sense of loss, for *having the Source of all things he has in One all satisfaction, all pleasure, all delight.* Whatever he may lose he has actually lost nothing, for he now has it all in One, and he has it purely, legitimately and forever."[38]

HOLY POSSESSIONS

Bondservanthood is not about perfection. Perfection means no mistakes, no defects, no imperfections. But we make mistakes. We wrestle with numerous character defects. We are clearly imperfect. Thus, bondservanthood is in no way about perfection. It's about possession. *We wholly belong to God.*

From Old Testament to New Testament, God has unashamedly declared His covenant people His treasure, His special holy possession.[39]

> "6 For you are a holy people belonging to the Lord your God. *The Lord your God has chosen you to be his own possession out of all the peoples on the face of the earth.* 7 The Lord had his heart set on you and chose you, not because you were more numerous than all peoples, for you were the fewest of all peoples. 8 But because the Lord loved you and kept the oath he swore to your ancestors, he brought you out with a strong hand and redeemed you from the place of slavery, from the power of Pharaoh king of Egypt." (Deuteronomy 7:6-8, CSB; *emphasis added*)

> "8 When He had taken the scroll, the four living creatures and the twenty-four elders fell down before the Lamb, each one holding a harp and golden bowls full of incense, which are the prayers of the

saints. 9 And they sang a new song, saying, "Worthy are You to take the scroll and to break its seals; for You were slaughtered, and *You purchased people for God with Your blood* from every tribe, language, people, and nation. 10 You have made them into a kingdom and priests to our God, and they will reign upon the earth."" (Revelation 5:9-10, NASB; *emphasis added*)

I'm not sure how you receive that, but it blows me away. God's people are God's prize! We are Jesus' treasure! This is why Scripture repeatedly explains God as jealous for His people and abhorring idolatry because His people are His purchased prize. And, as if it couldn't get any better, it does. Under the new covenant, believers are now God's temple!

"16 Don't you yourselves know that you are God's temple and that the Spirit of God lives in you? 17 If anyone destroys God's temple, God will destroy him; for God's temple is holy, and that is what you are." (1Corinthians 3:16-17, CSB)

God wanted His people in His presence so much that He gave the best of Himself to make that happen. First, He sent the Son to die for our sins so we can be made holy and able to enter His personal presence forever. Second, He sent the Holy Spirit to dwell within us to make us holy and be among His presence all the time. Think about that, the Spirit of God turns our mortal, fallen frames into a sacred place when He indwells us.

Remember, our bondservanthood is *the characterization of a willing and intimate spiritual servanthood to God where one's heart, mind, will, and body is under the authority of God.* Bondservanthood is not brute subjugation. It is possession as God's cherished treasure and is to be reciprocated in us. The presence of the Holy Spirit means our intimate spiritual servanthood is a holy possession for God. The Spirit's role is to work in and through our broken vessels and fallible submission unto the glory of God.

I need you to use your imagination here. Think of us as a holey water pitcher. No matter how much liquid we have, it will leak out because the pitcher is damaged. These holes represent the sin and deficiencies we were born into and struggle with while we're in this fallen earthly frame. Enter Christ and the Holy Spirit. In this illustration, Christ is a much larger pitcher and the Holy Spirit is the water. Our salvation places our holey pitcher inside Jesus' all-encompassing shatterproof pitcher. Furthermore, our salvation grants us the indwelling presence of the Spirit who unceasingly pours into our holey pitcher. As redeemed bondservants, our pitchers are now the possession of God. He holds the handle to use this damaged pitcher however He desires, which means our part will still be messy and inadequate—(picture water leaking out on God's hands as He uses our pitcher). Nevertheless, since we're in Christ's pitcher, it catches whatever leaks out, and the Holy Spirit recycles that water while continually adding freshwater because nothing is lost in Christ.

Can you picture this illustration in your mind? That's possession, Christian. And what makes this possession holy is two things: One, we are never not in the presence of God. We are always in Christ and the Spirit is always in us. Two, our bondservanthood is for God's use and glory. Our life has been purchased at a price, and we are now God's prized instruments, reserved for His sanctifying sacred use unto His glory—He's the Potter, we're the clay.

> "How good it is to have the consciousness that we belong to the Lord and are not our own. There is nothing more precious in the world. It is that which brings the awareness of his continual presence, and the reason is obvious. *I must first have the sense of God's possession of me before I can have the sense of his presence with me.* When once his ownership is established, then I dare do nothing in my own interests, for I am his exclusive property."[40]

Power to Succeed

Apart from the Holy Spirit, we are inadequate for God in every way (Rom. 8:5-15, 1Cor. 2:1-16). Thus, to be God's holy possession means we have been regenerated, sealed, and empowered by the Holy Spirit to be and do what we can't without Him. If you do comic books, comic cartoons, or have seen any Marvel movie from 2008-2019, think Captain America. Without the super-soldier serum, Captain America is just plain ol' Steve Rogers. Wholly inadequate as a superhero. That's us apart from the Spirit. What it takes to be *with* God, to be *used by* God, and to *live for* God requires the supernatural. Notice how Peter starts his second epistle,

> "1 From Simeon Peter, a slave and apostle of Jesus Christ, to those who through the righteousness of our God and Savior, Jesus Christ, *have been granted a faith* just as precious as ours. 2 May grace and peace be lavished on you as you grow in the rich knowledge of God and of Jesus our Lord! 3 I can pray this *because his divine power has bestowed on us everything necessary for life and godliness* through the rich knowledge of the one who called us by his own glory and excellence. 4 Through these things he has bestowed on us his precious and most magnificent promises, *so that by means of what was promised you may become partakers of the divine nature*, after escaping the worldly corruption that is produced by evil desire. *5 For this very reason, make every effort to add* to your faith excellence, to excellence, knowledge; 6 to knowledge, self-control; to self-control, perseverance; to perseverance, godliness; 7 to godliness, brotherly affection; to brotherly affection, unselfish love. *8 For if these things are really yours and are continually increasing, they will keep you from becoming ineffective and unproductive in your pursuit of knowing our Lord Jesus Christ more intimately.*" (2Peter 1:1-8, NET; *emphasis added*)

Peter's reference in verse 3 to Jesus' "divine power" is regarding the working of the Holy Spirit (Luke 24:49, Acts 1:8). Did you catch what this "divine power" produces? It's the result of this divine power that we've become partakers of the divine nature. It's this divine power that provides us with everything we need for life and godliness. Moreover, it's only after having this divine power bestowed upon us are we able to build upon the saving faith that has been granted to us through the righteousness of Jesus. Apart from the working of the Spirit, we are inadequate for God in every way. We were dominated by the corruption of this world produced by evil desire. However, because of the Spirit indwelling us, we can now build upon our faith and continually increase our pursuit of knowing our Lord more intimately as His bondservants.

Covenantal bondservanthood separate from the grace of God is impractical and leads to vexation (Gal. 3:10-14, Jam. 2:10). But with the Holy Spirit, we become something more. We become a "super-soldier" that's supernaturally enabled to be used by God and for God as His bondservants. The Holy Spirit fills in our deficiencies and supplies us with everything we will need to joyfully submit, live a godly life, and accomplish whatever and however God chooses to use us. The Holy Spirit is our "super-soldier serum." He takes what's inadequate and makes us suitable holy possessions of God.

Not Without a Fight

As Christians, we're all well aware that just because we're God's possession does not mean we're free from resistance—internally and externally. We live in a dual reality. We belong to God and we also live within a fallen frame in a fallen world. Our flesh and the world try to tell us we can do whatever we want and believe whatever we want. Many times we agree with it and do so. Yet, we have been redeemed. Our life belongs to God. We are slaves of Christ. We don't get to do what we want. We do what God wants. We don't get to believe what we want. We believe God's truth according to His Word. He is our Master. Therefore, we have to remind ourselves and submit to our new reality constantly. Our brother Watchman Nee, again, captures this well.

> "My giving of myself to the Lord must be an initial fundamental act. Then, day by day, *I must go on giving to him, not finding fault with his use of me, but accepting with praise even what the flesh finds hard*. That way lies true enrichment. I am the Lord's, and now no longer reckon myself to be my own but acknowledge in everything his ownership and authority. That is the attitude God delights in, and to maintain it is true consecration."[41]

While we know this and continue to grow in our knowledge of this, so does our enemy. And our enemy is clever. Since the end of the 20th century and the dawn of the 21st century, our enemy adjusted his tactic. Today, his target of attack is our allegiance—are we going to openly and continually declare ourselves as God's possession, as God's bondservants, or are we going to cave into social pressure and believe what the world says and teaches. The culture, in whichever direction any segment may be leaning, they all now assert: *"agree with me, or you're my enemy"*; *"tolerate my view— regardless if I tolerate yours—or you're my enemy."* That's a challenge for allegiance. American society regularly challenges Christians to do or say or choose based on what it approves, or they threaten to persecute us by way of ostracizing us, and/or sabotaging us, and/or boycotting us, and/or hounding and ridiculing us wherever the public square is. This isn't new to the global Church across history to the present, but it is newer to Christians in the U.S. in the decade of 2020.

Brethren, don't be manipulated or intimidated to deny being God's possession. Only God truly treasures us and proved it. This world doesn't, our family doesn't, our friends don't, our fans don't. Only God identifies us as His special people and proved it. Society and the culture identify us according to whatever is their agenda. Our redeemed nature affords us the privileged obligation of being God's bondservants. Our fleshly nature wants nothing but enslavement to sin and death. Don't be manipulated or intimidated to deny being God's possession. The alternative is to be the possession of what desires to destroy us. So, with the power of the Holy Spirit, we have to be vigilant to *not* sell out God or our allegiance to Him for acceptance from this wicked world, from its unstable societies, and from its capricious cultures. Instead, by the Spirit, we have to be vigilant *in* treasuring God and His possession of us no matter the cost.

To be a bondservant of the Lord is to be an unashamed worshiper of the Lord in everything and everywhere. And this is merited, seeing what we *were* once slaves of and *now* Who we are slaves to. Bondservanthood is a one-track mind fixated on Jesus and violently fights anything that would come between it. We should not be hiding or justifying sin. We should not constantly cave into whatever is around us, tempting us away from God. Again, this doesn't mean we won't battle and fall to these things at times. But being Spirit-filled bondservants means we *can* admit to these things without condemnation, we *can* repent from these things without question, and we *can* abstain from these things without fear. This proceeds from knowing who our Master now is and who our previous master once was. Christian, amid the resistance we face within ourselves and in this world, let us be known more for God's possession of our lives as His bondservants over everything else.

Now What?

In January 2000, I joined the United States Marine Corps. Entirely the providence of God. Total lifesaver. I learned so many lessons. Of course, it wasn't until after I got saved that I saw several parallels between being a Christian and being in the military.

As Marines, regardless if we're in peacetime, we are trained for wartime. Part of our training consist of submitting and following our chain of command, top-down. From the Commander in Chief in the White House to whichever NCO or Staff NCO is in the squadron, soldiers submit and follow orders. No soldier from any branch is a doormat, nor are they blind followers. The reason soldiers submit to their chain of command, even if they don't always agree or understand the order, is that their lives and other lives may depend on it during wartime. Options are for games. Discipline is for life. This is the way of the military.

Do you see the parallel between the military and being Christian? Apostle Paul did. He told Timothy,

"3 Share in suffering as a *good soldier of Christ Jesus.* 4 No one serving *as a soldier* gets entangled in the concerns of civilian life; he seeks to please the commanding officer." (2Timothy 2:3-4, CSB; *emphasis added*)

As bondservants of the Lord, we are very much spiritual soldiers enlisted into the Creator's work in our lives and the world (locally to globally). Just as military members take an oath of allegiance to our country, bondservanthood is our oath of allegiance to God over everything. No matter the branch of military each soldier pledges themselves to the same oath:

> "I, _____, do solemnly swear (or affirm) that I will support and defend the Constitution of the United States against all enemies, foreign and domestic; that I will bear true faith and allegiance to the same; and that I will obey the orders of the President of the United States and the orders of the officers appointed over me, according to regulations and the Uniform Code of Military Justice. So help me God."[42]

Similarly, every bondservant of Christ pledges themselves to the same oath as well.

> Covenantal bondservanthood is *the willing and intimate spiritual servanthood to God where one's heart, mind, will, and body is under the authority of God*—in joyful submission, devoted to a life of godliness, trusting Christ's rule over our life as preeminent, and set-apart as His holy possessions.

For a Marine like myself, I see these parallels and get pumped up. I get the relationship of how this works. I understand the consequences and benefits that follow immediately and in the long run. But not all believers get excited about their bondservanthood. In fact, from the churches I've pastored, to the professing Christians I know personally, to the professing Christians I see online, here's what I observed: *Many professing American Christians don't live their lives with their bondservanthood in mind.* I wonder how many are even aware or care that this is our identity in Christ. I see few and only know a remnant of believers whose lives proudly profess to be a slave of Christ. What about you? How many do you see and know? Would you consider this to be true of yourself?

If we're honest, the crux of why bondservanthood is foreign to so many Christians is they don't really want to own and live from the identity of wholly belonging to God. Our bondservant identity directly targets the authority and allegiance of our life. Too many of us have become entangled in the civilian affairs of this life. Frankly, it's pitiful when Christians are better bondservants of something else than they are of God while arguing how they can't live like this for God. Indeed, distraction is a killer of dedication. What did Jesus say in the parable of the sower? Good seeds can be choked out by the cares of this world and the deceitfulness of wealth (Matt. 13:22). Too many believers are consumed with whatsoever other than God. It would appear that everything else is more interesting than being a slave of Christ.

Bondservanthood confronts this faulty kind of thinking forthrightly. To be a bondservant of the Lord means we are no longer the ruler of our life, no longer the sun of our solar system. There's a new Commander in Chief, and it's not us, someone else, or anything else. Our salvation in Christ pledged us in a blood oath allegiance to Christ, for we were bought at a price.

Therefore, like soldiers, bondservants aim to please our Commander in Chief, Christ Jesus, above all else. We don't do so because we signed a contract like the military. We do because our Savior signed a contract for our eternity in His blood. It's from the gratitude of our salvation and love for our Savior that we aim to please Him. For as Calvin rightly expresses, *"Godly affection strives after obedience to the divine will."*[43] Think about it, we have been redeemed *by* Jesus *for* Jesus; we have been delivered *from* God's enemy and *from* God's judgment *for* God's pleasure. What greater aim or person to please is there for the Christian?

Also, like soldiers, bondservants serve and live for our Commander in Chief and His kingdom during wartime, not peacetime. Peacetime is our eternity with Christ. It's been wartime on this earth since Adam sinned in the Garden. Hence, we're equipped by the Holy Spirit to submit to Jesus' Lordship and follow His orders amid hostility—to include when we don't always agree or understand the orders—because our lives and other lives depend on it. Since our God knows all and works it all together for His glory and our good, why would we ignore His authority or order? For when we do, we return to Adam and Eve's sin and believe the lie of the serpent, giving into his temptation to be "like God."

Christian, let us not squander our bondservanthood for a purposeless and powerless life by being entangled in the affairs of this world. Let us not take the freedom we now have in Christ and willingly return to pleasing our old ownership with it. Our whole life belongs to God as a holy offering with a sweet-smelling aroma to Him. Every area. Every nook and cranny. Nothing is off-limits *to* God or *for* God. Be excited to be God's bondservant! If our life isn't safe and best used in the Master's hands, it will never be safe or best utilized anywhere outside His hands.

> "If there were nothing else to do but praise the Lord God with all your heart and voice, if you have never to eat, or drink, or sleep, but could praise God always and occupy yourself solely with spiritual pursuits, how much happier you would be than you are now, a slave to every necessity of the body! Would that there were no such needs, but only the spiritual refreshments of the soul which, sad to say, we taste too seldom! *When a man reaches a point where he seeks no solace from any creature, then he begins to relish God perfectly. Then also he will be content no matter what may happen to him.* He will neither rejoice over great things nor grieve over small ones, but *will place himself entirely and confidently in the hands of God,* Who for him is all in all, to Whom nothing ever perishes or dies, for Whom all things lives, and Whom they serve as He desires. *Always remember your end, and do not forget that lost time never returns.*"[44]

CHAPTER 3

Sojourners

My wife is a professional photographer. The week leading to her 39th birthday, she did a maternity shoot for my second little sister, pregnant with her first child. After the photoshoot, the three of us went to dinner at Olive Garden. It was fun to spend some one-on-one time with my little sister. I used to do that with her when she was a teenager. She would come to our home and hang out for days.

When we dropped my sister off, my wife remarked about her living situation. She was pondering that my siblings would probably come over more if we were in our own house because wherever we've lived had always been a safe place for them. This turned into an insightful conversation on our drive home. Along the way, my wife made a perceptive statement about us. She said, "We've been a transient family for so long."

My wife and I have three children and have been married now for twenty years. We've bounced around a lot over these twenty years. (I, myself, grew up bouncing around. The only home that was ever stable was my grandparents). We lived in Baltimore City, MD, and in the suburbs of Baltimore County for about five years. We rotated being homeless and living with others throughout those five years until we got into an apartment.

After those five years, we moved to California and lived in a city called Hemet for a year. It was high heat, cows, and mountains. Yup, hot and smelly. Then we moved to Los Angeles for another year and some change. We lived about a stone's throw from USC. Later, we migrated to the suburbs of East Los Angeles County for four years, but not before sleeping on people's couches with a family of five until a new place presented itself.

Those four years were significant in our journeying. Afterward, we made our way to Bakersfield, CA, for four more years. That time in Bakersfield, though socially and culturally challenging, was surprisingly rewarding. Finally, the Lord called us back to Maryland. This time to live on the border of Baltimore County and Carroll County—two counties that could not be any more culturally opposite.

I'll never forget what my oldest son told me when he was in seventh grade. "Daddy, I've been to seven schools in seven years." That cut me deep. His youthful comment filtered through my adult ears: *we hadn't given him stability*. The reasons we moved varied. The costs we endured were inestimable. The lessons we learned, immeasurable. Nonetheless, my wife was spot on. We were a transient family.

What we didn't realize until later in life, God mightily and advantageously used our transient seasons to expose, educate, realign, redefine, humble, and mature us. Our transience wasn't categorically bad. It was simply a matter of fact, a reality with much more significant meaning and implications than our experiences of being a transient family.

THE TRANSIENT BEGINNINGS OF GOD'S PEOPLE

In Scripture, we see another family like this, the family of Abraham, Isaac, and Jacob. Before entering the promised land, the people God chose for Himself would start out nomadic. They, too, would be transient. Abraham lived in Ur of the Chaldeans (Gen. 11:31). For around the next six to seven hundred years, the family of Abraham, Isaac, and Jacob moved and lived throughout the Mediterranean region in Asia Minor and Egypt.

"2 And God said to Moses, "I am Yahweh—'the Lord.' 3 I appeared to Abraham, to Isaac, and to Jacob as El-Shaddai—'God Almighty'— but I did not reveal my name, Yahweh, to them. 4 And I reaffirmed my covenant with them. Under its terms, I promised to give them *the land of Canaan, where they were living as foreigners.*" (Exodus 6:2-4, NLT; *emphasis added*)

From Genesis 11 on, we can read and assess their journey of being transient. Not sure if you've read Genesis. Wowzers. Talk about drama. A transient life is not without dramatics in the details, unsuspecting interjections, plot twists in the storyline, progressive or regressive character development, so on. Reading Genesis, then reflecting on my story and others, makes me wonder if God designed a transient component in humanity. Ecclesiastes does say, *"Everything on earth has its own time and its own season."*[1]

The transient story of the family of Abraham, Isaac, and Jacob doesn't conclude in Genesis, does it? Their exodus from Egypt and additional forty years in the wilderness of Sinai and Paran is also part of their story of transience. God called this from the very beginning.

"Then the Lord said to [Abram], "Know for certain that for four hundred years your descendants will be strangers in a country not their own and that they will be enslaved and mistreated there." (Genesis 15:13, NIV; brackets added)

Transience in God's Economy

God doesn't waste His people's experiences in His economy. I'm not sure how many of us have ever realized that the contents of Exodus to Deuteronomy took place while the people were in transit. The law of God came to the people of God not when they were settled but when they were transient.

"*1 In the third month from the very day the Israelites left the land of Egypt, they came to the Sinai Wilderness. 2 They traveled from Rephidim,* came to the Sinai Wilderness, and camped in the wilderness. *Israel camped there in front of the mountain.* 3 Moses went up the mountain to God, and the Lord called to him from the mountain: "This is what you must say to the house of Jacob and explain to the Israelites: 4 'You have seen what I did to the Egyptians and how I carried you on eagles' wings and brought you to myself. 5 Now if you will carefully listen to me and keep my covenant, you will be my own possession out of all the peoples, although the whole earth is mine, 6 and you will be my kingdom of priests and my holy nation.' These are the words that you are to say to the Israelites.."... 10 and the Lord told Moses, "Go to the people and consecrate them today and tomorrow. They must wash their clothes 11 and be prepared by the third day, *for on the third day the Lord will come down on Mount Sinai in the sight of all the people.*" (Exodus 19:1-6, 10-11, CSB; *emphasis added*)

God gave every command, instruction, warning, and blessing from Exodus 20 to Leviticus 27 while the people of God camped at Mount Sinai (Lev. 26:34). During Numbers and Deuteronomy, they move closer toward the promised land. They pick up and set down camp along the way while continuing to receive more commands, corrections, instructions, warnings, and promised blessings from God. Even here in the Old Testament, we see God demonstrating some good ol' discipleship on the go.

Interestingly, situated in the laws God gave Moses, we find traces of Him reminding His people of their transience. Of course, this made me wonder why? But God knows best what His people need to be reminded of and why. God, through Moses, uses Israel's transient family heritage and their recent exodus experiences to anchor how they are to treat others and how they are not to live unenlightened when they settle in the promised land.

"*Do not* mistreat or oppress a foreigner, *for you were foreigners in Egypt.*" (Exodus 22:21, NIV; *emphasis added*)

"*Do not* oppress a foreigner; you yourselves know how it feels to be foreigners, *because you were foreigners in Egypt.*" (Exodus 23:9, NIV; *emphasis added*)

"17 For the Lord your God is the God of gods and Lord of lords. He is the great God, the mighty and awesome God, who shows no partiality and cannot be bribed. 18 He ensures that orphans and widows receive justice. He shows love to the foreigners living among you and gives them food and clothing. *19 So you, too, must show love to foreigners, for you yourselves were once foreigners in the land of Egypt.*" (Deuteronomy 10:17-19, NLT; *emphasis added*)

"17 True justice must be given to foreigners living among you and to orphans, and you must never accept a widow's garment as security for her debt. 18 *Always remember that you were slaves in Egypt and that the Lord your God redeemed you from your slavery.* That is why I have given you this command. 19 When you are harvesting your crops and forget to bring in a bundle of grain from your field, don't go back to get it. Leave it for the foreigners, orphans, and widows. Then the Lord your God will bless you in all you do. 20 When you beat the olives from your olive trees, don't go over the boughs twice. Leave the remaining olives for the foreigners, orphans, and widows. 21 When you gather the grapes in your vineyard, don't glean the vines after they are picked. Leave the remaining grapes for the foreigners, orphans, and widows. 22 *Remember that you were slaves in the land of Egypt.* That is why I am giving you this command." (Deuteronomy 24:17-22, NLT; *emphasis added*)

In Exodus, and then in Deuteronomy, right before the Israelites are about to enter the promised land, God has Moses compare them to the foreigners among them because they were once foreigners. God is reminding His people who they once were, where they once were, and how they once lived, so they don't mistreat the foreigner. "Remember, Israelites, you used to be foreigners in Egypt. Remember your family's heritage, Israelites, you've spent hundreds of years as a nomadic people." Whether they realized it or not, or even wanted to accept this fact, the Israelites could relate to the foreigner.

✦ Lessons from transience.

There is a dual emphasis by God through Moses to His people here in these passages. The first is in the positive: *recall compassion to respond with compassion.* As the Israelites received grace, mercy, and compassion from God throughout their transient history, they were to extend the same to those not born from their people but living among their people. As ye have received, ye shall give. Jesus echoes the same point to the disciples in a parable,

> "32 Then, after he had summoned him, his master said to him, 'You wicked servant! I forgave you all that debt because you begged me. 33 Shouldn't you also have had mercy on your fellow servant, as I had mercy on you?'" (Matthew 18:32-33, CSB; *emphasis added*)

The second is an implied warning: *don't settle in the provision and forget where you came from.* God is the one who made sure the Israelites entered the promised land. God even tells Moses that after all He has done, is doing, and will do for His people, they will nevertheless rebel against Him and bring judgment upon themselves (Deut. 31:16-21). Yet in still, God provides what He promised. Every time God reminds the Israelites of the past He brought them from, that is a warning to them not to forget what they have and where they are is not by their own doing but by His hand alone.

Sometimes forgetfulness is evidence of entitlement. For example, the former adult generation that came out of Egypt were eyewitnesses of the Divine, but they missed the promise. Whereas the latter adult generation about to enter the promised land—and the subsequent generations born in the promised land—will inherit a privilege the former generations didn't possess, but they won't see the Divine at work. Thus, the presence of foreigners is to serve as a reminder of where they came from and help them remain humble while they settle and live in what God has blessed them with—a fulfilled promise they inherited.

Later in Deuteronomy, after issuing the blessings for covenant obedience and curses for covenant disobedience, God through Moses uses their transient experiences for another educational warning.

> "16 You yourselves *know how* we lived in Egypt *and how* we passed through the countries on the way here. 17 You *saw* among them their detestable images and idols of wood and stone, of silver and gold. 18 *Make sure* there is no man or woman, clan or tribe among

you today whose heart turns away from the Lord our God to go and worship the gods of those nations; *make sure* there is no root among you that produces such bitter poison." (Deuteronomy 29:16-18, NIV; *emphasis added*)

The transience of the Israelites afforded them a unique window into how other countries and people groups lived and worshiped, which contrasted how the children of Israel were truly being set-apart as God's special people. Oftentimes, the beauty and benefit of holiness is better realized when measured to the ugliness and detriment of unholiness. Have you ever said or heard, "You don't know what you have until it's gone"? What are we communicating when we say this? We often don't know how good something is until something bad or less good comes along and accentuates the good we overlooked or discounted. The transience of the Israelites living as foreigners in Egypt and as nomads post-Egypt—as they journeyed to the promised land—highlighted God's holiness revealed to them and called to be among them by the unholiness they saw and experienced. "Israel, you know firsthand, you saw firsthand, so make sure not to follow their wickedness; don't even entertain it."

What beginnings for the people of God! The calling of Abraham coincided with the calling to a nomadic life for himself, Isaac, and Jacob. God later gives Israel His law during their exodus from Egypt. Then, God also used their transient experiences as a teaching tool for how they are to live and treat those who would be in a similar social status as they once were, and how to spot what's despicable in His sight because He pointed it out as they traveled. Transience is in the roots of God's people, and He didn't waste a single one of their experiences.

ALL OF GOD'S PEOPLE ARE SOJOURNERS

The transient, nomadic, resident alien beginnings of the people of God are descriptives of *life as sojourners*. "Sojourner," like beloved, begotten, and bondservant, is not a term we use often. Of the 204 times the three Hebrew terms for "sojourner" are used in the Old

Testament,[2] they're usually translated into about four different words: *alien, foreigner, immigrant,* and *stranger.* In the core and contextual meanings of these three Hebrew terms for "sojourner," they all convey *temporary dwelling, whether long-term or short-term, distinguished from a native and without inclusive rights.*

To be a sojourner is to be a guest, not the homeowner, not the living resident. This is who the people of God were in the Old Testament before they entered the promised land. And, paradoxically, this was true for that first generation who did enter the promised land and took ownership of regions they did not originally establish or cultivate. Furthermore, this is also who they were after their exile from their land. Thus, the people of God in the Old Testament spent more time as sojourners than they did as residents of the promised land of Israel.

The portrayal of the people of God in the Old Testament as sojourners is not for them alone. Sojourner is a marker of all God's people, past, present, and future. While the Old Testament is littered with sojourner language, that's not the case in the New Testament. The Greek term for "sojourner" is only used a handful of times. There are two Greek terms used and both of their meanings convey *temporary dwelling as non-natives; foreigners from another land residing in a place that's not their homeland.*[3]

Of the handful of times "sojourner" is used in the New Testament, two of them are referencing the people of God in the Old Testament (Acts 7:6, 29, Heb. 11:13). Two more are referencing the dispersed Christians at that time and how to live while scattered (1Pet. 1:1; 2:11). The last one references how we were to God's kingdom before we were redeemed (Eph. 2:19). Notwithstanding the minimal usage of the term, the concept of believers "sojourning" here on earth is taught in multiple places. Thus, the New Testament further explains and applies God's people as sojourners without stating the term "sojourner." It's almost as if the New Testament writers assume it is common knowledge that God's people are sojourners, hence no need to state the obvious.

From Old to New, there is no change with the meaning of the term "sojourner"; neither is there much difference with God's people under the old covenant or the new covenant in being sojourners. Sojourner is a marker of all God's people, past, present, and future.

The Promise Land: on Earth or with God?

Depending on your age, you might have watched the 1980s cult classic "E.T." I remember watching that movie as an adult and recalling how it freaked me out when I was younger, but I couldn't stop watching it. Other than E.T. calling for "Elliot" as one of the more memorable lines of the movie, most fans can clearly remember "E.T. go home" with the finger point. And if you're anything like me, you probably read that under your breath in your best E.T. impersonation. Those who've seen the movie know why he says this. The very name he is called, E.T., stands for extra-terrestrial. His name is demonstrative of where he's from, which is not earth.

Guess what? Christians are no different than E.T.

God's people as sojourners are indicative of to Whom they belong. If the covenant people belong to God, then where God resides is where their true home is; and that's regardless of which covenant they are under because it's the same God who established the covenant with His people. Therefore, across every age, wherever the covenant people of God lived and live while on earth will always be temporary. We will always be the foreigners, the strangers, the non-natives because our true home is with our Covenant God.

The Holy Spirit in the book of Hebrews tells us that even though the Old Testament people of God were always looking ahead to the promised land or after exile looking to return to the promised land, it was actually never intended to be their true home. The promised land was a designated earthly location for the Israelites but not a permanent place for all of God's covenant people. The promised land was a foreshadow of God's heavenly homeland for all of His beloved and begotten children.

"13 All these people died still believing what God had promised them. They did not receive what was promised, but they saw it all from a distance and welcomed it. They agreed that they were foreigners and nomads here on earth. 14 Obviously people who say such things are looking forward to a country they can call their own. 15 If they had longed for the country they came from, they could have gone back. *16 But they were looking for a better place, a heavenly homeland. That is why God is not ashamed to be called their God, for he has prepared a city for them.*" (Hebrews 11:13-16, NLT; *emphasis added*)

Under the new covenant, our promise land is rightly understood as the same "promise" for God's children in the Old Testament, that is, not any earthly homeland but a heavenly one.

"18 *You have not come* to a physical mountain, to a place of flaming fire, darkness, gloom, and whirlwind, as the Israelites did at Mount Sinai. 19 For they heard an awesome trumpet blast and a voice so terrible that they begged God to stop speaking. 20 They staggered back under God's command: "If even an animal touches the mountain, it must be stoned to death." 21 Moses himself was so frightened at the sight that he said, "I am terrified and trembling." 22 *No, you have come to Mount Zion, to the city of the living God, the heavenly Jerusalem*, and to countless thousands of angels in a joyful gathering. 23 You have come to the assembly of God's firstborn children, whose names are written *in heaven. You have come to God himself*, who is the judge over all things. You have come to the spirits of the righteous ones *in heaven* who have now been made perfect. 24 *You have come to Jesus*, the one who mediates the new covenant between God and people, and to the sprinkled blood, which speaks of forgiveness instead of crying out for vengeance like the blood of Abel." (Hebrew 12:18-24, NLT; *emphasis added*)

After Adam disobeyed God and ushered sin and death everywhere in this creation, the earth ceased from being our home. God's redeemed people past, present, and future have been and will always be sojourners on earth until we reside with God where He is. Ergo, the Christian's eternity with Christ is our promise land (John 14:1-3; 17:24).

↳ We are guests.

Our time here on earth is as guests, not homeowners. We are passing through, not planting roots. Regarding the ever-changing currents of society and the culture, our time here is as foreigners not natives. Society's culture is of this world, and we are not. Hence, we will always be foreigners to the culture. *Always*.

James, in his letter, speaks more forcefully and says that we place ourselves in opposition to God when we are friends or seek to be friends with the world (Jam. 4:4). It's the trojan horse tactic. Many Christians desire to befriend the very society and culture that only welcomes them to unleash a hidden agenda for their selfish gain and the erosion of our Faith. **"The gifts of the ungodly are often attached to deadly strings."**[4] For example, Dr. Howard Vos, when recounting what believers were facing in the 3rd century, writes, **"Evidence shows that the design was not to destroy Christians but to reconvert them to the state cult."**[5] Early church father Augustine of Hippo, in his classic work "City of God," warned believers in the 5th century after Roman Emperor Constantine wooed them, and when the city of Rome was crumbling, that **"the citizens of the earthly city prefer their own gods."**[6] Then later he traces believers' foreigner status with earthly societies and cultures to Cain and Abel. He explains that Cain killing Abel was somewhat foreshadowing for God's people as sojourners **"what iniquitous persecutions [they] would suffer at the hands of wicked and, as it were, earth-born men, who love their earthly origin, and delight in the earthly happiness of the earthly city."**[7] What I tell you? We will *always* be foreigners to the culture.

We must understand, we became citizens of a new home-land *when* we became born-again. It was not optional. Our former citizenship on earth *with* the world's ways has been exchanged for our new citizenship *in* Christ and His ways. Dr. John Walvoord notes,

> **"Because of the new union and new position of the Christian,"** our **"former association with the world is altered, and by grace**

the Christian may be delivered from the power of the world system, though remaining in the world and being subject to its government."[8]

"18 "If the world hates you, keep in mind that it hated me first. 19 *If you belonged to the world, it would love you as its own. As it is, you do not belong to the world, but I have chosen you out of the world.* That is why the world hates you." (John 15:18-19, NIV; *emphasis added*)

"14 I have given them your word and the world has hated them, for *they are not of the world any more than I am of the world.* 15 My prayer is not that you take them out of the world but that you protect them from the evil one. *16 They are not of the world, even as I am not of it.*" (John 17:14-16, NIV; *emphasis added*)

"*20 Our citizenship is in heaven, and we eagerly wait for a Savior from there, the Lord Jesus Christ.* 21 He will transform the body of our humble condition into the likeness of his glorious body, by the power that enables him to subject everything to himself." (Philippians 3:20-21, CSB; *emphasis added*)

"12 And you will joyfully give thanks to the Father who has *made you able to have a share in all that he has prepared for his people in the kingdom of light. 13 God has freed us from the power of darkness, and he brought us into the kingdom of his dear Son.*" (Colossians 1:12-13, NCV; *emphasis added*)

The new, naturalized citizenship believers have been reborn into is not of this world because our God and Savior is not of this world. Moreover, for those whom the Holy Spirit has truly regenerated, God **"has inspired us with a love which makes us covet its citizenship."**[9] Therefore, as we live in this world—from the U.S. to other countries—we live as sojourners until we enter our promise land where our God and Savior resides.

CITIZENSHIP AS SOJOURNERS

For believers living in the U.S., whether we want to admit this or not, comprehending ourselves as non-natives, as foreigners, is tougher than it reads. Historically to presently, citizenship in the U.S. has been treated and acted on by professing Christians as sacredly as is being Christian, probably more so for some. If you have ever heard or said, "America is/was a Christian nation," you have proved the point. Sociology scholars Emerson and Smith pinpoint this wonderfully,

> "Many American values—freedom, individualism, independence, equality of opportunity, privacy, and the like—derive *largely from the confluence of evangelical Protestant Christianity and Enlightenment philosophy*, within the context of conditions encountered in the new world. Like a smoothly blended soup, the flavors of American values so well combined these traditions that both evangelical Christians and secularists could ladle from the same kettle. Historically, evangelical Protestantism was an "insider" religion, and was the mainstream religion for the first century and a quarter of American history."[10]

News flash, America is not and never was a Christian nation or country. Go look up the definition of "nation" and "country." The *only* "Christian nation" that exists *is* the Church, which *is* the Body of Christ. The U.S. was not a country of people purely established on biblical principles. The *only* country of people founded solely on biblical principles was the covenant people Israel. The Law (the Torah) was their actual God-prescribed constitution for them as a nation. The U.S. cannot claim to be a "Christian nation" founded on biblical principles and then slaughter, purchase, steal, enslave, and malign different people groups for colonial and economic advancement.[11] That's wicked, not Christian. Did "Judeo-Christian" principles and values influence the foundation of the U.S.? Certainly, in some ways. Has God sovereignly brought about and used the U.S.? Undoubtedly! However, what God allows and uses does not mean He claims it as His own possession. In the Old Testament, we see God used other nations as His instrument of discipline against His people in one season that He would later righteously judge for their wickedness in another season. But none of those nations did God ever claim as His people. They were simply nations He used for His purposes.

The seeds of this thinking that the U.S.A. is a Christian nation were planted by the countries that colonized America. What happened is the European colonists—France, Spain, Great Britain—were incognizant of a deeply embedded old heresy regarding the union of the Church and the State. In many ways, that has continued to this day. Many believers treat American citizenship reminiscently of how Christianity was first introduced in Armenia at the beginning of the 4th century and how the Church was with the Roman Empire in the late 4th century.

It is said that King Tiridates of Armenia became Christian and then made all his citizens become Christian as well.[12] George Thomas Kurian declared, **"Armenia is the oldest Christian nation in the world."**[13] Afterward, membership with the Catholic Church was citizenship with Rome, and vice-versa.

> "This New Testament faith became harder to recognize after Constantine embraced the faith.... By the year 325, when the Council of Nicaea made the alliance of church and empire clear for all to see, the nature of faith had been severely corrupted."[14]

> "Christianity's uniquely diverse constituency afforded Constantine a mechanism with which to unite the empire under a new *religio*. Roman Christian leaders adopted and expanded on the role of Christianity as a vehicle for imperial order."[15]

> "The beginning of an alliance between Christianity and the Roman Empire under Constantine profoundly influenced the history and development of religion and the state. In 381 Christianity was officially decreed the religion of the Roman state by Emperor Theodosius (378-95)."[16]

"Theodosius makes Christianity the religion of the empire with the edict of Thessalonica.... The emperor decrees that all imperial subjects must become Christians."[17]

"In 391 he closed all pagans temples. "It is our will," he decreed, "that all the peoples we rule shall practice that religion that Peter the apostle transmitted to the Romans.""[18]

"Overwhelmed by the favor that the emperor was pouring on them, many Christians sought to show that Constantine was chosen by God to bring the history of both church and empire to its culmination, where both were joined."[19]

"Europe was regarded as Christ's kingdom—Christendom. Thus, Christian baptism was not only spiritually but socially and politically significant: It denoted entrance into society. Only a baptized person was a fully accepted member of European society."[20]

This is a historical snippet. Far more can be said and quoted about the history of the Church and the State. Embarrassingly, in the 21st century, much of American Christianity still resembles this. One example would be Dr. John MacArthur's interview in August 2020 with Ryan Helfenbein of Liberty University's "The Falkirk Podcast."[21]

Dr. MacArthur, in this interview, makes several comments revealing this unsuspecting, deeply embedded heretical view of the union between the Church and the State. These statements represent the thoughts and beliefs of a multitude of professing believers in the U.S.

"certainly from a biblical standpoint, *Christians could not vote* Democratic."

"I said [to Trump] '*any real, true believer* is going to be on your side in this election,' because it's not just an individual, it's an entire set of policies that *Christians cannot* in any way affirm,"

"Joe Biden said the other day he's going to fill his cabinet with Muslims. That is as *anti-Christian a statement* as you could possibly make. That is a *blasphemy* of the true and living God."

Dr. MacArthur is one of a handful of Bible teachers I've learned and grown greatly from, so in no way is this an attack against him. But do you see what happened here?

- ✓ Is there any single political party that is purely Christian? *No.*
- ✓ So then, can what MacArthur said be the same regarding the other political parties? *In some way, yup.*
- ✓ Why is it blasphemous for an American president to bring Muslims into his cabinet? *It's not, unless America is a "Christian nation" under the theocratic rule of God.*
- ✓ Is this what America is? *Nope.*

This, consequently, is how we end up with heresy such as "Christian nationalism" because generations have been taught and reared in the ideology that the U.S. is a Christian nation. Thus, they genuinely believe fighting for specific fundamental "American values" is fighting for God and Christianity. But that's false. These kinds of problems are birthed from wrongly believing any country or nation of this world is a Christian nation. As one writer put it, in the U.S., **"we don't live in a theocracy. We live in a democratic society that celebrates pluralism."**[22]

I wonder. What if some Christians in the U.S. stopped treating this country like a theocracy? Maybe then they would stop being slaves to its politics. American Christians, you are not swinging the pendulum; you are the pendulum being swung by the politics of this world based on how you view and support things. In a democracy, your vote is power for those in power. Nevertheless, your vote is also your choice, not theirs. You don't "have to" choose one of the two evils. Would you vote for Hilter, or Nero, or Pharaoh? What if Hilter ran on pro-life talking points? What if Nero were pro-black lives matter? What if Pharaoh was for freedom of worship? You wouldn't vote for the enemy of your Faith; you would trust God. To adapt a line from the "Social Dilemma" movie: *voters are the users.* They're selling us on promises simply to get our votes because *our* votes equate to *their* power (or whatever power we believe we'll share in). Don't be a slave to politics. The U.S. is not a theocracy.

How does the maxim go, "those who fail to learn from history are doomed to repeat it"? This is the case for American Christianity. The American view of citizenship has at best muffled, and, at worst, suppressed many believers' heavenly citizenship and sojourning as earthly citizens. For many Americans, their political party is their "messiah," and their political views are their "holy scripture." Christian, don't let this be you.

Understanding Our Dual Citizenship

Citizenship as sojourners is about understanding the nature and priority of our dual citizenship—the heavenly and the earthly. Only the heavenly citizenship is primary and permanent. All earthly citizenships are provisional and missional.

When we hear or read "citizenship," we all have ideas that come to our minds. Let's get on the same page with what this means, at least in this book.

Citizenship consists of what it means to be a citizen of one's residing country or nation. After surveying a couple of the New Testament Greek terms and contexts of "citizenship" and "citizen," our "heavenly citizenship" can be biblically defined as *a redeemed people in communion with God and one another, living under God's government and blessings as inhabitants of His kingdom.*[23] If this sounds like a theocracy, that's because it is. We are not heavenly citizens of a democracy or any other human form of government. We are the Body of Christ. Therefore, wherever and however the Head (Christ) rules and resides, so goes the Body (the Church)—we are the bondservants. As for the "earthly citizenship," a general, working definition would be *the legally recognized status of a person living in a country/ nation under the authority of its government and recipients of certain rights, responsibilities, privileges, and opportunities afforded by it.*

115

Did you notice the difference between the two citizenships? Heavenly citizenship is about *who* we are and to *Whom* we belong. Earthly citizenship is about *what* we are part of and *what* we belong for. Earthly citizenship is transactional, changeable, debatable, and temporary. Heavenly citizenship is exclusive, familial, and eternal. This is why only heavenly citizenship is primary and permanent, while all earthly citizenships are provisional and missional.

If you have ever read or heard anything about our heavenly citizenship being a future, spiritual only reality, reject that noise. Such a devious invention was fed to you so that you would focus and invest more in this world, more in your earthly country of citizenship than rightly live in your heavenly citizenship. Our heavenly citizenship is not beyond us. It's now and forever. It is lived both in this world and the next world. Our promise land is our eternity with Christ, and our eternal life started when we were born-again (John 17:3). **"When Jesus defined eternal life as knowing God through Himself,** *He placed the ultimate reality—living forever—in the dimension of relationship,* **not the space-time continuum."**[24] This is why Scripture identifies believers as both sojourners and ambassadors. We live on earth *as citizens of another kingdom* (i.e., sojourners) and *as official representatives of that same kingdom* (i.e., ambassadors). The Christian's heavenly citizenship is a spiritual and physical, right here, right now, and all for eternity reality.

Have you ever flown on an airplane before? Took a greyhound or Amtrak? If so, then you have experienced how our citizenship is to be lived here. Our heavenly citizenship is the itinerary of how we live out our earthly citizenship. We live here as a one-way journey from earth to eternity with Christ. Our layovers are our missionary outposts. Some of us may have one stop on our itinerary. Some of us will have more. Nonetheless, the stops—i.e., wherever we may live, whatever country we may be citizens of—is simply a layover, not the destination. And yet, so many believers plant their roots at the layover as if it's the end destination.

Do you know the movie "The Terminal"? I haven't watched it. But shockingly, I remembered there was a movie about a guy living in an airport. So I looked it up.

Tom Hanks plays a guy from an Eastern European country trying to leave his politically unstable home and come to America. The main character, Victor, manages to leave his country and land in New York. Upon entering JFK airport, Victor's official papers are invalid because his country's government collapsed and is no longer recognized as a nation. Talk about bad luck. Since he can't make it past customs to officially enter the U.S., and he cannot be deported back to his country because they're in a civil war, he's stuck in the airport terminal. They thought he was going to attempt to escape from the airport. But he doesn't. He wants to enter properly. In turn, he decides to convert the international terminal's transit lounge into his home until he can leave. Bear in mind, he can barely speak or understand English. And he wasn't there for a couple of days either. He was there for months. Then, right when it appears he could be getting his wish of coming into America, he's blackmailed to go back to his country.

For Victor, this was all accidental; and he never reaches his end destination. For many American Christians, however, this is intentional. Many believers choose to live in the "terminal" of this world as if this is their end destination. But this is not to be us!

We are sojourners. This world and the earthly countries where we're citizens are not our home. The people around us who are unredeemed, this is *their* home. Therefore, *they* should invest in, fight for, give all, and get as much from it as *they* can. This is all *they* have. This is *their* heaven, *their* kingdoms. But that is not the case with us since this is not our home. It is adulterous of us to live on this earth like this is our heaven, to live in our earthly countries like they are the kingdom of God. We are foreigners here—the non-natives. We cannot do both. We cannot treat earth like heaven without undervaluing heaven. We cannot treat our earthly countries like the kingdom of God without disavowing God's kingdom.

EARTHLY ≠ HEAVENLY
EARTHLY < HEAVENLY
~~EARTHLY~~ HEAVENLY

✤ The wrong lenses.

Allow me tangent. I am a pastor, after all, and I do believe this needs to be said here.

While there are many errors in modern-day Christianity, especially in the U.S., I think one we rarely notice is how believers in this country have developed a nationalistic hermeneutic. First, this nationalistic hermeneutic has caused many American Christians to interpret the U.S. as the modern version of the Israelites. Therefore, certain civil and moral laws governing Israel in the Old Testament are to be applied to the U.S. That's not a biblical hermeneutic. That's a falsehood. Second, this nationalistic hermeneutic has caused many American Christians to interpret the U.S. as the Church. Therefore, where the Old Testament's moral and civil laws for governing Israel, along with the New Testament's teachings, best serve some agenda, these are to be applied to America's socio-political policies and practices. However, when Scripture conflicts with any social or political agenda, it demands it should be reinterpreted or dismissed. This, too, is unbiblical.

In no manner whatsoever is the United States of America the covenant people of God, nor is any one ethnicity represented in America the covenant people of God. In absolutely no way! To ever assume this is the real tragedy of blasphemy of the true and living God. Scripture teaches that God chose Abraham, Isaac, and Jacob and made a covenant with them and the one ethnic people that would come from them—the Israelites (Gen. 17:1-22; 35:1-12). They were the first and last monoethnic, singular nation to be God's covenant people. Later, because of the atoning work of Christ, there is now and forever one new covenant community made up of redeemed men and women from different nations, tribes, peoples, and tongues.[25]

Furthermore, the Church in America does not and is never to serve the will of the U.S. or its people, nor is the Church in America ever a social, political, or cultural movement for social, political, and cultural ends. This is also blasphemous to the Head of the Church, who has His own kingdom where its government rests upon His shoulders.[26] As R.C. Sproul Jr. once tweeted, **"In a wicked land either the state will judge us for loyalty to Christ, or Christ will judge us for loyalty to the state."**[27]

The point of my tangent, many believers in the U.S. have made their earthly citizenship the lens and rubric by which they interpret and apply Scripture, by which they presume upon the Church *and* America, and by which they live as Americans first, then Christian. But this world, this country, is not our home. Scripture was written *by* and *for* God's covenant people under the old covenant and new covenant. Please stop misinterpreting and misapplying God's Word *to* America.

We are foreigners here—the non-natives. Hence, what you as a believer biblically understand or not about the nature and priority of our dual citizenship—the heavenly and the earthly—will influence how you rightly or wrongly live as a sojourner on earth.

> **"There's no middle ground between these two things: either earth must become worthless to us, or we must remain bound by the chains of extravagant love for it. If, then, we care for eternity, we must make every effort to free ourselves from those chains."**[28]

Sojourning as Earthly Citizens

By now, you may be wondering am I implying that we abandon where we live to the evil one, that we not be involved in the betterment of our earthly countries in any way? Absolutely not. Sojourning is living *with* and *from* the knowledge of our permanent, primary identity as a citizen of the kingdom of heaven while we temporarily reside and participate as a citizen in the kingdoms of earth.

Recall the Israelites. They were always citizens of God and His promised land for them. God prophesied this Himself (Gen. 15:13-16; 17:6-8). Throughout all their journeying, they were still required to live according to their covenant citizenship—*the legally recognized status of a member of God's covenant people, under the authority of His law, and recipients of certain rights, responsibilities, and privileges*

119

afforded by it. And keep in mind, their journeying included before and after their exodus when they traveled across other countries, their later exile in Babylon and Mede-Persia, and finally being scattered about the Roman empire. This was the life of God's old covenant people as sojourners in other lands.

Living as a sojourning citizen of earthly countries is not much different for believers today, except we're under the new covenant and our geography isn't the same. Like the Israelites, Christians are perpetually required to live according to our heavenly citizenship *over all* our earthly citizenships. When we don't, it will always lead to spiritual adultery and idolatry. We see this repeated lesson with the Israelites, which is what brought God's loving judgment upon them. Realigning what's out of order is never without pain to what is fractured.

↯ The question & the answer.

So, what does our sojourning citizenship look like played out? As sojourning Christians who are citizens of America, should we engage in civic duties—e.g., voting; volunteering; campaigning; protesting; non-profiting; serving in government or military or other civil services; creating, passing, overturning, and enforcing laws, bills, policies, and propositions? Should we participate and invest time, labor, and resources to advance and improve this country?

Yes, we should engage, and participate, and invest in our country. We live here. It wouldn't be good stewardship of us not to. When Augustine addressed believers sojourning on earth as citizens of God's kingdom, he noted, **"For how could the city of God either take a beginning or be developed, or attain its proper destiny, *if the life of the saints were not a social life*?"**[29]

What we do and should do as sojourning citizens in this country is open for our involvement. However, "open for our involvement" excludes whenever being a citizen is contrary to Scripture or competes against our carrying out the mission of God. Whenever this choice is laid before us, we must choose to obey God over man—our heavenly citizenship over the earthly citizenship. Furthermore, "open for our involvement" doesn't mean overindulgence of involvement.

Overindulgence is a fruit of the flesh (Gal. 5:19-21, Col. 3:5). **"Anything you indulge in that contradicts the obedient worship of Christ is a wrongful worship."**[30] Moderation, on the other hand, is a fruit of the Spirit (Gal. 5:22-24). Our involvement as citizens is to be buffered and filtered by the fruit of the Spirit because the Holy Spirit wars against our unholy flesh to keep us from fulfilling its ungodly desires (Gal. 5:16-17).

One of the blessings of the New Testament's 1st century context is that we now have multiple examples and instructions for believers sojourning as citizens of earthly nations. Our 1st century brethren could relate to whatever difficulties we face trying to live as disciples of Jesus in countries hostile to who we are and what we believe. Hence, when Paul, Peter, and James gave believers practical marching orders for living as sojourning citizens of the countries on earth, they experienced firsthand the difficulty and success of doing so. This removes whatever excuses we may have with obeying these instructions, especially for Christians living in a free republic like the U.S., where we have much more opportunity for involvement and influence in its democracy—which tends to birth entitlement over obedience.

"1 *Everyone must submit to governing authorities.* For all authority comes from God, and *those in positions of authority have been placed there by God.* 2 So anyone who rebels against authority is rebelling against what God has instituted, and they will be punished. 3 For the authorities do not strike fear in people who are doing right, but in those who are doing wrong. Would you like to live without fear of the authorities? Do what is right, and they will honor you. 4 The authorities are God's servants, sent for your good. But if you are doing wrong, of course you should be afraid, for they have the power to punish you. They are God's servants, sent for the very purpose of punishing those who do what is wrong. 5 *So you must submit to them, not only to avoid punishment, but also to keep a clear conscience.* 6 *Pay your taxes, too, for these same reasons.* For government workers need to be paid. They are serving God in what they do.

7 *Give to everyone what you owe them*: Pay your taxes and government fees to those who collect them, *and give respect and honor to those who are in authority.* 8 Owe nothing to anyone—except for your obligation to love one another. If you love your neighbor, you will fulfill the requirements of God's law. 9 For the commandments say, "You must not commit adultery. You must not murder. You must not steal. You must not covet." These—and other such commandments—are summed up in this one commandment: "Love your neighbor as yourself." *10 Love does no wrong to others, so love fulfills the requirements of God's law.* 11 This is all the more urgent, for you know how late it is; time is running out. Wake up, for our salvation is nearer now than when we first believed. 12 The night is almost gone; the day of salvation will soon be here. So remove your dark deeds like dirty clothes, and put on the shining armor of right living. *13 Because we belong to the day, we must live decent lives for all to see.* Don't participate in the darkness of wild parties and drunkenness, or in sexual promiscuity and immoral living, or in quarreling and jealousy. 14 Instead, clothe yourself with the presence of the Lord Jesus Christ. And don't let yourself think about ways to indulge your evil desires." (Romans 13:1-14, NLT; *emphasis added*)

"1 First of all, then, I ask that requests, prayers, petitions, and thanksgiving be made for all people. *2 Pray for kings and everyone who is in authority* so that we can live a quiet and peaceful life in complete godliness and dignity. 3 This is right and it pleases God our savior, 4 who wants all people to be saved and to come to a knowledge of the truth." (1Timothy 2:1-4, CEB; *emphasis added*)

"Religion that God accepts as pure and without fault is this: *caring for orphans or widows who need help, and keeping yourself free from the world's evil influence.*" (James 1:27, NCV; *emphasis added*)

"5 Listen, my dear brothers and sisters! God chose the poor in the world to be rich with faith and to receive the kingdom God promised to those who love him. *6 But you show no respect to the poor. The rich are always trying to control your lives. They are the ones who take you to court. 7 And they are the ones who speak against Jesus, who owns you.* 8 This royal law is found in the Scriptures: *"Love your neighbor as you love yourself." If you obey this law, you are doing right. 9 But if you treat one person as being more important than another, you are sinning.* You are guilty of breaking God's law. 10 A person who follows all of God's law but fails to obey even one command is guilty of breaking all the commands in that law. 11 The same God who said, "You must not be guilty of adultery," also said, "You must not murder anyone." So if you do not take part in adultery but you murder someone, you are guilty of breaking all of God's law. *12 In everything you say and do, remember that you will be judged by the law that makes people free. 13 So you must show mercy to others, or God will not show mercy to you when he judges you.* But the person who shows mercy can stand without fear at the judgment." (James 2:5-13, NCV; *emphasis added*)

"13 *For the Lord's sake, submit to all human authority*—whether the king as head of state, 14 or the officials he has appointed. For the king has sent them to punish those who do wrong and to honor those who do right. *15 It is God's will that your honorable lives should silence those ignorant people who make foolish accusations against you.* 16 For you are free, yet you are God's slaves, so *don't use your freedom as an excuse to do evil. 17 Respect everyone, and love the family of believers. Fear God, and respect the king.*" (1Peter 2:13-17, NLT; *emphasis added*)

Many of us are familiar with these passages. But pause and really notice what's commanded and explained in these passages. Maybe circle them. Shucks, number them if necessary. Then consider that fellow believers wrote this to other believers living in political and social conditions that persecuted believers.[31] Fast forward and imagine Christian citizens scattered worldwide, focusing on obeying simply this handful of passages and nothing more. Do you think this would make every disciple of Jesus in every country benefit the people of that society, even if their society doesn't see it that way? I do, no doubt about it. You may not know, but this is partly why believers were persecuted during those earlier centuries. Those early Christians did not participate in the normal yet evil practices and

Roman worship of the day. Instead, they served and defended the lowly.[32] Augustine again hits the nail on the head,

> "No man has a right to lead such a life of contemplation *as to forget* in his own ease the service due to his neighbor; nor has any man a right to be so immersed in active life *as to neglect* the contemplation of God."[33]

When we do what we're supposed to as sojourning citizens will we still be hated by the world? Of course. But not because we deserve to be hated. Rather, it'll be because they innately hate the God and Savior we profess, worship, and represent (John 15:18-23).

⚘ The problem.

Many American Christians seem to think these kinds of biblical instructions aren't enough for their citizenship. "More must be done," they say. Many believers in the U.S. either have not known or have forgotten they are sojourning as earthly citizens. **"By craving to be more, man becomes less; and by aspiring to be self-sufficing, he fell away from Him who truly suffices him."**[34] And so, whether some believers realize it or not, they have become idolatrously invested in their earthly citizenship, believing this is what's primary and permanent.

Ponder that point with me. Could this be you, or someone you know, or someone you've seen online? So often the idolatry we personally struggle with is the hardest to spot and even harder to be called out on. **"For I am aware what ability is requisite to persuade the proud how great is the virtue of humility."**[35] Thanks be to God for the inner work of the Holy Spirit! May He help us as we explore this some.

The first example to ponder: Those who have become idolatrously invested *would be* the professing Christians that treat other Christians online and offline as enemies of God's kingdom simply because they vote or protest differently. Think of the brutish reactions to hearing or reading subjects like President Trump, BLM, Women's Rights, Pro-life, or kneeling for the national anthem. What about, "If you vote Democrat, you're not Christian because they support abortion and same-sex marriage." As if you know the reason why every Christian that votes Democrat votes Democrat. Or, "If you voted for Donald Trump in 2016 and 2020, you're not Christian (or you're racist) because he supported or emboldened white supremacy." As if you know the reason why every Christian voted for Donald Trump.

What was one of the lessons from Israel's sojourning pre-promised land that God wove into the law? *Don't settle in the provision and forget where you came from.* For us, that would be not settling in the provision of these earthly citizenships and forgetting that we were once spiritually dead and tyrannical citizens of this earthly kingdom,

> "2 *in which [we] used* to live when [we] followed the ways of this world and of the ruler of the kingdom of the air, the spirit who is now at work in those who are disobedient. 3 All of us also lived among them *at one time*, gratifying the cravings of our flesh and following its desires and thoughts. Like the rest, we were by nature deserving of wrath." (Ephesians 2:2-3, NIV; *emphasis* & brackets added)

More allegiance to any political party or ideology than to Christian-gospel unity is idolatrous. It's choosing the temporary earthly citizenship over your blood-bought heavenly citizenship.

The next example to ponder: Those who have become idolatrously invested *would be* the professing Christians that treat the very neighbors they are commanded to love and win to Jesus as enemies via the ridicule and disdain they spew online and offline simply because their neighbors vote or protest differently. Does getting their political ideology correct matter more than their lost soul being saved? Oh, and let's keep in mind that "correct" is subjective because it's "correct" according to *your* political ideology. Every proponent of a political ideology says theirs is "correct" or better than the others.

What was another lesson from Israel's sojourning pre-promised land that God wove into the law? *Recall compassion to respond with compassion.* For us, we must recall the compassion we've received from God and respond to one another and our neighbors with the same compassion we received. Grace is always appropriate; because if not for the grace of God, where would we be? *"But God, who is rich in mercy, because of his great love that he had for us, made us alive with Christ even though we were dead in trespasses. You are saved by grace!"*[36]

Have you noticed, because it never ceases to amaze me, that believers will call out others for the parts of the Bible they aren't obeying while failing to see and call themselves out for the parts of the Bible they aren't obeying (or even believing)? John Calvin would agree. He delivers a dagger to the heart of the matter.

> "Each of us thinks we have just cause for elevating ourselves and despising all others in comparison to ourselves—our self-love ruins us with such blindness…. We carefully conceal our abundant vices from others—and we pretend they're small and insignificant. In fact, we so delude ourselves that we sometimes embrace our vices as virtues…. Everyone flatters himself and carries, as it were, a kingdom in his breast. Consider arrogant men who, in order to gratify themselves, criticize the character and morals of others. And when contention arises, their venom erupts."[37]

More allegiance to any political party or ideology than to the mission of God is idolatrous. It's choosing the temporary earthly citizenship over your redeemed participation with God.

The final example to ponder: Those who have become idolatrously invested *would be* the professing Christians who have taken Satan up on his offer to Jesus for *"the kingdoms of the world and their splendor."*[38] Many American Christians have become consumed by the ownership and power in America's political kingdom over our position and responsibility in God's kingdom. Believers sojourning in the U.S. have to be honest with themselves. Some of them genuinely prefer this earthly kingdom over God's kingdom because, in this earthly kingdom, they have a sense of power in its democracy. Their "right" to choose has deceptively consumed them with the pursuit of their own will. It has robbed them of the true freedom as God's people living surrendered to God's revealed will in Scripture while sojourning as earthly citizens.

An excellent expression of this problem that has ensnared so many believers comes from Rick Holland. He states,

> "Idols have come between you and the Son of God, eclipsing His glory in your life…. Jonah 2:8 says, "Those who regard vain idols forsake their faithfulness." But the term *vain idols* there literally means "false vanities." The word for "idol" is the same word used in Ecclesiastes for "vanity." An idol is a lying, temporary experience, a false vanity telling you that a temporary, fleeting pleasure will satisfy you, last just as long as you need it to, and give you just precisely what you want. That's what idols do."[39]

What was the final lesson of God we saw from Israel's sojourning pre-promised land? *They received a unique window into how other countries and people groups lived and worshiped, contrasting how and why they were truly set-apart as God's special people.* For us, we reside in a country with a front-row seat to observe and examine how all kinds of people live and falsely worship. Like Israel, this is meant to cause us to appreciate and better comprehend why and how we are set-apart as God's special people, and cause our distinction as God's people to stand out even more.

> "9 But you are a chosen people, a royal priesthood, a holy nation, God's special possession, that you may declare the praises of *him who called you out of darkness into his wonderful light.* 10 Once you were *not a people, but now you are the people of God;* once you had not received mercy, but now you have received mercy. 11 Dear friends, I urge you, *as foreigners and exiles,* to abstain from sinful desires, which wage war against your soul. 12 Live such good lives *among the pagans* that, though they accuse you of doing wrong, *they may see* your good deeds and glorify God on the day he visits us." (1Peter 2:9-12, NIV; *emphasis added*)

More allegiance to any kingdom of man than to the kingdom of God is idolatrous. It's choosing the temporary earthly citizenship over your heavenly citizenship with God.

Have any of these examples been you? Have you become idolatrously invested in your earthly citizenship, buying into its vanity? Do you know someone like this? Have you seen professing Christians like this? Tragically, I can call to mind several times I've witnessed believers I know treat other believers and their unsaved neighbors just like those examples. I have also noticed others bow their knee to Satan's offer without ever realizing they have. Many of these believers I once pastored or currently pastor. Hence, one of the reasons why I wrote this book.

I began writing this book toward the end of 2020. 2020 was a wild year, y'all! *Wild!* I don't have time to list out how bananas that year had been. But do you know what I think was the most disheartening part of 2020 (and honestly, from 2014-2021)? The jumbo-screen view of the American Christian's idolatrous political affair played round the clock like a reality TV series. On social media. On the radio. On the news. In the pews. In the blogosphere. You would've thought, with as much airtime as we were getting via viewership, we would've been smart enough to capitalize by proclaiming and demonstrating the biblical gospel. Alas, we did not. Instead, Americans and the watching world got an unhealthy dose of the "American evangelical gospel," not the gospel of Jesus Christ. What a disgraceful and distasteful representation of Christ as His disciples.

"We labor and fret for a small gain, while loss of the soul is forgotten and scarcely ever returns to mind. *That which is of little or no value claims our attention, whereas that which is of highest necessity is neglected*—all because man gives himself wholly to outward things. And unless he withdraws himself quickly, he willingly lies immersed in externals."[40]

↳ The resolution.

Recall that handful of passages from a couple of pages ago. Suppose American Christian citizens would have simply practiced:

- *"keeping yourself free from the world's evil influence"*
- *""Love your neighbor as you love yourself." If you obey this law, you are doing right."*
- *"if you treat one person as being more important than another, you are sinning."*
- *"must show mercy to others"*
- *"don't use your freedom as an excuse to do evil."*
- *"Respect everyone, and love the family of believers. Fear God, and respect the king."*

If believers would've spent a quarter of the time and energy that was wasted on political pandering and social bickering to focus on merely obeying these instructions, our witness would have been more credible to a world that needs our soul-saving message.

Remember, earthly citizenship is provisional and missional. The "rights" and "liberties" American Christians possess and fight for so aggressively can be lost or renounced for the sake of our heavenly citizenship at any given moment. For example, America's democracy could change or God could call you to another country that doesn't have the same "rights" and "liberties." This is why believers who are U.S. citizens, engaging in civic duties, participating and investing in the advancement and improvement of America, must do so from our identity as sojourners. We are the guests here, not the homeowners. We are passing through, not planting roots. Moderation. Not over-indulgence of involvement.

Homeowners have a different degree of investment, involve-ment, and ownership in the upkeep of their house. Guests are not compelled or affixed to the same degree of maintenance because guests can leave at any time. But guests should seek to be helpful in the upkeep out of gratitude for their stay. Thus, they are not without some responsibility and benefits. Similarly, this is the case with be-lievers as sojourners.

The unredeemed have a legitimate reason as citizens to always be doing more, constantly pushing the envelope, continually progressing, and regularly fighting for whatever they think will retain what made or makes their life and country great. This is *their* home, *their* heaven, *their* kingdoms. For them, they're building towers of Babel. We, who have been redeemed, know they won't succeed. But think about the mixed messages we send them when we vigorously join them in building these towers of false hope, these kingdoms where they are the false gods who rule, the false messiahs who rescue and deliver, the false prophets who declare and decree. Sojourning citizens understand that whatever is built here on earth is but sand-castles. Only what is done for God's mission and glory is what will ever matter.

> "A culture or an individual with a weak base can stand *only when the pressure on it is not too great*.... Culture and the freedoms of people are fragile. Without a sufficient base, when such pressures come only time is needed—and often not a great deal of time—before there is a collapse."[41]

"25 Be careful that you do not refuse to listen to the One who is speaking. For if the people of Israel did not escape when they refused to listen to Moses, the earthly messenger, we will certainly not escape if we reject the One who speaks to us from heaven! 26 When God spoke from Mount Sinai his voice shook the earth, but now he makes another promise: "Once again I will shake not only the earth but the heavens also." *27 This means that all of creation will be shaken and removed, so that only unshakable things will remain. 28 Since we are receiving a Kingdom that is unshakable, let us be thankful and please God by worshiping him with holy fear and awe. 29 For our God is a devouring fire.*" (Hebrews 12:25-29, NLT; *emphasis added*)

Scripture does not promise believers "rights" and "liberties" as sojourning earthly citizens. Remember, the old covenant people of God lived as sojourners without possessing or fighting for any "rights" or "liberties" in the lands where they were exiled and scattered. Our 1st century brethren also lived as sojourning citizens without fighting for any "rights" or "liberties." We do see in Paul's case that he utilized the "rights" of being a Roman citizen. But he did so for two reasons, and neither was for personal or political gain. First, he used his "rights" for the sake of being God's moral light exposing certain secrets of the dark by demanding the Roman authorities do what is just to their citizens according to their law (Acts 16:35-39; 22:22-29). Second, he used his "rights" for the sake of being missional (Acts 21:37–22:16; 23:11-30). In both instances, Paul was resourceful as a sojourner. He prioritized the heavenly citizenship *in* the earthly citizenship, not the other way around.

> "This is great progress in the Christian life—that we nearly forget ourselves, that in all matters we hold our own concerns in less esteem, and that we faithfully strive to devote our energies to God and His commands. For when Scripture orders us to disregard our own concerns, *it eradicates from our souls the desire to possess things for ourselves, to love power, and to long for the praise of men.* Moreover, *it uproots our appetite for ambition as well as our appetite for all human glory and other more secret evils.*"[42]

Whatever we do here sojourning as citizens of America (and anywhere else), we must do so with our identity, trust, and hope *in* God, not this country or this world. Think about the varying outcomes of our earthly citizenship: persecution, success, disappointments, peace, change (good, bad, neutral), conflicts, enjoyment, rejection, collapse, etc. In the face of such capriciousness, the reason we can continue confidently reflecting Christ and remain on mission for Christ would be because we aren't tethered to and swayed by this earthly citizenship.

> "15 Do not love the world or the things of the world. If someone loves the world, then love for the Father is not in him; 16 because all the things of the world — the desires of the old nature, the desires of the eyes, and the pretensions of life — are not from the Father but from the world. 17 And the world is passing away, along with its desires. But whoever does God's will remains forever." (1John 2:15-17, CJB)

As sojourning citizens whom the Holy Spirit indwells, we don't ever need to be afraid of changing regimes, changing politicians, changing laws, changing social movements and issues, changing national citizenships, and so on. Change is not an enemy to sojourners. On the contrary, change is a tool in the hands of our sovereign King orchestrating His agenda in His Creation. A sojourner understands this because earth is but a layover, not our end destination. A sojourner does not establish and settle on what is fragile and passing away but on what is unshakeable and forever.

Do you remember Jesus' parable of the talents (Matt. 25:14-30)? There were three servants who each received a certain amount of "talents" (or currency) from their master. Each servant was supposed to make good on their master's investment. Two did, one didn't. The two received more and a blessing. The one lost what he had and was judged. Christian, invest your earthly citizenship "talents" wisely while you sojourn here, lest you prove yourself to be an unprofitable servant and suffer whatever the consequences.

Christianity is a sojourning spiritual movement that impacts societies through the salvific transformation of its people via the gospel of Jesus Christ. Additionally, as a sojourning spiritual movement, Christianity impacts societies by practically serving the people as demonstrations of that same gospel—i.e., grace in action, mercy in action, compassion in action, forgiveness in action, and so on. This is our heavenly citizenship invading our earthly citizenships. If it's not for the mission of God and the glory of God, it will be a waste to God. So don't waste the time and earthly citizenship God has provisionally entrusted to you as a sojourner on building up sandcastles that will not last (which unknown to your unsaved neighbor is their tower of Babel). Sojourning is living with and living from the knowledge of our primary and permanent identity as a citizen of the kingdom of heaven while we temporarily reside and participate as a citizen in the kingdoms of earth. For *"since we are receiving a Kingdom that is unshakable, let us be thankful and please God by worshiping him with holy fear and awe"*[43] in our earthly citizenships.

"There is, therefore, something in humility which, strangely enough, exalts the heart, and something in pride which debases it. This seems, indeed, to be contradictory, that loftiness should debase and lowliness exalt. *But pious humility enables us to submit to what is above us*; and nothing is more exalted above us than God; *and therefore humility, by making us subject to God, exalts us*. But pride, being a defect of nature, by the very act of refusing subjection and revolting from Him who is supreme, falls to a low condition.... *And therefore it is that humility is specially recommended to the city of God as it sojourns in this world*, and is specially exhibited in the city of God, and in the person of Christ its King; while the contrary vice of pride, accor-ding to the testimony of the sacred writings, specially rules his adversary the devil. *And certainly this is the great difference which distinguishes the two cities of which we speak*, the one being the society of the godly men, the other of the ungodly, each associated with the angels that adhere to their party, and *the one guided and fashioned by love of self, the other by love of God*."[44]

THE JOURNEY OF SOJOURNERS

Sojourners are in a constant state of journeying until we come to our heavenly homeland and can wholly rest with our Savior and King. Therefore, the life of a sojourner cannot be lived in a bubble, sheltered from harm or obstacles or conflict or messiness. Our sojourning is a journey of faith, following Jesus each day He gives us a heartbeat and breath in this fallen world where we temporarily reside. Yes, some of you may never travel geographically. But that's not what's promised in our sojournership. The journey of sojourning is about saying "yes" to God's daily lead and directions without always knowing what's on the other side of that "yes" as we are passing through this world.

Do you know what a journey is? A journey is an act of traveling from one place to another; it's going from here to there and over-coming whatever obstacles are in between to get where you're going.

133

So, if the life of a sojourner is a journey of faith in following Jesus, that means every day is an opportunity to travel with Jesus; an opportunity to progress forward in our life and with other people, tackling whatever obstacles are along the way as we follow God's lead.

To "follow" is to exercise faith that causes us to obediently put one foot in front of the other in the direction God is leading according to His Word and however He leads us personally. Interestingly enough, the majority of what we are to obey in Scripture involves other people in some way; it involves getting out of our bubble of safety, comfort, and familiarity. That's following. Conversely, the opposite of follow is "stagnation." Stagnation is the state of not flowing or moving, the lack of activity or growth.

While "follow" is an indication of us exercising our faith, "stagnation" in the life of a sojourner is an indication of a lack of trust in God. Trust is what produces our pursuit of God in our sojourning. We follow what or whom we trust. Thus, if we aren't growing in our faith, then we aren't trusting God—we're not as desperate for Jesus as we need to be. If we aren't moving around in obedience day-to-day, person-to-person, and within ourselves—tackling whatever the obstacles are along the way—then we're not trusting God. Stagnation reveals we are not trusting that God's wisdom is better than ours, that His instructions are better than our feelings, and that His plan is better than what we think is best. Moreover, stagnation can be a telltale sign that we've forgotten our identity as sojourners. It is evidence of settling in this earthly reality and becoming too invested in our earthly citizenship.

As sojourners on a journey of faith following Jesus, our obedience to God is vital in distinguishing us as sojourners in our earthly citizenships and no longer as natives of this world. Moralism, which is largely defined and evaluated subjectively today, is a fool's gold fruit of the Spirit. There will be moralistic people going to hell. There will *not* be immoralistic people going to heaven. Biblical morality is different from worldly morality, for obedience to God is distinct from merely being a "good, moral person." Apart from God, moralism glorifies humanism—which is the center of worship in all earthly citizenships.

Obedience to God only ever glorifies God because He's the reason why we obey Him—for Christ's atoning sacrifice on our behalf, for His worship, for His glory, for His love toward us, so on. Biblical morality isn't about humans as the centerpiece nor the betterment of humanity. Biblical morality is about obedience to God as the centerpiece and His worship as the betterment for humanity's sake.

We all know obedience isn't easy. We have two natures warring against each other in our being (Rom. 7:21-25, Gal. 5:17). Consequently, fighting to be faithful in our obedience to God is a strenuous trek, so sometimes it is easier to settle with being seen as a good, moral person. Nonetheless, with the power of the Holy Spirit present within us, we must fight on![45] The joy of grace is that it covers our mistakes while we strive onward in our obedience. Therefore, don't let stagnation distort your identity as a sojourner to those around you. Don't let your attachments to the things of this world grow greater than your loyalty to God. *"Since you call on a Father who judges each person's work impartially, live out your time as foreigners here in reverent fear."*[46] The journey of faithfully following Jesus in our sojournership will mark us differently to those around us.

Wherever you currently are in your Christian walk, own it. You can't move forward in denial. Sojourning is not a journey for the fainthearted. It constantly clashes with our earthly nature. It relentlessly goes against the grain of our deeply embedded earthly heritages. So, if this is where you are, cry out each day, *"Lord, I believe; help my unbelief."*[47] Then trust-fall follow your Savior with the confidence that He knows best who you are, where you are to go, how you are to be, and what you are to do.

NOW WHAT?

At the beginning of this chapter, I shared how my wife is a professional photographer. She's also a missionary. She read David Platt's "Radical" in 2011, and it rocked her world. The Lord would later use her photography business to get her on the international mission field. That was the beginning of the end. She's been to southern India, Ghana, and two provinces in Thailand. She hasn't been the same since. According to her, she would live on the international mission field if she could. Of course, she has asked me to go with her. And I would reply, "At some point, I may."

Those mission trips changed her life. Her sense of urgency and missional IQ is astute now. At the end of 2018, in our previous church, my wife was on the missions team going to Thailand in January 2019. Our oldest son was supposed to go with her. It would've been his first time leaving the country. Unfortunately for him, but fortunately for me, he wasn't able to go. So I was asked to go in his place. Looking back, by the grace of God, I'm so glad I obliged.

God ministered to me profoundly on that Thailand mission trip. Challenge. Conviction. Lots of introspection. Tremendous encouragement. It reframed several areas in my thinking and understanding. Who could've known the very thing I was reluctant to do would've been as rewarding for my soul as it was. My words to follow will fail to accurately capture the profundity and all the stories.

Before this trip, if you would've asked me about our sojournership as Christians, I would've given you a biblically quaint answer. Nothing incorrect, but a crucial element would've been missing. Since this trip, my biblical understanding of our sojournership has been colored in with personal experience. The biblical picture of a sojourner is no longer a blank outline. For me, it's now vivid and evocative. What it means to be a sojourner has come alive.

During the first half of our trip, we spent our time with the children of missionaries scattered throughout Asia—as north as Mongolia, as south as India, and as west as Jordan. Humbling and enlightening are an understatement. Their ages ranged from first-graders to teenagers. We were supposed to serve them. But, instead, they taught us. Never say who you can't be discipled by.

These children are called "third-culture kids"—TCKs. They are born from parents native to one country's culture but reared in another country's culture while being raised in a Christian household. Three cultures—Christian, their parents' home country, the current country they reside. And you thought your life was complicated. Most of them were born on the mission field, in countries where they don't speak the language nor look like the natives. Some of them move frequently because they live in closed countries, and deportation or incarceration looms over their heads if their parents are discovered as Christian.

TCKs experience so much. The particular kids we served were predominantly Anglo. They were not always able to communicate the complexities of what they encountered as minorities and foreigners, nor how it parallels minorities and foreigners in America. However, they knew and could express it doesn't feel good and isn't right. Surprisingly, they were understanding of why the natives treat them that way. These kids learned the culture and language to live among, befriend, and win their peers to Jesus, just as their parents were doing in the places they worked and lived. Think about what I just said. These were school-age kids who never enlisted to be missionaries. Yet, they display resilience through what they endure, extend grace to the natives, and possess patience and dedication to adapt. These kids should inspire us. It can be done! It's not without its challenges. But it can be done because these kids are doing it.

TCKs are the modern-day epitome of what it means to be sojourners. It is their life. They don't try to be because they have no choice but to be a sojourner. These kids are natively from the country of their birth parents but born in another country as foreigners. Technically, this means they're native to neither. They are raised Christian, and American, and whatever other culture they occupy. To make matters more trying, when these kids returned to the states, they didn't feel at home here either. Besides their extended families, they have no friends and didn't quite fit in American culture. In essence, they don't entirely fit anywhere and thus can live wherever God sends their parents. Transience is not unusual for them. And yet, these kids live like this and remain childlike—unhardened, finding fun wherever they can, being organically missional, and trusting their parents wherever they go.

What life is for TCKs is to be the sojourning life of every Christian. We were initially born natives of an earthly homeland. Now

137

that we have been beloved and begotten from the Heavenly Father, our new native home is His heavenly one. Though we have a new homeland, we currently reside in our former homeland, but as foreigners, no longer natives. While we were raised according to the culture of our birth country or residing country, in Christ we are new creations being raised in His likeness—which is countercultural. Yes, we can relate to the natives of these earthly homelands because we were once natives and still possess an earthly citizenship. But we are to use our familiarity and citizenship to win them to Jesus, not be won again to the former (2Pet. 2:20). Like TCKs, since we are the guests, we should not entirely fit wherever we are civilians nor their cultures. Only Christians are free to move about this earth navigating its citizenships with independence from its political, social, and cultural entrapments, going unburdened in any direction our Heavenly Father leads and sends, enjoying Him and trusting Him all along the journey. For, **"if [our] 'Christianity' only works in America,"**—or only works in whatever country we live in—**"it's not Christianity."**[48]

This is the life of a sojourner. We don't try. We have no choice. *We are not of this world.* Christians are third-culture kids. Our lives should be so foreign to the world that their only rationale is we don't belong to this world. The sooner we accept this reality and stop resisting it, the more liberated we will become from the things of this world. The sooner we welcome this reality and stop fighting it, the more flexible we will become in our earthly citizenship in this world. The sooner we trust this reality and stop challenging it, the more useful we will become for the mission and glory of Jesus as we pass through this world.

CHAPTER 4

Ambassadors

Have you ever heard of a brand ambassador? I have. But I never gave it much thought until about 2016. I have a close friend who lives in Northern California. He started as an Uber driver and got some investments to purchase a Tesla. Over time he became an unofficial but recognized Tesla brand ambassador with Uber. I remember him coming to visit us in Bakersfield with his Tesla. It was like he drove in on Santa Claus' sleigh. If magic was real, his Tesla was magical.

Tesla kind of sells itself. But our friend did a great job telling us about it, posting constant pictures of it, doing live videos with it, and answering questions. So much so my wife became enamored with Tesla. Now she can spot a Tesla while we're driving and tell you what model it is. She even has an annual date on our shared calendar of when I said she would never get one as motivation for her to get one. My friend was terrific at being a brand ambassador, if for nothing else than converting only one person because my wife is a true believer in Tesla. She even purchased an official Tesla jacket from an actual dealership to wear as inspiration for getting a Tesla.

I'm not poking fun at my wife, more so highlighting the effect our friend had at being a brand ambassador for Tesla. And he didn't do anything remarkable. He really enjoyed his job and his car to the point where he couldn't help himself. He was always talking about it, marketing for it, and representing the brand well enough that others would take interest. I don't even think he was paid for it. Being a brand ambassador isn't so hard when you believe in and enjoy the product because it effortlessly flows from a place of delight.

My friend represents a truth about all of us. We're all unofficial and unpaid brand ambassadors and evangelists for several categories—our cars, our sport's teams, our colleges, our politics, our social causes, our cultural traditions, favorite video games, favorite music, favorite artists, favorite devices (Apple or Android, Mac or PC), etc. We are constantly talking about these things, unknowingly marketing for these things, and representing these things well enough that others may have taken an interest in them with us. All because it effortlessly flows from a place of delight.

Do you know where I'm going next? Yup, the heart check. As a Christian, can you honestly say this is true of you with the official ambassadorship God has actually assigned to you? I'm not sure how many of us can say "yes," myself included. Some of us might can answer "here and there." This is where I can raise my hand. Nevertheless, with our "here and there," it's probably still not close in comparison to our other ambassadorial categories. I'd be curious to see a poll of how many professing believers even know what it means or looks like to be an ambassador as a Christian.

If we're honest, that heart check exposes a problem, doesn't it? When our official ambassadorship outranks our unofficial, unpaid brand ambassadorships, and yet the latter outperforms the former, we have to own that we have a problem living out our identity in Christ.

WHAT IS AN AMBASSADOR?

Do you know what an actual ambassador is? Please humor me and quickly think of an answer. What did you come up with? I normally answer, "an official representative." I tend to think of movies I've seen and try to picture the "ambassadors" I saw depicted in their role at the embassy. Shucks, my wife has watched so much "Law & Order: SVU" that I'm sure I've seen episodes of ambassadors accused of sex crimes but covered by their diplomatic immunity.

My typical answer and mental image are not incorrect. However, it is too simplistic. It's possible that what may have come to your mind could be too simplistic also. The actual definition is much weightier, and the professional role is more distinguished.

According to Dictionary.com and Encyclopedia Britannica, "ambassador" is defined as *a diplomatic official of the highest rank sent by one national government to another country as its resident representative and/or sent by one national government to another country to represent it on a temporary mission.*[1] If you were to look up "ambassador" as a career, you might come across how ambassadors work in foreign countries as diplomats with temporary citizenship while still retaining citizenship in their home country.[2]

Think about those descriptions:

1. *Sent by a home government to a hosting country as the home government's resident representative.*

2. *Government official of the highest rank on foreign soil.*

3. *Sent on a mission.* (As a matter of fact, the National Museum of American Diplomacy says U.S. ambassadors **"all have the same mission—to represent the interests and policies of the United States."**[3])

4. *Working with temporary citizenship in a foreign country while retaining their home citizenship.*

Can you read the weight in those descriptions? Do you sense the seriousness of the role? Did you catch the similarities with us as Christians?

This is the meaning and description of ambassador from extrabiblical sources. What about the Bible? How does the Bible speak to what is an ambassador? Is it different, comparable, or both?

Ambassador in the Old Testament

The Bible mentions "ambassador" in both testaments. In the Old Testament, there are four Hebrew terms used in numerous passages to describe an ambassador. These terms in context indicate *an official messenger (an envoy) who carries out a task for their country's leaders*

and/or communicates a message from their superior or people.[4]
Notice this in a few passages.

"1 Now when all the kings west of the Jordan heard about these things—the kings in the hill country, in the western foothills, and along the entire coast of the Mediterranean Sea as far as Lebanon (the kings of the Hittites, Amorites, Canaanites, Perizzites, Hivites and Jebusites)—2 they came together to wage war against Joshua and Israel. *3 However, when the people of Gibeon heard what Joshua had done to Jericho and Ai, 4 they resorted to a ruse: They went as a delegation*[5] *[pretended to be ambassadors]* whose donkeys were loaded with worn-out sacks and old wineskins, cracked and mended. 5 They put worn and patched sandals on their feet and wore old clothes. All the bread of their food supply was dry and moldy. *6 Then they went to Joshua in the camp at Gilgal and said to him and the Israelites, "We have come from a distant country; make a treaty with us.""* (Joshua 9:1-6, NIV; *emphasis* & bracket added)

"Listen, Ethiopia—land of fluttering sails that lies at the headwaters of the Nile, that *sends ambassadors in swift boats down the river. Go, swift messengers*[6] *[ambassadors]! Take a message* to a tall, smooth-skinned people, who are feared far and wide for their conquests and destruction, and whose land is divided by rivers." (Isaiah 18:1-2, NLT; *emphasis* & bracket added)

"13 For I have sworn by my own name," says the Lord, "that Bozrah will become an object of horror and a heap of ruins; it will be mocked and cursed. All its towns and villages will be desolate forever." 14 I have heard a message from the Lord that *an ambassador was sent to the nations to say,* "Form a coalition against Edom, and prepare for battle!" 15 The Lord says to Edom, "I will cut you down to size among the nations. You will be despised by all."" (Jeremiah 49:13-15, NLT; *emphasis added*)

"11 Then this message came to me from the Lord: 12 "Say to these rebels of Israel: Don't you understand the meaning of this riddle of the eagles? The king of Babylon came to Jerusalem, took away her king and princes, and brought them to Babylon. 13 He made a treaty with a member of the royal family and forced him to take an oath of loyalty. He also exiled Israel's most influential leaders, 14 so Israel would not become strong again and revolt. Only by keeping her treaty with Babylon could Israel survive. 15 Nevertheless, this man of Israel's royal family rebelled against Babylon, *sending ambassadors to Egypt to request* a great army and many horses. Can Israel break her sworn treaties like that and get away with it! 16 No! For as surely as I live," says the Sovereign Lord, "the king of Israel will die in Babylon, the land of the king who put him in power and whose treaty he disregarded and broke.'" (Ezekiel 17:11-16, NLT; *emphasis added*)

"A wicked *messenger*[7] *[ambassador]* falls into trouble, but a trustworthy *envoy*[8] *[ambassador]* brings healing." (Proverbs 13:17, NIV; *emphasis* & brackets added)

Do you see how "ambassador" was used and portrayed? Being identified as an ambassador meant to be an official messenger and representative of a superior or people sent to another country for a specific purpose. Did you notice in the Joshua 9 passage that the people of Gibeon faked being ambassadors? If you read through verse 15, you'll see they were received as officials from a faraway land and made a treaty with them. That is the high regard for ambassadors, and it's akin to the respect of ambassadors today.

Compared to the extrabiblical sources, what's not in the Old Testament is temporary citizenship awarded to these ambassadors or a long-term residency on foreign soil. Instead, they came, delivered or received, and returned home once the work they were sent for was complete.

Here's a more fascinating and obscure detail. Of the handful of Hebrew terms used for ambassador, the term *malak* (מַלְאָךְ) is equally translated throughout the Old Testament as "angels," because it also captures who and what the angels of God came to earth to do for God. Angels are ambassadors of heaven sent to earth by God as His official messengers and representatives to declare His specific messages and perform His specific duties. What weightiness and seriousness of ambassadorship! The Holy Spirit used such a description for a role filled by both humans and angels.

But wait until you see how the Spirit describes ambassadors next.

Ambassador in the New Testament

Unlike the Old Testament, the New Testament only expressly references the term "ambassador" twice.[9] Both are from Apostle Paul. And he doesn't change the Hebrew description of ambassador. As a matter of fact, Paul uses what was customary to the Old Testament as a base to legitimize and enhance the believer in Christ's ambassadorship from God.

> "14 For the Messiah's love has hold of us, because we are convinced that one man died on behalf of all mankind (which implies that all mankind was already dead), 15 and that he died on behalf of all in order that those who live should not live any longer for themselves but for the one who on their behalf died and was raised. 16 So from now on, we do not look at anyone from a worldly viewpoint. Even if we once regarded the Messiah from a worldly viewpoint, we do so no longer. 17 Therefore, if anyone is united with the Messiah, he is a new creation – the old has passed; look, what has come is fresh and new! 18 And it is all from God, who through the Messiah has reconciled us to himself *and has given us the work of that reconciliation,* 19 which is that God in the Messiah was reconciling mankind to himself, not counting their sins against them, and *entrusting to us the message of reconciliation.* 20 *Therefore we are ambassadors of the Messiah; in effect, God is making his appeal through us.* What we do is appeal on behalf of the Messiah, "Be reconciled to God! 21 God made this sinless man be a sin offering on our behalf, so that *in union with him* we might fully share in God's righteousness."" (2Corinthians 5:14-21, CJB; *emphasis added*)

> "19 And pray for me, too, that *whenever I open my mouth, the words will be given to me to be bold in making known the secret of the Good*

News, 20 for which I am an ambassador in chains. Pray that I may speak boldly, the way I should." (Ephesians 6:19-20, CJB; *emphasis added*)

Notice the portrayal of an ambassador by Paul. It's the same description and definition from the Old Testament. A task. A message. A representation. All delivered from a superior and for a superior. Thus far, ambassadorship in the Bible is consistent across both testaments and akin to the extrabiblical explanation. While these two are the lone passages for Christians being mentioned explicitly as ambassadors in Scripture, they are more than enough. I can recall reading something from Dr. Elmer Towns where he said, **"The importance of any doctrine is not determined by how many verses discuss it. If God said it once, it is enough."**[10]

The Holy Spirit unveils something uniquely profound about Christian ambassadorship in Paul's brief exposition. In 2Corinthians 5:14-21, Paul masterfully weaves the genesis and enterprise of being ambassadors of Christ.

Love is where Paul begins. The new life Christians have, united with the Messiah, is a product of His love. Jesus came to sacrifice His innocent and holy life to rescue us from our deadness in sin. Life for the believer is consequently a two-fold gift of God—our birth and rebirth. Therefore, we are undeniably under the authority of He who gave us life. *"For the Messiah's love has hold of us"* (v14). We are the Lord's bondservants.

From love, Paul then plunges into incarnation. The Christian's new life united with the Messiah was God's work through Christ to reconcile us to Himself. After reconciling us as a product of His love, God then gives us the same work of reconciliation as ambassadors of Christ. Thus Paul submits, similar to how the Incarnate Jesus was the Trinity's ambassador to humanity to accomplish reconciliation, God is now sending us into the world as His official messengers and representatives of the reconciliation He accomplished.

What I tell you, masterfully woven. From love, Jesus incarnationally came to reconcile us. Now, as products of that love, God specifically appoints us to the work of reconciliation as ambassadors of the Incarnate Son. This is how the Holy Spirit has Paul introduce believers as ambassadors in Scripture!

In the Old Testament, the Spirit relates ambassadors with angels. A high honor. In the New Testament, the Spirit emerges Christian ambassadorship from Jesus' ambassadorship. The highest honor. Our ambassadorship is God's designated representation of the Incarnation of Christ to the world. To be an ambassador of Christ, Paul audaciously says, is *"in effect God making His appeal through us"* (v20).

⚑ Greater than you think.

Though only mentioned twice in Scripture, we see the Christian's ambassadorship is not some minor kingdom role. We are the official proxies of our Incarnate Savior in this world. *"What we do is appeal on behalf of the Messiah"* (v20). I don't know about you, but I am tremendously excited and immensely humbled by this. What a *selah* moment.

There is no greater King. There is no greater kingdom. Therefore, there is no higher, more honorable service in God's kingdom or any kingdom. We will never have a greater work to do in all our life, nor will we ever possess or proclaim a greater message or cause in all our life. Thus, no leader, no country, no government position, no nobility, no royalty, no status, no career, no political cause, no social cause, no cultural identification, no relationship, not a single thing from this world is more excellent than this! Our ambassadorship is preeminent over everything we do in this world. You name it or think it, it's included. In *whatever* we do, *wherever* we are, the precedence for *why* God has sovereignly placed us there and doing that thing is *to leverage it all* for our ambassadorship of Christ.

The Triune God has designated believers in Christ—His Church—as His official vehicle for His ongoing divine work of reconciling others to Himself and for His ongoing representation in this world of the magnificent reconciliation accomplished in Christ. Hence, as ambassadors of Christ, we are:
- *heralds and portraits* of reconciliation (His work).
- *heralds and portraits* of the Incarnation (His Person).

- *heralds and portraits* of His kingdom (His union with believers and rule as their King).

No one in the world bears this ambassadorship but born-again believers in Jesus, and there is nothing greater.

"Truly, truly, I say to you, *whoever believes in me will also do the works that I do; and greater works than these will he do*, because I am going to the Father." (John 14:12, ESV; *emphasis added*)

By now, you should know that our ambassadorship coincides with our so-journership and great commission from Jesus. Like a multi-colored, multi-strand rope, sojournership and mission are inter-woven in ambassadorship. Each classifies a different aspect of being an ambassador for Christ while here on earth.

> Sojourner = Our Relocation
> Ambassador = Our Post
> Missionary = Our Assignment

I covered being sojourners in the previous chapter. We saw we are citizens of a heavenly kingdom though temporarily residing here in the kingdom of this world. That's the ambassador's diplomatic relocation. I will explore being missionaries in the following chapter, which is our assignment of carrying out the ongoing divine work of God reconciling others to Himself. That's the ambassador's diplomatic mission from our King. Hence, being Christ's ambassadors is our diplomatic post here on earth. Our ambassadorship is our privileged duty of being our King's official representatives and missionaries in this foreign world where we temporarily reside as sojourners. Whether this world wants it, recognizes it, or not, we are the official proxies of our Incarnate Savior, His heralds and portraits in this world. Therefore, our ambassadorship is an honorably designated and purposeful role of the infiltration and representation of Christ in this world.

HERALDS & PORTRAITS OF RECONCILIATION

To be an ambassador of Christ is to be a herald and portrait of His reconciliation work. In 2Corinthians 5:18 (CJB), when Paul writes, "*God... through the Messiah has reconciled us to himself and has given us the work of that reconciliation,*" what does he mean by reconciliation?

When some hear or read "reconcile" or "reconciliation," what we may think is bring back, make amends, or rejoin something that's been separated. Paul has something more significant in mind here. The Greek term Paul uses for "reconciliation" means *the change of two divergent parties into coming together.*[11] Think of two one-way streets going in the opposite direction being rerouted to merge into one one-way street going in the same direction. This is reconciliation. However, Paul contextually adds that instead of the two divergent parties coming together, God restores the divergent party together with Himself. To use the illustration, God is the One who reroutes the one-way street going in the wrong direction to merge with His one-way street going in the right direction. That's what Paul means with this reconciliation. It is the quintessence of the gospel. Thus, *"the work of that reconciliation"* is introducing those going in the wrong direction—the wrong way, the wrong truth, the wrong life—to the Great Rerouter who can merge them into His one-way street going in the right direction—His way, His truth, His life.

Obviously, this is predominantly toward unbelievers. However, this reconciliation is also for believers. Once we've reconciled to God through and in Christ, another reconciliation takes place. Union with Christ has reconciled believers together in Christ (John 17:20-26, Eph. 2:11-22). The Great Rerouter not only reroutes us with Himself but also with one another. No longer are our one-way streets going in opposite directions from one another because of external distinctions. In Christ, there is no segregation or division or partiality because of ethnicity, or culture, or class, or sex, or nobility, or anything else we can add here. What does Paul write in Galatians 3:27-28,

"27 For those of you who were baptized into Christ have been clothed with Christ. 28 There is *no* Jew or Greek, slave or free, male and female; *since you are all one in* Christ Jesus." (CSB, *emphasis added*)

Is this reconciliation between one another something we practice well? Not all the time. We tend to more easily find reasons to divide and segregate than we do to unite. The fact that something as eternally trite as politics can divide Christians is pitiful. In my opinion, our default is partiality (favoritism) because it's easier than the unity we have with one another in Christ (e.g., Jam. 2:1-9). D.A. Horton, in his book "Intensional," has a whole chapter on the sin of partiality. He writes,

"Partiality happens when one person superficially evaluates another person's worth and judges them before getting to know them or their story. We practice partiality when we make judgments about a person's character based on all things external: their accent, clothing, gender, hair, height, tattoos, skin color, etc. and then treat that person as if our judgment is true.... When we purposefully give extra attention to some people we prefer, we are by default neglecting those we do not. This evil can become so normal in our practice that we won't even understand the reason when it's called out. The flesh is tricky because we're most comfortable around those who are like us."[12]

The enemy deceives Christians into believing we are each other's adversaries. In no way is this true. We have been irrevocably reconciled together in Christ. We are collectively one new man, one body, one temple of the Lord. The wall of hostility is forever gone. Therefore, firstly, the work of reconciliation is also for believers to pursue reconciliation—united on the same one-way street in Christ, going in the same upward direction—with one another where there is division, disunity, or partiality among or toward each other (Matt. 18:21-35, Col. 3:12-15, Eph. 4:1-3). Secondly, we all know believers who have drifted back onto the wrong way, back believing some wrong versions of truth, and back into wrong living. Thus, this reconciliation work would additionally include longsuffering in rerouting those believers back to our Savior's way, truth, and life (Gal. 6:1-2, Jam. 5:19-20).

To be an ambassador of Christ is to be a herald and portrait of His reconciliation work primarily to unbelievers and also with believers.

Gospel-Mindedness

So what does being a herald and portrait of this reconciliation look like? Since I'll be addressing our mission directly in the next chapter, I'll answer this question from a different aspect: Gospel-mindedness. Being a herald and portrait of reconciliation looks like being gospel-minded in all things. Gospel-mindedness is *being conscious and focused on the gospel and its result in either salvation or sanctification*.

Think about what's been happening in our country and the world merely since the dawn of the 21st century. For example, the extent of dissenting voices available everywhere online, the post-modern progressive view of Christianity, the sexuality and Bible debate, the stark political divide and fanaticism, the social protesting and unrest, and the apparent racial tension merely within the American Church. Think about how Christians and the gospel are unbiblically or unpleasantly spoken of during this time. Now, more than ever, how Christians live and communicate with one another and unbelievers is utterly critical to our effectiveness or ineffectiveness *with* the gospel and *for* the gospel. Since we are ambassadors of Christ and profess the name "Christian," we must always be mindful that both unbelievers and other professing believers see us—whether fairly or not—as representatives of Jesus and His gospel.

There is never a time where we're not heralds and portraits of reconciliation. *Ever.* Being conscientious of this reality means gospel-mindedness includes utilizing the speculation and expectation of others regarding what they think of Christians, Jesus, and His gospel to be opportunistic in our representation of reconciliation. That's a free, recurring platform to represent the narrative of Jesus' reconciliation rightly. Ambassadors don't shy away or hide from their foreign and possibly hostile audience. They speak and do with the protection and authority of their country for the sake of their superior's agenda. The same is true in our case. James says,

> "19 *be swift to hear, slow to speak, slow to wrath;* 20 for the wrath of man *does not produce* the righteousness of God." (James 1:19-20, NKJV; *emphasis added*)

Paul says,

> "Let no harmful language come from your mouth, only good words that *are helpful in meeting the need,* words that *will benefit those who hear them.*" (Ephesians 4:29, CJB; *emphasis added*)

> "15 *be very careful, then, how you live—not as unwise but as wise,* 16 *making the most of every opportunity,* because the days are evil. 17 *Therefore do not be foolish, but understand what the Lord's will is.*" (Ephesians 5:15-17, NIV; *emphasis added*)

Elsewhere, Paul adds,

> "5 *Behave wisely toward outsiders, making full use of every opportunity—* 6 *let your conversation be gracious and attractive so that you will have the right response for everyone.*" (Colossians 4:5-6, NLT; *emphasis added*)

Instructions like these should ring more loudly and be heeded more solemnly now in light of the weight of our ambassadorship. Our voice and presence carry great weight because there is never a time where we're not heralds and portraits.

There are immediate and relevant implications that proceed from this aspect of our ambassadorship. For example, one area of significant ramifications is the things for which we contend. Recall how I briefly mentioned our unofficial brand ambassadorships at the beginning of this chapter. Here is an implication of our official ambassadorship in this area many Christians sadly never consider: Whatever things we contend for in this life, we are battling for them from our diplomatic post where we're always on duty as heralds and portraits of reconciliation, never as our own person separate from our ambassadorship. Have you ever followed someone on social media with two accounts, their official business one and their personal one? Why do they do this? Because there are things they cannot say on their official business account since they represent their company or government office. As ambassadors of Christ, we do not have two accounts. We are never not in our official ambassador role. We're always on duty as heralds and portraits of reconciliation, never as our own person separate from our ambassadorship.

Our official ambassadorship determines what is most important during our time here on this earth. Think for a moment, what are the Christians you know personally and see online contending for in America? Here's my quick list: social justice, politics, pro-life, second amendment rights, capitalism, socialism, freedom of religion. What is most important *is not* fighting for our agendas, the social and political views of this country, or even contending for what we think is right and worth the fight. This doesn't mean we never engage in these things. But it does mean we never elevate them to or above what is most important.

For the ambassador, in being a herald and portrait of reconciliation, the most important is always the gospel's effectiveness not being quenched by our words and actions. We are to be strategically influential with introducing those going in the eternally wrong direction to the Great Rerouter. Only He can merge them into His one-way street going in the eternally right direction. Helping people that are still dead in their sins and separated from God only achieve a better life in this world is a fool's pursuit and the most hateful thing we can do. We know for those apart from Christ, there is an afterlife that's eternally worse than whatever joy, pain, prosperity, poverty, justice, or injustice they experience here. If Jesus, when talking to the Pharisees, said, "*on the day of judgment people will have to account for every careless word they speak. For by your words you will be acquitted, and by your words you will be condemned,*"[13] how much more consequential is our carelessness as heralds and portraits of His reconciliation?

152

Being Gospel-minded in the Difficult

Being gospel-minded is seeing every interaction, every conversation, and every opportunity through the lens of our representation of reconciliation. Of course, this is easier said than done. Though, that doesn't mean it's undoable. In some ways, we experience how un-demanding this is with those who are agreeable with us. It's less intimidating and thorny talking about Jesus and what we biblically believe with those who share similar visceral views that can often be contentious with someone who doesn't. Yet, we know the difficulty with those whose deeply held beliefs are different or clash with ours. Nonetheless, that doesn't mean it's undoable with them either. Jesus wouldn't have told His disciples to love our enemies or forgive the brethren seven times seventy if being gospel-minded with people we're at odds with was unattainable.

If seeing every interaction, every conversation, and every opportunity through the lens of our representation of reconciliation is problematic but doable, then how can we do this?

• *First, we must know what keeps us from being gospel-minded with others and adjust accordingly.*

You can't fix what you don't know. For example, fear and pride are different. Whatever adjustments you would make for fear may not be the same for pride. Adjusting from fear may mean taking risks in being bold with others about Jesus' work of reconciliation. Alternatively, adjusting from pride may mean being humble in your presumptive estimation of others and being humble in your cynical approach to disagreeing with their views. You can't truly adjust if you aren't willing to be brutally honest with why you aren't gospel-minded either at all, or that much, or with certain people.

Your effectiveness in being gospel-minded will always be limited if you don't know what's hindering you. **"Learning what you control and what you don't helps your witness,"** explains Dr. Alvin Reid. **"When you choose wisely regarding those things over which you have control, it affects all your life, including your witness."**[14]

- *Second, we must regularly remind ourselves of the weight of our voice and presence as an ambassador of Christ in this world.*

Let's recall how we got to this point: With love, the Father gave up the Son for a creation that rejects Him. With love, the Son willingly came into His creation to save them by dying for them, despite them still rejecting Him. From this love, our spiritual death was overturned and our whole life was restored. From this love, our eternal separation from God was eternally reconciled. Then, via the same love, we have been appointed ambassadors of this reconciliation of love. So, you tell me, is there anything about this that is not weighty?

There is not a particle of our redeemed lives decoupled from Jesus and not appointed for the sake of Jesus. Remember, we are the Lord's bondservants. You own nothing of you because it all belongs to Jesus. Our life is to be spent for Jesus, just as Jesus spent His life on us (2Cor. 5:14-15, Phil. 2:6-8). Therefore, *"let this mind be in you which was also in Christ Jesus."*[15] Your voice, your views, your agendas, your presence, your choices, your actions, and whatever else you deem is a part of you, it all belongs to Jesus and is under ambassadorship for Jesus in this world. This is the epitome of gospel-mindedness. Christians are eyeglasses through which the world sees our wonderful Savior and His magnificent work as either beautiful or repulsive, in focus or out of focus. Discipline yourselves to remember the weight of our voice and presence as an ambassador of Christ in this world.

- *Third, focus on being winsome, not winning.*

I'm not sure how often you may do this, but I've wasted a lot of time trying to "win" arguments only to have "lost" the person in the process. Ergo, as an ambassador of Christ, did I actually "win" if I lost the person? Nope. And it's a more substantial loss because of my ambassador role. For example, Dr. John Davis, when exploring Abraham's intercession in Genesis 18:20-33 for the infamous Sodom, made a terrific remark to this point.

"It is extremely difficult, if not impossible, to pray effectively for lost souls if one *is not* convinced that lostness will ultimately result in literal, eternal punishment."[16]

Hence, being winsome is thinking other-person first, not proving points or correcting wrongs. Yes, there is a time and place for correcting errors. But there is also a winsome manner for correcting errors (2Tim. 2:24-26). The prevailing point, winning the person is the priority. Always.

To be winsome is to be singularly concerned with the long-term gain of eternal success. How can I best communicate God's truth? How can I best demonstrate God's love? How can I best extend God's grace? How can I best present life in Christ? How can I win this person toward the gospel or biblical truth? This is all winsome reasoning. Proverbs 11:30 (CJB) says, *"The fruit of the righteous is a tree of life, and he who is wise wins souls."* However, winning in any manner that does not include the person is merely a situational victory, a short-term earthly gain. As a herald and portrait of reconciliation, to focus on winning and not being winsome is self-centered. Any thought of "how can I personally win?" elevates your knowledge, ability, agenda, and satisfaction. It does not elevate Jesus' reconciliation in the slightest. That is purely self-centered and in no way gospel-minded. Self-centeredness is a glaringly ugly and yet deceptively subtle sin that we all struggle with. Don't lose sight of who you are in your interactions with others, whether in person or online. Focus on being winsome, not winning.

- *Fourth, consciously lean on the Holy Spirit.*

In the winter of 2020, I taught a message entitled "Hope in the Coming of the Holy Spirit." A point I made was, maybe the reason we feel like we're drowning in our trying to live for God is that we do it in our willpower. Trying to live for God in our willpower is like breathing underwater through a snorkel—can't go too far or last too long with only a snorkel. While living for God by the power of the Holy Spirit is like being in a fully geared scuba suit—you can go wherever you want for the length of the air you have in the tank, and you're equipped for whatever you may encounter. That point applies here also. We can't be a herald and portrait of reconciliation in our willpower. Our lungs alone are not strong enough to handle the waters of the world we live in. Hence, why many professing believers succumb to the world, they give up from swimming against the current. We need oxygen and gear from an outside entity to help us survive these rough waters. The Holy Spirit is that support! He is our internal power source to rightly representing Jesus in this world (2Tim. 1:7-14).

As we previously explored in the bondservants chapter, we will never be successful in any form of living for God—in this case, being heralds and portraits—apart from the Holy Spirit. Therefore, *ask Him* daily for His help. Shucks, throughout the day we need to be asking the Spirit for help. Furthermore, *trust Him* daily to help. Faith knows the Holy Spirit is involved in whatever good we do, in however well we communicate and demonstrate the gospel. It is never by our willpower, abilities, or intellect. It's always because of the Spirit. Lastly, *strive to live out His fruit* in our interactions with others, and He will meet us there to represent Jesus as His herald and portrait. This is how we can consciously lean on the Holy Spirit.

To be a herald and portrait of reconciliation is to be gospel-minded in all things because it's worth everything. Gospel-mindedness is vital to our effectiveness with the message of reconciliation, specifically in our culturally challenged era today. If people are turned off or turned away because of, let's say, the exclusivity of Christ in the gospel, that's one thing. But to be turned off or turned away because of our carelessness with the gospel is solely our fault.

What we evangelize for, if not the gospel, screams what we prioritize and possibly idolize. Remember, being a brand ambassador isn't so hard when you actually believe in and enjoy the product; it effortlessly flows from a place of delight. This is to be the case of our ambassadorship with the message of reconciliation. Yes, as we've seen, this will still have its share of difficulties. However, these four points of being gospel-minded will aid us in being able to better see every interaction, every conversation, and every opportunity through the lens of our representation of Jesus' reconciliation.

HERALDS & PORTRAITS OF THE INCARNATION

To be an ambassador of Christ is to be a herald and portrait of the Incarnation (His Person). In 2Corinthians 5:19-20, Paul writes,

> "19 God *in the* Messiah was reconciling mankind to himself, not counting their sins against them, and entrusting to us the message of reconciliation. 20 Therefore we are ambassadors of the Messiah; in effect, God is making his appeal *through us*. What we do is appeal *on behalf* of the Messiah..." (CJB; *emphasis added*)

When Paul says, *"God in the Messiah was reconciling mankind to himself,"* he's noting the Incarnation. The eternal Son came in the flesh as the Messiah of God to not merely invite people separated from Him into His kingdom. He came to also clear every obstacle and cover their atoning fare for entrance into the kingdom. God didn't accomplish His reconciliation from afar. Nope. He did it in an up-close and personal way. The Son became what He was reconciling.

Thus, when Paul declares we're ambassadors of Christ and *"God is making his appeal through us,"* again he's noting incarnation. This time instead of God *in the* Messiah, it's God *through* us. That "appeal" here in the Greek is communicating *God, through us, is coming alongside others to urgently call them via invitation to be reconciled to Himself.*[17] Picture someone served with a subpoena. But not a subpoena to appear or testify, rather a subpoena to receive a plea bargain. And to add a caveat, when Paul states, *"What we do is appeal on behalf of the Messiah,"* it's not serving the subpoena like some legal messenger. Instead, it's serving it as someone who was once in their shoes, imploring them to accept the plea because they fully know the charges and evidence against them. This is the tone of the "appeal" God is making through us, just as He did through Jesus.

Similar to how God the Son came in the flesh to accomplish reconciliation, God is now working through us in the flesh to actively reconcile people to Himself. We don't do the reconciling. God does. We are the reconciled vehicles God inhabits to continue meeting people in an up-close and personal way to reconcile them to Himself. Since it was the Incarnate Son who accomplished this reconciliation, as His ambassadors, our lives are to reflect and represent this firsthand experienced reality. Hence, we are heralds and portraits of Christ's Incarnation in this world.

Life, Light, & Darkness

So what does being a herald and portrait of the Incarnation look like? Being a herald and portrait of the Incarnation looks like *us being the incarnational lights of Christ in the darkness we live among*. To be ambassadors of the Incarnation is to represent how Jesus Himself was incarnational unto reconciliation.

I believe Apostle John gives us a superbly concise and cogent explanation of Jesus' Incarnation unto reconciliation (John 1:1-5, 14-18; 3:16-21). In the opening of his gospel account, John articulates that Jesus is the eternal Word (*Logos*) of God and possessor of life. The life He possesses brought light to humanity, which shines into their darkness. Then He became flesh and dwelt among the darkness to lead those in darkness into His light. That's Jesus' Incarnation—the wholly human embodiment of the divine Word, Life, and Light. It is infinitely beyond us to represent the Incarnation of the divine Word. However, in the New Testament, Jesus and other passages explain that we do represent "the light"—and His light is of His life.[18]

To know how we are to be the incarnational lights of Christ in the darkness we live among, we must first understand what John was explaining about life, light, and darkness in John 1:4-5.

> "4 The Word gave life to everything that was created, and his life brought light to everyone. 5 The light shines in the darkness, and the darkness can never extinguish it." (NLT)

Regarding "life" (*zōē*),[19] absolutely no created thing comes into being apart from the divine Word—that's existence in every fashion and form, and salvation for those who believe (John 1:12-13). This "life" here in context also includes moral life. Therefore, the reality of humans' innate sense of right, wrong, good, bad, justice, and injustice exists because of the divine Word. What does Apostle Paul tell us?

> "14 Even Gentiles, who do not have God's written law, *show that they know his law when they instinctively obey it, even without having heard it.* 15 They demonstrate that God's law is written in their hearts, *for their own conscience and thoughts either accuse them or tell them they are doing right.*" (Rom. 2:14-15, NLT; *emphasis added*)

However, since man's conscience is warped because of sin, people define right, wrong, good, bad, justice, and injustice all subjectively. Hence, though the sense and ability to consider these moral concepts come from this "life" provided by the divine Word, that does not mean it's always in agreement with the divine Word. Yet, even the most crooked moral compass is still evidence of its Creator, because broken clocks are still right twice a day.

Regarding "light," this is a revelatory light. John is capturing in this one term what I call *the trinity of truth.* "Light" here in context in the Greek (*phōs*) means *the truth, the knowing of truth, and the right living in agreement with truth.*[20] This trinity of truth is only provided to humanity from the life of the divine Word. Think of a lightbulb and lamp. A lightbulb possesses light. But disconnected from a lamp, no one can see the light of the bulb. As soon as you connect the lightbulb with a plugged-in lamp and turn it on, the light from it is visible. In this illustration, the lightbulb would represent the trinity of truth and the lamp would represent the life from the divine Word. The trinity of truth has always existed in the Holy Trinity. But there was a problem. This "light" wasn't visible to humanity until the life from the Word illuminated it to humanity.

Initially, the divine Word provided this "light" in the Law of God to the Jews only. The Law was the truth of God, the accessibility of knowing this truth, and the commands for right living in agreement with this truth.[21] Paul, much earlier before the Gospel of John, would write in Galatians 3:24 that the Law was the light (a "tutor") that was to lead to Jesus Christ so that men may be justified by faith. But John means more than just the light of the Law of God here. The divine Word, no longer through the Law but through Jesus, is this "light" (the trinity of truth) given to all people, not only the Jews. In and through the Person of Jesus is the whole truth of God, the knowledge of the whole truth of God, and the right living in agreement with the whole truth of God revealed and made available to humanity (2Cor. 4:6, 2Tim. 1:9-10). Apart from Jesus, no person can possess this "light." Nevertheless, this "light" will still shine in their darkness because the darkness cannot overcome it.

Enter "darkness." "Darkness" here in context in the Greek (*skotia*) is actually the antithesis of the trinity of truth.[22] I call this *the trinity of absence*—the absence of God's truth, the absence of knowing God's truth, and the absence of the right living in agreement with God's truth. So when John says, *"the light shines in the darkness,"* he's kind of alluding to what Paul communicates in Romans 7.

> "...in order that sin might be recognized as sin, it used what is good to bring about my death, so that through the commandment [*the light of the law*] sin might become utterly sinful." (Romans 7:13, NIV; brackets added)

Darkness (*the trinity of absence*) is unknown as darkness until the light (*the trinity truth*) shines in the darkness and brings awareness that it's dark. Once the light is present and shining, the darkness cannot overcome it—i.e., it cannot lay claim of ownership or authority over the light.[23] The divine Word has been making His light shine amid the darkness of humanity in particular ways:

- *by way* of the Law (the Torah) via God's people in the Old Testament;
- *by way* of Himself appearing in the flesh;
- *by way* of the new covenant seen via Christians and the Holy Scriptures (Old and New Testament);

- and also, *by way* of other humans who from their consciences speak, decide, create, govern, whistle-blow, protest, police, and morally live in agreement with God's truth (though they may not know it personally nor do so as worship of God).

Thus, for darkness to be more clearly seen as darkness, the light of God must shine brightly in the darkness. In order for man to see what man is lacking, the trinity of truth must shine brightly in the absence of truth. Otherwise, without the light, all there is for humanity is darkness and the cluelessness of being in darkness.

The Gravity of the Light

Before we get to the practical—the "how"—we once more need understanding. This time we have to understand the gravity of the implications of professing Christians as the incarnational lights of Christ in the darkness we live among.

Ponder the gravity of this with me. Think how more chaotic and wicked our world would be without any presence of the light (the trinity of truth) in it. Think how more vicious and conniving humans would be to one another without any presence of the light (the trinity of truth) represented among them. And not to bum us out, but we can't gloss over pondering this gravity in the negative.

There is a grim reality of how "Christians" regrettably participate in the deeds of darkness while operating as representatives of the light. Think how much damage and death have been caused in the name of the light (the trinity of truth). For example, the wars by the historic Church; the imperialism and colonization in the name and cause of Christianity; the involvement from Christians in the enslaving, torturing, murdering, segregating, and discrimination of Africans and African Americans. Think of the atrocities committed against Native Americans, Africans, African Americans, Asians, Asian Americans, and other Europeans on U.S. soil since the 15th century done in the name of Christianity, in the name of light. Does any of this sound like the light of Christ? Absolutely not! Any form of racism, any form of ethnic supremacy, and any form of murder and abuse is evil no matter the generation, institution, or person. It is darkness, and it is not from God. Deeds like this done in the name of the light or by an ambassador of Christ are disguises of darkness.

Nevertheless, the atrocities in Christianity's history do not negate God's truth, nor does the wake of chaos from Christian history disprove God's truth. In fact, they both affirm and prove His truth that humans are entirely depraved, we all need Jesus as Savior and Lord, and only God knows what's best. That's His light shining in the darkness.

"While we cannot condone [sin]," notes Dr. Davis, **"we must recognize that God can overrule the errors of men in fulfilling His ultimate purposes (cf. Ps. 76:10)."**[24] As horrifying as the past has been and at times when the present is, without any presence of God's light shining through numerous forms, the world would be far worse. We would've had far more wars, far more holocausts, far more genocides, a far more extended period of slavery and segregation, far more abortions, far more deaths by violence, far more corruption and abuse, far more social and ethnic-based injustices, and so on. It is only because of the divine Word bringing light to humanity that darkness has not wholly overtaken all of humanity. No doubt darkness abounds all around, yet it cannot overcome the light. And part of the reason why darkness cannot overcome God's light, because He shines through His heralds and portraits of the Incarnation. God has designated us the incarnational lights of Christ in the darkness—from our smallest deeds to our largest successes, even our failures. As hip-hop artist Propaganda summarized, *"God really does use crooked sticks to make straight lines."*[25]

What this looks like: Incarnational Lights

Now to the original question, how are we as heralds and portraits of the Incarnation to be the incarnational lights of Christ in the darkness we live among? I'll answer this twofold. First, we'll start with what it means to be incarnational lights of Christ.

Without question, our model of what it looks like to be incarnational comes from the Incarnate Christ Himself. Jesus crossed over and became fully human to reach humans (Phil. 2:5-8). He entered our world of darkness to tangibly be light in the darkness and rescue people from their darkness. Have you ever heard or said, "Jesus was countercultural"? I have for both. While this is true, it's also a serious understatement. Jesus wasn't merely countercultural; He was *contra-darkness*. He entered into darkness but was not part of the darkness. Neither did He add to the darkness. Instead, he subtracted from it by adding His light via His presence, His interactions with others, His teachings and corrections, His actions, and His atoning work.

That is how we are to be incarnational lights, by being *contra-darkness*. Darkness cannot be subtracted by darkness because it equals more darkness (Rom. 6:19). Yes, God has and will continue to sovereignly work through the conscience of unredeemed humans. In this way, He shines His light in areas of darkness via whatever means they possess for His purposes to be accomplished. However, they are still in the dark, so their work will never rescue anyone from their darkness. We, on the other hand, are not of the darkness but the light. Only we who are beloved and begotten bondservants are the incarnational lights of Christ sojourning all over this world with the message and mission of reconciliation. Therefore, only we can add in the light of Christ to subtract the darkness around us. And how do we do this?

- ✓ By our Christlike presence—i.e., the fruit of the Spirit.
- ✓ By our Christlike interactions with others (online and offline).
- ✓ By our Christlike actions and service.
- ✓ By the Christlike use of our influence, privileges, and resources.
- ✓ By our Christlike humility and repentance before others.
- ✓ By our Christlike forgiveness of others.
- ✓ By our Christlike love for our neighbor.
- ✓ By our Christlike love for one another.
- ✓ By our Christlike obedience to God.
- ✓ By our Christlike witness.

This kind of living is *contra-darkness*.

Our incarnational light can't be forced. It is lived out from the personal experience of Christ's light shining into our darkness, rescuing us. When we live out what His light accomplished in our lives, His light then shines through. His light turned our captivity and despair into freedom from the penalty, power, and soon to be, the presence of sin and death. His light continually exposes and heals other areas in our life still in the dark—our ignorance, foolishness, carnality, hurts, habits, hang-ups, etc. We went from being slaves of the darkness and its casualties to experiencing the liberation, peace, and joy of the Lord. Since the world can only fabricate an insufficient and flawed experience of life compared to what we receive and experience in Jesus, when we live from the personal experience of our reconciliation, Christ's light is present and shining in whatever darkness is around. **"The integrity and honesty of a child of God are among his most potent weapons in spreading the gospel."**[26]

This is why we cannot live our Christian life in a bubble only around other Christians. Christian fellowship and community are a must and necessary component of our discipleship. In no way forsake assembling together to stir each other up to love and good works (Heb. 10:24-25). But light shines brightest in the dark. We understand that the reason for humanity's problems is sin, and until Christ returns, problems will persist. However, human problems are podiums to portray and proclaim a wholeness only found in Jesus contrary to the empty hope offered by the world's solutions. The Light of the world came for those in the darkness of the world, as we once were. To be incarnational as Jesus was incarnational, for the purpose of reconciliation, is to be among the darkness as Jesus was among the darkness.

Hence, as incarnational lights of Christ, we need to be spending time with those in darkness as Jesus did. I'm not implying putting yourself in harm's way, or in knowingly tempting situations, or in unwise friendships and partnerships. For example, I'm not going to a strip club to be the light in that dark place. That's moronic for me; so, I'm not doing it. But going to my unsaved family's or neighbor's house or party, that I can do. Spending time, moral support, and assistance helping homeless families get settled somewhere, that I can do. Doing coffee dates and conversations with people living a hard season of life I previously survived, that I can do. During our church plant in 2013-

2015, my wife and some women from our church partnered with a local ministry to go love and serve working girls in South Los Angeles. That, they can do. Letting struggling locals from the community have a place to come, talk, be treated with dignity, get out of the heat or cold, grab something to eat, drink, and so on, that's something local churches can do.

Ambassadors are to build bridges into the darkness with the light on account of the agenda of the Light. Incarnational is about opening up our lives to be light in the dark and being willing to enter into other people's darkness for the sake of the light that can lead them to reconciliation with God (1Cor. 9:19-23). So invite folk into your life, your homes, your spaces, and your time. Allow them to see how you live as a believer in your context (e.g., 1Thess. 2:7-12). Even more, be open to opportunities to spend time with them in their context on their terms without expecting or insisting they adjust for you (e.g., Luke 5:27-32).

⚓ The light of love.

Considering the temperament of the days we're living in, I believe a potent luminescent of our incarnational light is Christ's way of love—another model of *contra-darkness*. Like grace, Christ's way of love is never out of season and always pierces through the darkness.

Jesus' incarnational love was in humility, empathy, and sympathy (Heb. 2:9, 14-18; 4:15). Empathy is *"the ability to understand and share the feelings of another."*[27] Sympathy is *a common feeling of understanding between people.*[28] Sympathy is like kneeling to console and support someone who's fallen. Empathy is more than kneeling; it's getting on the ground with them, figuratively putting on their shoes to see and understand it from their perspective, to feel it how they feel it. John Calvin describes this more emphatically. He wrote,

> "Something more is required from Christians than wearing a cheerful face and rendering their duties attractive by friendly words. First, they should imagine themselves in the situation of that person who needs their help, and they should pity his bad fortune as if they themselves both bore it and felt it. Thus they

will be compelled, by a feeling of mercy and humanity, to give him help as if it were given to themselves. One who has this mind-set and approaches the task of helping his brothers will not contaminate his duties to others with arrogance or resentment."[29]

Did not Jesus model this first? Jesus humbled Himself, entered our broken world, into our broken lives, and empathized and sympathized with us. For us to love like this requires that we humble ourselves and enter the world of those in darkness we're trying to reach, to share in their joy and pain, try to feel what they feel, try to see and understand their life from their perspective, all the while radiating the love Jesus showed us. On this kind of incarnational love, D.A. Horton adds this,

> "Diane Langberg once said, *"the trauma of this world is one of the primary mission fields of the twenty-first century."*…. As the body of Christ, we must better empathize with those who risk opening up about their trauma, and we must create pathways of healing from within the church…"[30]

What were some stressful things that happened in your life this year? Who was there with you and for you? What did their presence mean to you? How much did it help you? Now assume this was you being there for your unbelieving neighbor or coworker or friend in stressful situations, maybe like a lost loved one, or a crisis, or a deep hurt like a family falling apart, or fear like during a pan-demic, or an injustice, or unmet needs. Assume our local churches were there like this for the unbelieving, the impoverished, and the overlooked within our reach. Can you see how our light could shine brightly by doing this? As believers, we are *broken-but-being-made-whole* people because our Savior is *shalom*.[31] He is wholeness. In Him, nothing is missing and nothing is broken. This kind of incarnational love is being among other broken people, showing them the gentle, gracious potter hands of our Savoir, who can make them whole as He is making us whole.

Our world is filled more with unbelievers than believers. Imagine the impact Christians could have with simply loving the unbelievers around us. Here's an unassuming and compelling act of love we probably don't consider much but is painless for being incarnational lights of Christ: Stop holding unbelievers to the standard in the Word of God. Stop expecting them to agree or follow or submit to the wisdom and commands of God in His Word.

In the U.S., Christians have this tendency to assume other Americans are under the authority of the Bible and thus judge them by the Bible. This is wrong and a deterrent. Psalm 50:16-17 (ISV) says, *"As for the wicked, God says, "How dare you recite my statutes or speak about my covenant with your lips! You hate instruction and toss my words behind you."* Paul wrote in Romans 6:20 that unbelievers are slaves to sin and free regarding righteous living. Spiritually dead people in darkness cannot follow a living God of light. Instead of imposing the light upon them, focus on you living as the light among them. Love them right where they are, just as you used to be right where they are until Jesus' love rescued you. It'll be through your demonstrative and verbal example of Christ's love toward them they may see and hear of God's saving grace and be reconciled through Jesus. Dr. Rick Taylor, regarding this point, explains,

> "Compassion is not just doing good things. Living the life God is working out in you involves compassion with both your actions and your words. There is as much danger in only sharing your words without actions as there is in doing actions without ever speaking any words."[32]

⚶ Loving the difficult.

Another compelling act of love for us as incarnational lights of Christ is how we interact with the difficult people in our lives and around us. No one is exempt from dealing with difficult folk, whether believer or unbeliever. Shucks, in a world of social media, trolling appears everywhere. Loving the difficult to deal with people definitely sets Christians apart. Not because unbelievers don't also do this, but the motivation behind why we do is distinct. Look at what Jesus taught on loving difficult people,

"27 "But to you who are willing to listen, I say, *love your enemies! Do good to those who hate you. 28 Bless those who curse you. Pray for those who hurt you.* 29 If someone slaps you on one cheek, offer the other cheek also. If someone demands your coat, offer your shirt also. 30 Give to anyone who asks; and when things are taken away from you, don't try to get them back. *31 Do to others as you would like them to do to you.* 32 "If you love *only* those who love you, why should you get credit for that? Even sinners love those who love them! 33 And if you do good *only* to those who do good to you, why should you get credit? Even sinners do that much! 34 And if you lend money *only* to those who can repay you, why should you get credit? Even sinners will lend to other sinners for a full return. 35 *"Love your enemies! Do good to them. Lend to them without expecting to be repaid. Then your reward from heaven will be very great, and you will truly be acting as children of the Most High, for he is kind to those who are unthankful and wicked. 36 You must be compassionate, just as your Father is compassionate."* (Luke 6:27-36, NLT; *emphasis added*)

As we sojourn here, we are to emanate salt and light wherever we are. Loving the difficult to deal with people for the reasons Jesus mentions is a heavenly flavor in a fallen world and illumination in the darkness we're passing through. Think about what it looks like to love the people on the opposite political and social aisle than you—online and offline. Think about what it looks like to intentionally seek understanding and common ground with those you disagree with (for whatever reason) rather than treating them as enemies. I didn't say capitulate and agree with something where you disagree. Being loving in disagreements is disagreeing with dignity and respect—where do we agree; what point can I affirm as a good point from their position; making sure our tone and responses are friendly and not attacking; so on. This is emanating salt and light with people we find difficult. This is being winsome. This is Philippians 2:14-15 (NLT), *"Do everything without complaining and arguing, so that no one can criticize you. Live clean, innocent lives as children of God, shining like bright lights in a world full of crooked and perverse people."*

Loving difficult people as incarnational lights of Christ is summed up in one word: *kindness* (Matt. 5:9). Be kind to people on the other side of your political, social, cultural, and religious views is a simple way of loving the difficult to deal with people—even more so during tense seasons when kindness is a rarity across differences. You don't have to agree or endorse to be kind to others. Kindness isn't determined by harmony with the recipient. Kindness proceeds from love and grace regardless of the recipient. The love and grace we've received from Jesus while we were still His enemies is to birth a stream of kindness in us toward others who also need to experience the love and grace of Jesus. You have no idea how God will work behind the scenes with your simple acts of kindness toward the people on the other side of the aisle who are expecting you to dislike them or berate them or argue with them or be aggressive, mean, or condescending to them. That's the joy of following our sovereign Savior. He's all-powerful, all-present, all-knowing, all-perfect, and always working to accomplish His purposes. We have no idea what He can do or will do through us being His little lights in the darkness by taking on the challenge of loving difficult people in our sphere as He did and still does.

We are to be the incarnational lights of Christ by following after the *contra-darkness* model of Christ. It is crucial for us to live conscientious of this royal reality. There is no other way for this dark world to see the glorious light of Christ but through us shining His light wherever we are all over the world.

> "God is using His church to be lights in the world to show the world what He is like and to be living, visible, tangible explanations of Him—the greater, invisible, intangible God. You are a light in the world, which means wherever you go in the world, where you live, work, play and see needs, you are designed to be a living demonstration of God to those around you."[33]

What this looks like: Representations of Truth

Back to the question: How are we as heralds and portraits of the Incarnation to be the incarnational lights of Christ in the darkness we live among? The second answer is in what it means to represent the trinity of truth (light) in the absence of truth (darkness) around us.

As a reminder, the trinity of truth ("light," *phōs*) is *the truth, the knowing of the truth, and the right living in agreement with the truth*. The fountainhead of the trinity of truth is the divine Word of God, which He's supernaturally disclosed for His people in His sixty-six inspired books of Scripture. The antithesis of the trinity of truth is the trinity of absence ("darkness," *skotia*)—*the absence of God's truth, the absence of knowing God's truth, and the absence of the right living in agreement with God's truth*. The fountainhead of the trinity of absence is sin and its effects—separation from God and His truth, rejection of God and His truth, opposition to God and His truth, ignorance of God and His truth, noncompliance to God and His truth, subversion of God and His truth, and reconstruction of God and His truth.

Jesus, the *Logos* of God, walked the earth as the trinity of truth personified (John 1:14-17; 5:31-47). He lived, spoke, performed miracles, worked wonders, and sacrificed Himself, all *as* the trinity of truth. He taught, affirmed, interpreted, and fulfilled the trinity of truth in the Old Testament.[34] He discipled His followers according to the trinity of truth and then told them to go do likewise.[35] Hence, why we have the trinity of truth in the New Testament.[36] Jesus even corrected many of the religious leaders for their absence of truth, in that they were cancerous with the truth of God for their personal gain and did not rightly live in agreement with God's truth (Matt. 23:1-36).

That was how Jesus represented the trinity of truth (the light) in the darkness during His days on earth. So, what about us? What does our incarnational representation of the trinity of truth look like among the absence of truth in our todays? For us, like Jesus, it's about abiding in it.

We abide in the trinity of truth similar to how Jesus is the trinity of truth. In John 8:31 (NKJV), Jesus said, *"If you abide in My word, you are My disciples indeed."* The Greek term for "abide" He uses is about *cleaving,* as in Genesis 2:24 when it says man shall *"be joined"* to his wife.[37] It's also the same Greek term for how the branch is to *abide or be joined* to the Vine in John 15:1-8. In a sense, Jesus is communicating that abiding in His teaching is like marrying His teaching, becoming one flesh with His teaching. And Jesus is the archetype of this. He is the Incarnation of the trinity of truth. Comparably to what He is instructing His disciples, Jesus married (cleaved, joined) His divine life and light with His humanity and became one. We are to abide in the truth of God, the knowing of the truth of God, and the right living in agreement with the truth of God in a similar incarnational manner.

Haphazardly knowing, handling, and living in agreement with God's truth is not abiding. You don't randomly enter marriage, do you? Nope. And if you are habitually haphazardous in your marriage, your spouse probably wants to do marriage counseling or you might be possibly heading for a divorce. Abiding is intentional. It's a regular, throughout the day decision to be made. Abiding is lived. It requires constant effort for it, attention to it, time with it, and reflection of it. Abiding is also enjoyable and desirable. The more you know and understand Whom you're abiding in and what you're abiding in, the more joy and desire for abiding that follows.

✦ The 1st way.

The first way we abide in the trinity of truth is *by learning and being grounded in God's truth*. The Bible—Old Testament to New Testament—is replete with verses for learning and being grounded in God's truth. Shucks, Apostle Paul speaks to this in every single chapter in his second letter to Timothy.[38] And that's merely one book!

As disciples, we must regularly read, study, meditate, memorize, and be taught Scripture. So go to your worship service every week ready to engage in learning and being grounded in God's truth. Go to your Bible study or discipleship class or small group, however frequently

171

it meets, always ready to engage in learning and being grounded in God's truth. Take notes, ask questions, probe deeply, and hold firmly what you are learning to ground yourself in what we biblically believe and why. I know this all sounds normative. But our abiding in the trinity of truth like this does shine in the absence of truth around us. We shine because we are not being like those Paul says won't submit to God's truth but will instead reject His truth for falsehood (2Tim. 4:3-4); nor are we being like those Apostle Peter calls "ignorant and unstable" who distort the Scriptures on purpose to their own destruction (2Pet. 3:16). This will always stand out in the absence of truth around us.

One might think that's all there is concerning this first way of abiding. But the complexity and concession of our day necessitate greater implications of abiding by learning and being grounded in God's truth.

I love Church history. It's one of my favorite subjects. Over the last few years, I've spent more time reading specifically on American Church history. It's so heartbreaking that just about anyone can say anything about the Bible and the majority of professing American Christians can't determine if it's true or not—which means anything anyone says about the Bible can arise and be accepted as valid. Why do you think this is? If you're like me, I'm sure you have some reasons in mind. But I do believe it boils down to a two-headed culprit.

The paramount sponsor for the trinity of absence, second to sin, is relativism. This insidious plant is at the heart of the absence of truth. Relativism isn't some recent historical philosophy. It dates to the fall of Lucifer and has been the slow death of epistemology throughout the ages, starting in the garden of Eden. As a result, the proper principles of sound biblical hermeneutics have been and are still being contorted by people, leaders, and scholars to justify whatever a person wants to believe regarding God's truth (e.g., 2Cor. 11:13-15).[39] Hence, the formation of the relativistic-subjective hermeneutic—the two-headed culprit. This is all darkness posing itself as light, and it has subtlety deceived many professing believers because they are not abiding by learning and being grounded in God's truth.

Anytime a Christian takes the wisdom of this world and uses it to interpret and apply Scripture, they are operating in relativism and not abiding in the trinity of truth. The truth and wisdom of God cannot be understood through the wisdom of this world (1Cor. 2:1-16). If so, it would then not be the truth and wisdom of God. Our 11th century brother and theologian, Anselm of Canterbury, articulates this like such,

> "I acknowledge, Lord, and I give thanks that You have created Your image in me, so that I may remember You, think of You, love You. But this image is so effaced and worn away by vice, so darkened by the smoke of sin, that *it cannot do what it was made to do unless You renew it and reform it.... For I do not seek to understand so that I may believe; but I believe so that I may understand.*"[40]

> "When beginners foolishly try to ascend intellectually to those things *that first need the ladder of faith* (as Scripture says: 'Unless you have believed, you will not understand' [Isa. 7:9]), *they sink into many kinds of errors by reason of the deficiency of their intellect.*"[41]

Regarding the truths and wisdom of God in Scripture, there's a reason "faith" comes before "understanding" (Rom. 10:16-17, Heb. 11:1-3, 6). What belongs to God requires God to understand it. This is why God chooses what is deemed foolish to shame the wise; because the supposed wisdom of this world sees "faith first" as foolish, yet in God's economy, faith is the key to the understanding and intellect regarding His truth and wisdom (1Cor. 1:18-31). Faith is abiding in the trinity of truth, and abiding requires that we confidently know and believe in what we're abiding. The moment our faith wanes, so goes the understanding and intellect regarding God's truth and wisdom. What then naturally lurks in its place is using the world's wisdom because it makes more sense to our natural mind (e.g., John 8:30-59).

When Christians use the wisdom of this world to interpret and apply Scripture, all you get is a worldly interpretation and application that always justifies the world's ways or fleshly thinking and not God's truth. For example,

- The wisdom of this world says it's justifiable to have contempt for or to cancel people who believe differently or disagree with you. Yet, God commands His people to love everyone—neighbor, enemy, and other believers—unbiasedly (Matt. 5:38-48, Rom. 13:8-10).

- The wisdom of this world says sexual identity is fluid and not biologically determined as God created in Genesis and instructed throughout His Word (e.g., Gen. 1:26-27; 2:18-25, Matt. 19:4-6). Nevertheless, God still says even sexuality belongs to Him and is to be submitted to Him in holiness (1Cor. 6:9-20, 1Thess. 4:1-8).

- The wisdom of this world says trust what or how you feel, follow your heart and believe whatever you want. However, God tells His people repeatedly that the heart is wicked and the natural human inclination is toward evil (Jer. 17:9-10, Matt. 15:10-20).

- The wisdom of this world says speak your mind, share your views. God's wisdom says, think before you speak and don't be rash with your words nor venting your opinions (Prov. 10:19; 13:2-3, Matt. 12:33-37).

- The wisdom of the world presupposes the Bible as we have it is untrustworthy—i.e., the content is either contradictory or something is missing or both—and therefore should not be believed as is. The writers of Scripture declare God is real, this is His holy inspired book, and thus it is authoritative and trustworthy in all its content and sufficient for God's people in every way (e.g., Prov. 30:5-6, 2Tim. 3:14-17).

See how relativism sounds a lot like what the serpent whispered to Eve, *"Did God really say...?"* And like Eve, many Christians, maybe unknowingly, subvert the trinity of truth for whatever else they see, hear, think, or believe is more desirable or more reasonable to them.

As ambassadors, being heralds and portraits of the Incarnation, we are not to make a habit of being turncoat abiders (Heb. 3:12-15; 10:35-39). Every year since 2015, I've noticed how professing American Christians are better politicians and social activists than they are disciple-theologians. It's telling when you know your politics and your social causes in the right context better than your Bible in the right context. Shucks, many use the Bible to justify their political, social, and cultural ideology over knowing and practicing sound biblical theology. How telling is it when you can defend your political, social, and cultural views better than you can defend what Scripture actually teaches or not (i.e., apologetics and polemics)? How telling is it when you can defend your political, social, and cultural views better than you can rightly interpret Scripture (i.e., hermeneutics)? How telling is it that many believers are better followers of their favorite politicians or social causes or cultural concerns over being better followers of Jesus? Or, how telling is it that many believers are better *anti-* whatever politician, or political and social view, and so on, over being more *anti-* their personal idols, diminishing of the truth, and silence with the gospel? Thomas á Kempis hits it spot on,

> "What *good* is much discussion of involved and obscure matters, *when* our ignorance of them will not be held against us on Judgment Day? *Neglect of things which are profitable and necessary and undue concern with those which are irrelevant and harmful, are great folly.*"[42]

Are you catching the point of my examples here? I'm not saying believers living in the U.S. should not have knowledge of their personal political, social, and cultural views, or that they can't disagree with other viewpoints, or that they can't support or champion specific causes. What I am saying is we must understand, no matter the reason, it is idolatry of darkness to do any of this more than abiding in the divine Word's trinity of truth.

175

Limit your load of intaking other information so you can retain what matters most. For instance, how often do you re-listen to sermons or reread non-fiction Christian books (e.g., doctrinal, spiritual growth, Christian living)? Now think about how much info you consume compared to how much Bible or biblical edification you consume. You re-watch the same movies. You re-listen to the same music. However, the majority of Christians think one sermon a week is enough. They think five to fifteen minutes here and there in their Bible is enough, and then without thoughtfully reflecting on whatever they did read. They think rarely to never reading Christian non-fiction books is acceptable. Too many Christians think this infrequency is enough to sustain them in a world that's pulsating the trinity of absence everywhere, all the time. Thus, one component of our incarnational representation of the trinity of truth is abiding by ever learning and being firmly grounded in God's truth. This way, we can uphold it thoroughly and untaintedly in our thinking and living, shining amidst the absence of truth all around us.

⚮ The 2nd way.

The second way is a natural consequence of the first way. We abide in the trinity of truth *by being on guard for error and deception.*

> "46 I have come as a light into the world, that *whoever believes in Me should not abide in darkness.* 47 And if anyone hears My words and does not believe, I do not judge him; for I did not come to judge the world but to save the world. 48 *He who rejects Me, and does not receive My words, has that which judges him*—the word that I have spoken will judge him in the last day." (John 12:46-48, NKJV; *emphasis added*)

> "6 *Let no one deceive you with empty words,* for because of such things God's wrath comes on those who are disobedient. 7 Therefore do not be partners with them. 8 *For you were once darkness, but now you are light in the Lord.* Live as children of light 9 (for the fruit of the light consists in all goodness, righteousness and truth) 10 and find out what pleases the Lord. *11 Have nothing to do with the fruitless*

deeds of darkness, but rather expose them." (Eph. 5:6-11, NIV; *emphasis added*)

"Therefore, dear friends, since you know this in advance, *be on your guard, so that you are not led away by the error of lawless people and fall from your own stable position."* (2Peter 3:17, CSB; *emphasis added*)

Jesus taught that true born-again believers do not abide in darkness (the trinity of absence). Both Paul and Peter urge believers to vigilantly keep a close watch out for error, deception, and sin lest we be led astray and fall into spiritual instability (i.e., fall away from faithfulness). What do you think that means for us today? It means we cannot be incarnational lights of Christ that are more cautious with other things than we are with unbiblical ideas, beliefs, and information we repeatedly ingest. Otherwise, our light will dim in the darkness and we will unknowingly become obese with falsehoods. Recall Paul's warning in 2Timothy 3:13 (CSB), *"Evil people and impostors will become worse, deceiving and being deceived."*

Often, we think of false teachings as only theological. But false teachings can take on many forms: philosophical, scientific, sociological, political, cultural, and bad hermeneutics (which leads to misinterpretations). Anything teaching or prompting you to believe something that is not in accordance with Scripture, rightly interpreted, is false teaching.

Evermore than any other time in the history of mankind are believers to be on guard for error and deception. Right about now, everywhere we turn, almost everyone who is communicating any kind of message is prompting or teaching us something unbiblical. It may make sense. It may sound right. You might even agree. Nevertheless, anything apart from the trinity of truth is poisonous and deadly.[43] Think about it, since the internet's presence, humans have become inundated with more output, more information, and more misinformation. This has not made humanity smarter. Instead, it has revealed and amplified the deep-seated gullibility of people, Christians included. Look at what Proverbs 14:15-18 says,

"15 *The one who is easy to fool believes everything,* but the wise man looks where he goes.16 A wise man fears God and turns away from what is sinful, but *a fool is full of pride and is not careful.* 17 *He who has a quick temper acts in a foolish way,* and a man who makes sinful plans is hated. 18 *Those who are easy to fool are foolish,* but the wise have much learning." (NLV; *emphasis added*)

I'm not sure how many of you know or think about this point: Every video you see, media segment you watch, website you visit, podcast you listen to, and article or book you read that supports the view of "_____" (insert whatever you want in that blank), there is another video, media segment, website, podcast, article, and book that will dispute it and declare the opposite. And just because they say it's true and you believe it's true doesn't mean it's actually true. Welcome to the digital age of relativistic information where there is abounding material that supports everyone's viewpoint, all made available to you via the internet. Death is now served at our fingertips 24/7. If you don't know how to detect the landmines of error and deception embedded all around, you are playing Russian roulette with what you think, watch, peruse, listen to, and read. And sadly, too many professing Christians in the U.S. have unsuspectingly become radicalized by the tribe they follow.

Enter the peril of tribalism. According to several dictionaries, *tribalism contains a strong loyalty to one's tribe (party, group, or people) above other groups.*[44] Encyclopedia.com provided a little more background and insight into tribalism. In short, it states,

> "Tribalism is the manifestation of a collective group identity based on common natural impulses such as fear, desire, necessity, or ethnic distinctiveness.... Tribalism, therefore, is a fluid concept with both positive and negative connotations that must be understood with reference to specific contexts."[45]

Consequently, tribalism is pseudo-validation; (also known by a theory called "identity-protective cognition").[46] Tribalism, unfortunately, influences what information people research and accept as valid and what information they reject as false or conflicting.[47] For example, if you find yourself always or mostly agreeing with a particular group of people while disagreeing with other groups that your group disagrees with, that's tribalism. Hence, tribalism also thrives in and enjoys echo chambers—which, with social media, is now a jumbotron for the world to see.

For point sake, the only "tribalistic" thinking and views Christians are to defend and promote is the trinity of truth from the King and kingdom of whom we are ambassadors. All other tribalism is idolatrous because it elevates another tribe over the one tribe Jesus created in Himself (Gal. 3:26-29; 6:14-15, Col. 1:19-22). Thus, examine your tribe: your cultural tribe, your social tribe, your political tribe, your media tribe, your social media tribe, your information tribe, your church tribe, your friend tribe. If your tribe is not Christo-biblio-missio-centric, either leave that tribe, or abandon their thinking, or be led astray by them and their ideology (e.g., Acts 13:4-10).

Notice what Kempis implores in the 14th century, reflecting on what Christ speaks to our soul regarding being aware of listening to the voice of others.

> "My child, *do not let the fine-sounding and subtle words of men deceive you*. For the kingdom of heaven consists not in talk but in virtue. *Attend, rather, to My words which enkindle the heart and enlighten the mind, which excite contrition and abound in manifold consolations…. Woe to those who inquire of men about many curious things, and care very little about the way they serve Me…*. I teach *without* noise of words or clash of opinions, *without* ambition for honor or confusion of argument. I am He Who teaches man to despise earthly possessions and to loathe present things, to ask after the eternal, to hunger for heaven, to fly honors and to bear with scandals, to place all hope in Me, to desire nothing apart from Me, and to love Me ardently above all things."[48]

What did Paul tell the Corinthians about the people they're around? *"Don't be fooled. "Bad company ruins good character.""*[49] Similarly,

Dr. John Davis again, when pulling a point from the story of Lot in Genesis 19:30-38, notes, **"Our moral environments significantly influences our lives."**[50]

Our abiding in the trinity of truth shines brightly in this kind of darkness *when* we're not being gullible and willingly ingesting anything. This absence of truth is expected for the unredeemed (2Cor. 4:4). For the people and leaders in the local churches who call themselves Christian but represent the "tares" that grow with the wheat, error and deception are their scapegoats for abandoning the appearance of belonging to Christ. But this is not the case with born-again disciples of Jesus. Jesus said His sheep know His voice, listen to His voice, and follow their Shepherd (John 10:1-5, 14, 27). Then He said we'd receive the indwelling presence and power of the Holy Spirit who will keep us on track in God's truth (John 14:26; 15:26; 16:13-15). As redeemed bondservants and ambassadors, it is totally within our power to choose either to ingest and digest the world's errors or to vigilantly abide in our King's Scriptures; because to do one is to reject the other.

> "34 "Your eye is like a lamp that provides light for your body. When your eye is healthy, your whole body is filled with light. But when it is unhealthy, your body is filled with darkness. 35 *Make sure that the light you think you have is not actually darkness.* 36 If you are filled with light, with no dark corners, then your whole life will be radiant, as though a floodlight were filling you with light."" (Luke 11:34-36, NLT; *emphasis added*)

> "21 *But examine all things; hold fast to what is good. 22 Stay away from every form of evil.*" (1Thessalonians 5:21-22, NET; *emphasis added*)

> "1 Dear friends, do not believe everyone who claims to speak by the Spirit. You must test them to see if the spirit they have comes from God. For there are many false prophets in the world.... 5 *Those people belong to this world, so they speak from the world's viewpoint, and the world listens to them.* 6 But we belong to God, and those who know God listen to us. If they do not belong to God, they do not listen to us.

That is how we know if someone has the Spirit of truth or the spirit of deception." (1John 4:1, 5-6, NLT; *emphasis added*)

"8 Watch yourselves so that you don't lose what we have worked for, but that you may receive a full reward. 9 *Anyone who does not remain in Christ's teaching but goes beyond it does not have God.* The one who remains in that teaching, this one has both the Father and the Son. 10 *If anyone comes to you and does not bring this teaching, do not receive him into your home, and do not greet him; 11 for the one who greets him shares in his evil works.*" (2John 1:8-11, CSB; *emphasis added*)

Knowing that every human is born into darkness (the trinity of absence) provides fundamental insight into understanding humanity, and that is: *Humans can convince themselves of anything, including how what is actually false or wrong is accepted as truth or appropriate.* This fundamental insight is an effect of the fall. It must be considered when interacting with others, along with what we choose to personally believe and accept as truth during our lives, because we, too, are not excluded from this effect. **"Our opinions, our senses often deceive us and we discern very little."**[51] Hence, why Christians must unequivocally anchor everything we believe in what is only divine, inerrant, and sufficient—God's Word. Praise God He provided His people with His divine transcript in these sixty-six books! Hearsay, subjectivism, and relativism are much easier to fall prey to without a transcript. But with a transcript, we can refer to and check what God "actually" said, did, commanded, explained, and established as His truth and wisdom over simply receiving whatever someone tells us or whatever we concoct in our reasoning. It is paramount for us as ambassadors to root and filter everything—our words, actions, attitudes, beliefs, and what we see, hear, read, think, and so on—through God's Word, properly interpreted. Nothing more, nothing less.

To be heralds and portraits of His Incarnation and not abide in our Incarnate Savior's teachings is self-destructive for us and ruinous for those still in the dark. We would be putting a shade over the light we claim. Abiding is not merely an instruction we must obey. Abiding is indispensable for us to be able to guard against error and deception.

Dr. John MacArthur makes a fantastic and pertinent point about this in the book "Fools Gold."

> "Scripture does not give believers permission to expose themselves to evil. Some people believe the only way to defend against false doctrine is to study it, become proficient in it, and master all its nuances—then refute it. I know people who study the cults more than they study sound doctrine. Some Christians immerse themselves in the philosophy, entertainment, and culture of society. They feel such a strategy will strengthen their witness to unbelievers. But the emphasis of that strategy is all wrong. Our focus should be on knowing the *truth*. Error is to be shunned. Granted, we cannot recede into a monastic existence to escape exposure to every evil influence. But neither are we supposed to be experts about evil. The apostle Paul wrote, "I want you to be wise as to what is good and innocent as to what is evil" (Rom 16:19). Federal agents don't learn to spot counterfeit money by studying the counterfeits. They study genuine bills until they master the look of the real thing. Then when they see bogus money they recognize it. Detecting a spiritual counterfeit requires the same discipline. Master the truth to refute error. Don't spend time studying error; shun it. Study truth. Hold fast the faithful Word."[52]

The actual battle of darkness the Church of this age is facing is not with political, social, and cultural issues—though they matter and are to be addressed as an implication and application of sound biblical doctrine. The war Christians are in today is a war of worldviews that undermine the absolute and objective trinity of truth as revealed in Christ, as revealed in His Scripture, and as revealed through proper hermeneutics. The political, social, and cultural issues of our todays and tomorrows stem from worldview roots. Abiding by being on guard for error and deception is how we represent the trinity of truth (the light) in the darkness. We won't be validating or furthering the progress of the trinity of absence.

✦ The 3rd way.

The third way we abide in the trinity of truth is *by reflecting Whom and what we are abiding in*. As explained earlier, we abide in the trinity of truth in a similar incarnational manner as Jesus did in His Incarnation. Namely, Jesus married (cleaved, joined) His divine life and light with His humanity and became one. In the Incarnation, Jesus was the expressed image of the invisible God in a physical body.[53] Those who laid their eyes on Jesus of Nazareth saw the exact reflection of God. In like manner, our abiding in the trinity of truth is to express the image of Whom and what we're abiding in. When people see us, they are to see Jesus and His truth.

How was it revealed that Jesus was God in the flesh? He said it. He taught it. He lived and characterized it by doing things only God could do. How is it revealed that someone is married? They talk about it and display it, right? They have a love for each other that they outwardly, verbally, and nowadays digitally express. Typically, they have a wedding band on. They're monogamous. They fully integrate their lives. They're only to be intimate (physically and emotionally) with each other. They date. And so forth. How is it revealed that a Christian is abiding in the trinity of truth? Not much different than the answer for Jesus and marriage.

To abide in the trinity of truth is to live like Scripture is the *only* truth, even when everything else around us may be trying to convince us that biblical truth is wrong, culturally bound, or antiquated. Belief directs conduct. Every human operates relatively according to what they believe, whether it's true or false, right or wrong, empirical, theoretical, or spiritual. What we believe charts the course of our conduct (Rom. 12:2). Therefore, how Christians openly live their lives is to be directed by God's absolute and objective truth that we claim to believe and abide in. We can't claim to abide in the trinity of truth and it not be evident that we do (1John 1:5-7).

- ✓ We are to *speak* (which includes what we say online) like we believe the truth we claim we abide in.
- ✓ We are to *reason* like we believe the truth we claim we abide in.

- ✓ We are to *choose* like we believe the truth we claim we abide in.
- ✓ We are to *behave* like we believe the truth we claim we abide in.
- ✓ We are to *lead and influence* like we believe the truth we claim we abide in.
- ✓ We are to *repent* when we're wrong or have sinned like we believe the truth we claim we abide in.
- ✓ We are to *forgive* when we've been wronged or sinned against like we believe the truth we claim we abide in.
- ✓ We are to *interact* with one another and others like we believe the truth we claim we abide in.

Are you catching the gist? Go through the New Testament, notice how every life application verse(s) precedes or proceeds from a revealed truth of God. God's truth distinctively roots a lifestyle. **"For it is a fact that the more powerfully sacred Scripture nourishes us with things that feed us by obedience, the more acutely we are drawn to things that satisfy us intellectually."**[54]

As herald and portraits of the Incarnation, our lives should declare we are happily and faithfully married to Jesus and His truth. People around us should be able to figuratively see a "biblical ring" on our lives—a visible token of a loving and monogamous commitment that identifies we are married to Jesus and all of His teachings and truths in all of Scripture. Our abiding should make Jesus attractive. It doesn't mean it will always attract people to Jesus unto salvation, as much as it means it should catch people's attention and interest like other attractive relationships tend to do. For instance, as dysfunctional as my marriage was in the past, some people that get to know us and our story walk away saying, "I want a marriage like that." Although those in the dark don't like Christ's light because it exposes their darkness (John 3:19-20); like insects to lights, there should be something about Whom and what we're reflecting that is both inviting and convicting to onlookers.

There are numerous parallels to our abiding by reflecting. The moon, for example. The moon doesn't glow on its own. Instead, the moon that appears visibly enough in the sky reflects the sun's light from its angle to the earth. That's how we are to be as ambassadors of Christ. We are moons for the Son—a reflection of His light on this planet. Or, likewise, lamps and mirrors. Abiding by reflecting is about being lamps or mirrors with legs, showing and shining God's truth everywhere we are. And this is not forcing it or bombarding people with it. Rather, it's reflecting it in how we live out the trinity of truth we claim to believe. Ever seen "Beauty and the Beast"? Remember the candlestick, Lumiere? He didn't force or bombard people with his little light. If you can recall, whenever he was around, his little light was always glowing. It goes unnoticed until when? The space he was in was dark. Then his little light shined brightly.

The point from every parallel I can make is this: *obedience to the truth of God emits the light of the truth of God.* **"In the spiritual realm,"** says Dr. Howard Hendricks, **"the opposite of ignorance is not knowledge, it's obedience. In the New Testament understanding, to know and not to do is not to know at all."**[55] Once more, our brother Thomas á Kempis has something valuable to add.

> **"I would rather feel contrition than know how to define it.** *For what would it profit us to know the whole Bible by heart and the principles of all the philosophers, if we live without grace and the love of God?* Vanity of vanities and all is vanity, except to love God and serve Him alone. This is the greatest wisdom—to seek the kingdom of heaven through contempt of the world. It is vanity, therefore, to seek and trust in riches that perish. It is vanity also to court honor and to be puffed up with pride. It is vanity to follow the lusts of the body and to desire things for which severe punishment later must come. It is vanity to wish for long life and to care little about a well-spent life. It is vanity to be concerned with the present only and not make provision for things to come. It is vanity to love what passes quickly and not to look ahead where eternal joy abides."[56]

Representing the trinity of truth amid the absence of truth is about reflecting the truth we abide in. Christians are to be a constant reminder in the darkness that the Light is near. As heralds and portraits of the Incarnation, we're never not glowing—never not portraying Christ's Incarnation. Yes, some days our light may be dim because of our own sin, selfishness, ignorance, or neglect. But if we're truly in Christ, whoever follows Him shall not walk in darkness. So even dim lights still glimmer because light is never dark, no matter how low the light may be. When the people, ideas, cultures, and environments around us are operating in the trinity of absence, our confident and graceful obedience to the truth of God will naturally shine brighter as the contrast. Consider then our light's reach in where and how we obey God's truth online and offline, in our words, actions, choices, attitudes, and demeanors, in our homes, schools, workplaces, with our influence and positions of authority, so on. There's a host of spaces and ways to reflect the truth amid its absence.

> "18 The way of the righteous is like the first gleam of dawn, which shines ever brighter until the full light of day. 19 But the way of the wicked is like total darkness. They have no idea what they are stumbling over." (Proverbs 4:18-19, NLT)

To be heralds and portraits of the Incarnation is to be lighthouses of Jesus and His truth. His light is shining in and through us to those lost in the sea of darkness. Hence, we have to stop willfully choosing the darkness because it's easier. We have to stop willfully choosing the trinity of absence over the trinity of truth because it doesn't fit our plans, preferences, politics, or lifestyle. It being too hard, too offensive, too out of touch, and so on are also not valid reasons. We don't merely hurt ourselves when we do this; we also become distractions for others from the truth. We reflect and shine the light of Christ in the absence of truth when we live according to the truth as revealed in Scripture.

Lights on the Move

As sojourners, we're the salt. We're sprinkling a little godly flavor everywhere we go as we pass through. As ambassadors—in being heralds and portraits of the Incarnation—we are the incarnational lights of Christ in the darkness we live among. We're shining God's truth and heart wherever He stations us. We are the reconciled vehicles God inhabits to continue meeting people in an up-close and personal way to reconcile them to Himself.

But there's more. We are powered by the very life of the very *Logos* of God. Therefore stop giving in and giving up so easily. We are powered by what can never be overpowered. We do more to hinder our own light than those around us do. So go, Church! Be the incarnational lights of Christ everywhere you are and in every space God allows you to shine His light. Go with power and be the representation of the trinity of truth. For when we are abiding in God's truth by knowing His truth, upholding His truth, proclaiming His truth, and rightly living in agreement with His truth, we are shining His light in the absence of His truth around us.

Remember, light will always contrast darkness. Light and dark are perpetual opposites. They are the antithesis of one another. Light and darkness can never blend, so it can never be light and dark. It's either light or dark. Choosing the light that we now are in Christ will always stand in contrast to the darkness around us because His light shines bright in the darkness. Shine as ambassadors of our Incarnate Savior, representing how Jesus Himself was incarnational unto reconciliation.

HERALDS & PORTRAITS OF HIS KINGDOM

To be an ambassador of Christ is to be a herald and portrait of His kingdom—i.e., His union with believers and rule as their King. In 2Corinthians 5:17, 21, Paul said,

> "17 Therefore, *if anyone is united with the Messiah, he is a new creation – the old has passed; look, what has come is fresh and new!*.... 21 God made this sinless man be a sin offering on our behalf, *so that in union with him we might fully share in God's righteousness.*" (CJB, *emphasis added*)

The Greek term Paul uses here for "creation" is a call back to the creation of the world.[57] God created the world brand new, something from nothing and something never done before. Those of us now "in Jesus" are created as something brand new—something never done before. Different and far greater than the world's creation, we are not a new entity; we are now in union with Christ!

Our union with Christ is a supernatural placement in God and under His rule. Recall how the Holy Spirit supernaturally placed the eternal Son in the womb of Mary to bring about something radically new—the Incarnation. Later, the Holy Spirit supernaturally places believers into Christ Himself to bring about something radically new— "a new creation." Like with the supernatural phenomenon of the Incarnation, have you ever thought about what this "new creation" fully entails? This "new creation" means (i)a *new* human-spiritual race (the Body of Christ, made up of born-again men and women from different ethnicities, cultures, and languages), (ii)an individual *new* birth into a *new* life, and now (iii)a born-again native and noble of a *new* kingdom. I hope reading that got you as fired up as it did for me! How's that for something *"fresh and new"*?

Paul is declaring that to be united with the Messiah is life-transforming in totality *of* our humanity, *of* our whole person (past, present, and eternity), and *of* our domain. Our immersion in Christ permeates everything. Nothing is left untouched. Nothing in our lives is not under His rule. We are not merely God's one-time creation, fearfully and wonderfully made in His image. We are God's two-time creation, fearfully and wonderfully in His image, and perfectly made anew in Christ (1Cor. 15:45-49). To be a herald and portrait of Christ's kingdom is about being the emissaries of life *in* the King and His kingdom while here on earth. We're the official envoys of this "new creation."

Kingdom Carriers & Representations

Wherever God lives and rules is His kingdom. He exists outside of time; therefore, eternity is His kingdom (Ps. 45:6; 90:2; 93:1-2). He sits on heaven; therefore, heaven is His kingdom (1Kin. 8:27, Isa. 66:1). He says He will rule and reign in the new heavens and new earth;

therefore, they are His coming kingdom (Isa. 65:17-19, Rev. 21:1-5). And, it has been made abundantly clear that God lives and rules in and through His beloved and begotten people. Therefore, Christians—the Church, the Body of Christ—are the kingdom of God on earth. Not that we are the possessors of the kingdom. Rather, because God is in possession of us, we are now His kingdom here.

Jesus declared our Triune God makes His home in us, and Paul says we are God's temple.[58] Ponder the weight of that reality. Our redeemed life is another throne of God where He rules and reigns via the indwelling presence of the Spirit and His Word as our constitution. As we've already explored, we no longer sit on nor own the throne of our lives. God does. He purchased it through the sacrifice of Jesus and sealed His purchase with the Holy Spirit. For this reason, being heralds and portraits of life in the King and His kingdom while here on earth means every Christian is a kingdom carrier and kingdom representation.

In the Lord's Prayer, when Jesus tells His disciples to pray, *"Your kingdom come, Your will be done, on earth as it is in heaven,"*[59] He was communicating this kingdom carrier and kingdom representation. In the context of this verse in the Greek, Jesus was explaining that the King does His will—i.e., His heart's desire, whatever He wants—within His kingdom.[60] In this context, Jesus is instructing His disciples to desire and willfully request in their prayers that their King rule His kingdom however He so desires on earth like how He rules His kingdom in heaven. Jesus is not saying pray for these things *to* happen, but that His disciples are to affirm they *will* happen—and not perfectly, but presently. For, it will *"be done"* through us, His kingdom carriers and kingdom representations, because those then and us today who profess Christ as our Savior and Lord are His kingdom on earth.

In this short sentence, Jesus taught His followers across every generation that in our prayers, we are to align our thinking to God's reality—He's the King that does His will in His kingdom, both in heaven and on earth. Thus, we, the born-again covenant people of God, need to accept and expect the King to rule His kingdom however He desires in and through our redeemed lives on the earth He created. But let's be honest, that's a challenge to every fiber of our controlling nature.

Is it not? Nevertheless, we can embrace this new reality without being gripped with fear of losing control or anxiety and concern. Indeed, we can do so with confidence because it's not ourselves or some earthly ruler we're submitting our lives to represent their kingdom. Our King's unchanging character is why we can accept and expect Him to rule however He desires in and through us with confidence.

⸎ Carriers.

Do you have a cell phone? Come to think of it, who doesn't have a cell phone right about now? Those of us with cell phones know that every cell phone with service has a cellular carrier—e.g., Verizon, AT&T, Sprint, T-Mobile. Every cellular carrier has a range of coverage. Whenever you're in their range of coverage, you have service. Being kingdom carriers is no different, but certainly better. Jesus is the cellular carrier with an eternal range of coverage. Every one of His born-again disciples is then the personal Wi-Fi hotspots of His kingdom. Wherever any believer in Christ physically is, there is God's kingdom. This is why we are to take the gospel of the kingdom to the ends of the earth, because the good news of the King and His kingdom is not solely before them *in* our words but also *in* our presence.

Each of us, everywhere we are—home, work, school, hanging out, doing hobbies, online, out and about, on the phone, gaming, so on—are to exhibit the presence of the life and rule of the King and His kingdom. The unredeemed people around us should detect a different Wi-Fi network from theirs, and with a much stronger signal. Something is to be significantly distinctive from how we are compared to how they are because our kingdoms stand in stark contrast to one another.

As carriers of Christ's kingdom, whether in the good or the bad, we portray the kingdom everywhere we are and in everything we do. Nothing is off limits. This then includes whatever may not typically come to your mind: In our parenting. In our neighborliness. With the abilities we possess. In the issues and causes we're passionate about. With certain privileges and/or wealth we have. In using our "rights" and "liberties." In the positions of authority and influence we hold. Everywhere and everything! Regardless if you want to or not, if you're aware of it or not, every Christian's life previews to others a place where God lives and rules. That's the reality of being kingdom carriers. Allen M. Wakabayashi explains it as such,

> "The community of faith is not meant to be simply a heavenly support group! No, the church is meant to be a community that witnesses to the truth and life of God. It's not just about our needs but about a whole world of people who need to see that God is alive and loves them. *Through our individual lives and corporate life together, God is at work to show the world his love and power, his justice and truth.* Often we become so self-absorbed with how the church is or is not meeting our needs that we forget that the church exists for the world."[61]

❧ Representations.

Picture your happy place. What does it look like? For me, this looks like sitting in a comfy chair with a good book (and a pencil), a nice hot cup of coffee, a blazing, crackling fireplace next to a big window overlooking a snowy field or lake, and my wife somewhere nearby. If you're married, picture a romantic place. On a riverboat in Paris in the fall. At a tropical destination in the summer. In a cozy cabin in the winter. Picture a place you would hate. Is it trashy? Is it too hot? Is it too cold? Is it smelly? Is it too noisy? If you played along, did you notice how each place evoked an image and triggered a sense? Your happy place might've made you smile. Your romantic place might've made you warm inside. A place you would hate might've made your face scrunch up. Each place we pictured represented something to us, and our response to it followed suit.

Now let's put ourselves up as the picture. What kingdom are you representing to those who are around you or watching you? What image is your life evoking before others? What senses and responses are being triggered by what you say (online and offline), your demeanor, your choices, your actions, and the use of your influence?

Does your life look like you are under the rule of King Jesus and part of His kingdom? If it doesn't, then at best, it's poorly representing His kingdom. The worst would be that your life becomes a distortion for what people think of Jesus and His kingdom. On the other hand, let's suppose you're tempered, gracious, honest, repentant, forgiving, generous, a peacemaker, and unashamed. When the people around you know or find out you're Christian, this preview of the kingdom before them is more attractive than repellent. Broken and fruitful living more accurately represents life in the King and His kingdom. It highlights our shortcomings, Christ's restorative grace, and the fruit that gradually follows living in and for Him.

Don't ever think your life as a Christian—how you stumble, how you fail, how you rise, how you follow, how you lead—is not representing the kingdom. It most certainly is. Hence, *how* we live for Jesus here on earth is so critical because it reflects the kingdom and the King we profess to represent. This means we do not simply reflect and represent a future hope to those in this world—eternal paradise with God *to come*. But also a present hope—eternal life in Christ *now*. We are to represent what heaven on earth looks like through our lives. We are to show and tell others what life in the King and His kingdom is like and how it's far better than life outside of God's kingdom. Notice Augustine's contrast in the "City of God."

> "If any man uses this life with a reference to that other which he ardently loves and confidently hopes for, he may well be called even now blessed, though not in reality so much as in hope. *But the actual possession of the happiness of this life, without the hope of what is beyond, is but a false happiness and profound misery.* For the true blessings of the soul are not now enjoyed; for that is no true wisdom which does not direct all its prudent observations, manly actions, virtuous self-restraint, and just arrangements, to that end in which God shall be all and all in a secure eternity and perfect peace."[62]

⚘ Mistaken representation.

Allow me to quickly address a way we mistake this kingdom representation. In the U.S., some of us tend to want to fight for what seems like everything. However, not every fight, not every cause, not every argument is our ambassadorial responsibility. Being a kingdom representation is not about imposing our kingdom values, kingdom ethics, or kingdom civics upon any government, society, or culture; nor is it about the official regulation of man's kingdoms under the authority of Scripture. Only Christians are responsible for and in control of how we are as kingdom carriers and kingdom representations. We cannot expect nor hold unbelievers responsible for representing our kingdom's values, ethics, and civics.[63] That is purely the Christian's duty and something we must hold one another accountable to.

As sojourning ambassadors of Christ, we have to divest ourselves from this notion that the nations and countries of this world are vassals of Christianity. We've already explored that the covenant people of God—made up of born-again men and women from all nations, tribes, peoples, and tongues—is the sole nation of God. The global Church—past, present, and future—is the only actual theocratic nation because we are exclusively God's kingdom on earth. Therefore, we cannot hold non-theocratic countries, societies, and cultures to the theocratic standard of Scripture. That's unreasonable and unfair. Nowhere in Scripture are we taught to demand, expect, or compel the people in the kingdoms of this world to live according to the kingdom of God. Can we infuse our kingdom values and ethics into man's kingdoms? Absolutely! This is why God appointed *us* as ambassadors of Christ and has sovereignly placed *us* wherever we are and in everything we are doing. It's for that very reason *we* are His kingdom carriers and representations.

God has chosen to display His kingdom to this world through those of us He's saved. Christian infighting shows a divided kingdom. Christian adultery with the world shows an unattractive kingdom. Christian segregation shows a tribalistic kingdom. But Christ in the Christian reigning as King everywhere we are, at every stage and season of life we traverse, and in every situation we face (especially the situations we dislike), demonstrates a hopeful kingdom.

> "We are God's chosen people in whom the Age to Come has taken root. As the Spirit enlivens our love and worship and empowers our truthtelling and actions, we give off the fragrance of the coming kingdom of God. We give people real tastes of the goodness, justice, power and mercy that will one day mark God's beneficent reign when Jesus returns and sets all things right."[64]

Kingdom Vision

As kingdom carriers and kingdom representations, we are to seek to bring God's kingdom into environments where there is no coverage or little connection to Jesus. Homogeneity is an obstacle to the great commission. If, as heralds and portraits of the kingdom, we only stay in comfortable and like-minded spaces—i.e., our same ethnicity or those culturally like-minded, politically like-minded, socially like-minded, and so on—then that's disobedience to the vision and mission of the kingdom. This doesn't mean we have to move if we live in a monoethnic neighborhood or leave our homogeneous church, nor does it mean we can't be friends or hang out with those who are like-minded and like-ethnic. What it means is the kingdom of light is designed to be among the diversity of the kingdom of darkness to lead those in darkness into the light. Thus, we cannot willingly segregate from cross-ethnic or cross-cultural environments and interactions, both among unbelievers and among the diversity represented by believers.[*]

⚘ Vision distortion.

God gives us a profile of His kingdom vision in the book of Acts. Though the book of Acts takes place in the 1st century, the challenges and lessons are timeless and seemingly always culturally relevant. For example, a lesson from their challenges appears to be a

---

[*]As a reminder, "ethnicity" means *the people group from which you were born.* "Culture" is *the traditions, customs, and ways of a certain group of people.*

reoccurring challenge for Christians across the centuries: We as Christians can have good intentions in carrying out the great commission but be blinded to our ethnic and cultural prejudices or inhibitors that hinder us from fulfilling it.

If you have your Bible nearby, take a moment and read Acts 10. Notice how God coordinates His kingdom vision between different people groups from different cultures so that His mission can be carried out accordingly. First, God came to Cornelius, a gentile, in a vision by way of an angel. Then God came to Peter, a Jewish Christian, through a vision of something far more graphic. God only gave Cornelius an instruction and nothing more about why. And Cornelius, the unredeemed God-fearer, responds promptly in faith to the vision of God (Acts 10:7-8). On the other hand, God gives Peter far more than an instruction. And Peter, the redeemed leader of the Church, was hesitant to the vision of God because of his cultural heritage and religion. It took three times just to get his attention, and even then, he still didn't respond in faith (Acts 10:11-16). While Peter was ethnically and culturally a Jew, by this time, he is no longer under his Jewish culture's religion. He was born-again in Christ. Yet, it was a battle at times for Peter to not think according to the Mosaic Law.

What we see and can learn from Acts is that sometimes God has to directly and repeatedly confront us to remove our ethnic and cultural inhibitors so we can truly see His kingdom vision. The vision of the kingdom is cross-ethnic and cross-cultural.[65] Christian, to be a herald and portrait of Christ's kingdom is to embrace and champion the vision of His kingdom over your allegiance to your country, ethnicity, culture, and traditions. Remember, we are God's official envoys of His new creation in Christ, and one aspect is that we are a new human-spiritual race—the Body of Christ, comprised of born-again men and women from different ethnicities, cultures, and languages. But again, let's be honest here. For many of us, this is beyond our limited perspective. The comfortability and favoritism of our personal ethnicity, culture, generation, socio-economic demographic, and political affiliation, or the hurt caused by one another's ignorance and prejudices that retreat us back to segregation, all limits our vision of the kingdom.

We can't make disciples of all nations and seek to reach the ends of the earth if we can't see and move beyond our comfortability and preferences. Shucks, the "of all nations," could be represented right in our own families, neighborhoods, cities, or churches if they're ethnically and culturally diverse. So, I wonder if some of the ethnic tension and socio-culture clashing in the U.S. and the Church is not solely because of political and media instigation. Maybe it's by the design of God coordinating His kingdom vision between different people, bringing attention to our ethnic and cultural prejudices and inhibitors so that His mission can be carried out accordingly by His Church in our country. Maybe God is the One up to something. If so, it is our responsibility as heralds and portraits of the kingdom to open our eyes of faith and follow Him. Let us not resist what He's doing just to fight for things that are perishing and of no eternal value.

↟ A hopeful vision.

When believers catch God's kingdom vision, there should be an expectation and readiness that accompanies it. Why? Because the gospel is for everyone! Thus, each Christian gets to play a crucial part in it reaching multitudes of people. And, equally as important, what's included in this crucial part we play is rightly representing united ethnic and cultural diversity in the kingdom. This testifies that the gospel is for everyone.

God's kingdom vision is a gloriously unique calling and most incredible privilege for born-again believers! We get to participate with God in His plan of cross-ethnic and cross-cultural redemptive reconciliation, both with unbelievers and believers. Then, to ensure our success, we are supported by the Holy Spirit. We don't have to attempt to muster up our own limited strength and wisdom, nor are we confined to human ingenuity. We are powered to participate by the divine. We can trust God and follow His ways unto success with His kingdom vision (Prov. 3:1-8).

On humanity's best day, with the most astute, brilliant, and compassionate minds, this kind of vision could never be achieved (Prov. 15:8-9, 26, 29). Even if it were in an ideal environment and unlimited resources, it still wouldn't matter. Any solution they came up with would constantly be subjective because mankind is wholly flawed and broken.[66] Whatever mankind creates or curates will always in some manner be faulty. I'm not implying it won't be good things. It will and has been. However, imperfect people cannot generate anything perfect or close to perfect. Nothing. No systems. No laws. No government. No plans. There will always be flaws, which means it won't be "good" for everyone. To deny this reality undermines biblical truth and our kingdom hope while giving credence to mankind's humanistic math that "broken + broken = something whole" is attainable. **"Mankind will not be able to solve the problem of mankind because mankind is the problem."**[67]

Only the impeccable Creator of humanity can bring about a vision like this. Only He can take what's flawed and broken and produce something entirely new and whole from it. Only He can take what's irreconcilable and reconcile it as one. That's the "new creation" we're to be envoys of.

Jesus modeled His kingdom vision in His Incarnation and His newly created human-spiritual race. He then deploys His redeemed people to be heralds and portraits of what can only be accomplished by Him, through Him, and in Him. God is reconciling different people to become one family scattered everywhere to work together with Him and each other. Therefore, if you don't expect with readiness that God is doing this and will use you to help do so, you have not caught His kingdom vision.

✝ Adjusting the lenses.

Let's clear up a possible misconstruction. The believers who live in monoethnic environments are not in any wrong for where they live, nor are they in the wrong for going to a homogeneous church if that's the demographic of their environment. Much of the countries around the world are monoethnic. We don't convict those believers of a wrong for living where they do. At the same time, believers are also not to treat this kingdom vision disingenuously. The vision of the kingdom is not a token project where you insert yourself into different ethnic spaces or invite others into your monoethnic space just to check a box. It's always about the heart. I saw a tweet that said something like, **"Diversity *is not* the goal; it's *a means* to the goal. Doxology is the goal."** Again, it's always about the heart.

Since the U.S. is probably the most ethnically diverse and culturally inclusive nation, those who live here have fewer excuses than our brethren in other countries. So, regarding this misconstruction, the kind of heart questions we must ask are:

◈ Do I choose to live where I live to intentionally segregate from others who are ethnically different from me?

◈ Do I choose to attend a church to intentionally segregate from others who are ethnically or culturally different than me?

◈ Do I choose to pursue cross-ethnic and cross-cultural engagement or inclusion because it's the popular thing to do or to not be mislabeled as a racist or something else?

These kinds of questions highlight what's counter to the vision of the kingdom, *the wrong heart.*

Are you involved in God's kingdom vision with the right motives—for the King's pleasure and mission? If not, then more than likely, you are sheltered in the comfortability or bias of your ethnicity, culture, generation, socio-economic demographic, political affiliation, etc. For those who are naturally engulfed in more homogeneous environments—neighborhood, school, work, church, so on—if you don't have any cross-ethnic or cross-cultural relationships or regular genuine interactions, your vision is limited. Not non-existent, just limited. We all need those across-the-spectrum relationships and genuine interactions. This way, we can experience the kingdom vision of God, see where our inhibitors are, and intentionally be on mission as His kingdom carrier and representation to those who look, think, and live differently than us. If you don't have these relationships or interactions, or care to pursue these relationships and interactions, then you have knowingly or unknowingly sheltered yourself from God's kingdom vision. Repentance, prayerful change, and someone to hold you accountable to this are required on your end. And amen that our King is gracious to grant this!

For my brethren who are exhausted from being the ethnic or cultural minority in the majority's space, drained from trying to build cross-ethnic and cross-cultural bridges to what seems like no avail, and worn out from discipling people who agree in word but not in their repentance, action, or thinking, I can empathize with your weariness. However, the vision of the kingdom is not to respond to ignorance, prejudice, ethnocentrism, or racism in the Church in kind or with more intentional segregation. That assists in perpetuating those problems because it abandons the vision. Responding to a wrong with a wrong doesn't make it right; it creates another wrong. Jesus instructs us to respond in the Christlike manner we desire for them to respond (Matt. 7:12).

Since the vision is cross-ethnic and cross-cultural inclusion, you can't respond to their lack of inclusion with withdrawal. If you're on the inside, you fight for inclusion to model what the kingdom vision looks like, and you keep fighting until the leaders and influencers of the majority catch it and follow suit. God sovereignly placed you there partly for that reason. How else would there ever be progress for God's kingdom vision if He didn't insert His ambassadors amid homogeneity? And to make sure I'm not mistaken, I am in no way saying remain in an abusive fellowship, ministry, or Christian organization. Abuse and suffering are different. Suffering for the gospel, or for Christ's sake, or for being Christian is to be expected and endured (Matt. 5:10-12, 1Pet. 4:12-19). Abuse is harm without the element of it being for the gospel, Christ, or our faith. So leave the abuse and report it if you can. But if it's not abuse, then we mustn't forsake suffering for the vision of the kingdom and retreat to segregation because it's easier or more comfortable.

Remember, these challenges aren't new in the Church. The New Testament highlights how Jewish Christians during the 1st century struggled with ethnocentrism, culturalism, and discrimination of the gentile Christians.[68] Thus, loving correction, longsuffering, and constant discipleship are how we respond. Paul had to do this very thing with Peter (Gal. 2:1-21), and the Lord does the same with us (Heb. 12:5-11).

As a multiethnic African American man with an urban, thuggish, and debauched past whom God has called into Anglo-American spaces, I get it. I have spent most of my Christian life and pastoral ministry as a minority in majority spaces. I have dealt with and at times still deal with the ignorance, arrogance, blindness, stubbornness, insensitivity, and self-righteousness from the majority. So please hear my heart when I say this: *we cannot afford to resign from contending for the vision of the kingdom.* No matter which ethnic minority you may be, we are further along than we've ever been, standing on the shoulders of those who labored before us to get us to where we are now. We must do the same for those to come. The beauty of the diversity and tapestry of Christ's kingdom is on display to the world. This is not some shoddy vision. It is a global vision with temporal and eternal ramifications. It's worth whatever lashes and sacrifices we experience in pursuit of it, especially since our King bore those stripes first in His body when He sacrificed His life to bring this kingdom vision into reality (1Pet. 2:21-25; 4:14-19).

> *"Therefore, my dear brothers and sisters, be steadfast, immovable, always excelling in the Lord's work, because you know that your labor in the Lord is not in vain."* (1Corinthians 15:58, CSB; *emphasis added*)

⚑ The vision keeper.

Christian, our God is sovereign. There is absolutely nothing powerful enough to derail the cross-ethnic and cross-cultural kingdom vision and mission of God. Not our free-will, nor our sin, not the world's way, nor Satan and his forces. Nothing. God will bypass our selfish and prejudiced choices, just as He has done with the racist, ethnocentric, and chauvinistic past (and sometimes present) of the Church. God will plow right over the enemy, just as He did on the Cross. And, through the power of the Holy Spirit, God will raise up more Stephens, and Philips, and Pauls, and Cornelius's, and Rhodas.

He will use them to agitate the religiosity of a complacent, biased, and disobedient Church, and use them to be prophets and trailblazers until the Church repents and realigns to the vision and mission of the kingdom.

This is our God, and He will not relent on His kingdom vision and mission. The question for you, Christian, is what are you going to do? Are you going to be willingly part of the problem in both kingdoms (the kingdom of darkness and the kingdom of light), or be willingly used by the Holy Spirit as an ambassador of the kingdom to participate with Christ in bringing about His cross-ethnic and cross-cultural vision?

In no way am I implying that embracing, championing, and being involved in the vision of the kingdom will not be daunting and injurious. It most certainly will. I am communicating that it can *only* be done by Christ through our representation of Him to the world. And it's worth far more than whatever we'll lose along the way.

Kingdom Justice

Being heralds and portraits of the kingdom means our responsibility is to live out our kingdom values, kingdom ethics, and kingdom civics. We infuse the kingdom of God into the kingdoms of man by us representing life *in* the King and His kingdom wherever God has sovereignly placed us to work, go to school, live, play, shop, and serve. Moreover, this infusion includes with our abilities, concerns, privileges, wealth, rights, liberties, and positions of authority. Also, as thorny as it is, social justice is another arena where we are to be kingdom carriers and representations; and not elusively, but according to Scripture applied in our particular contexts.

➤ **Social justice -v- Kingdom justice.**

Since I'm aware that seeing the phrase "social justice" will evoke some internal and external reactions depending upon your view, allow me to explain what I mean so we're on the same page. On September 14, 2017, I wrote a blog article entitled "A Biblical Response: Social Justice & the Christian." At the beginning of the article, I sought to clarify this messy phrase in a way I believe could be a common agreement, at least among believers.

"When we hear/read "social justice" don't always equate it to politics or social movements. It is always wise to first ask (or investigate) what context is this "social justice" referring to before assuming what you think the person meant. In my post I explained what I meant without ever using the term "social justice." I said "justice/change to be had/heard in social areas" and "justice/change in social areas to be had amidst the Church."

Social means *"relating to human society, or the interaction of the individual and the group, or the welfare of human beings as members of society"* (Merriam-Webster.com).

So my use of "social areas" would be "areas relating to the welfare of human beings as members of society."

Justice means *"the maintenance or administration of what is 'just' especially by the impartial adjustment of conflicting claims or the assignment of merited rewards or punishments"*; *"the principle or ideal of just dealing or right action"* (Merriam-Webster.com).

So my use of "justice" would be "the principle or ideal of just dealing or right action." Thus, my use of "justice/change in social areas" would then mean *"the principle or ideal of just dealing or right action in areas relating to the welfare of human beings as members of society and/or the Church."* This is what I mean whenever I communicate something regarding "social justice." (I also believe this is what it should mean for every Christian)."[69]

That's my working definition of "social justice." Thus, "injustices" would then be *wherever there is an absence of fair or just dealings or the absence of right actions*—i.e., individually, corporately, institutionally, or systemically. However, justice and injustice can be subjective because what one calls fair or unfair, just or an inequality, another may say differently. Only Christians have the objective standard of right and wrong disclosed by God in His Word (Rom. 7:7-13). Therefore, kingdom justice is *the kingdom's values, ethics, and civics applied by ambassadors where injustices are present in the social arenas we live in so that people see life in the King and come to believe the gospel of His kingdom*.

Any kind of justice promoted and employed by ambassadors of Christ can never be apart from the justice found and experienced only in the kingdom of Christ. Otherwise, we become ambassadors of worldly justice, not the justice of God's kingdom. As Augustine wrote, *"True justice has no existence save in that republic whose founder and ruler is Christ."*[70] This is but another reason why we have been appointed as herald and portraits of the kingdom. Christ's kingdom is the only place that can deliver on true, lasting justice and righteousness, which is something that will never be found or had in any of the kingdoms of man or by way of their justice. There's only one right way, and it's not man's way. Therefore, Christian, we cannot get swept up in the tragic setup of expecting what's promised regarding God's coming kingdom with being fulfilled here in the kingdoms of man.

> "While we shine His light brightly in this world (through our words & actions), *we must not lose sight* that this present darkness will not be completely vanquished until the culmination of His kingdom comes (1Cor. 15:23-26). It **is** in *that day*, and only in *that day*, that
> - every wrong will be righted,
> - every injustice will be righteously avenged,
> - every sin will be judged,
> - the prince of the power of the air that is deviously at work in the hearts of men will be eliminated,
> - death will be swallowed in victory,
> - and the pain caused by sin will be no more.
>
> There is *a day* where this will be the norm. But *that day* is not our todays. And if we lose sight of this, we set ourselves and our neighbors up with a false hope....

Between us shining the light of Christ and God continuing to extend to humanity His common grace, we can and we will see glimmers of what this coming kingdom will look like...

- *when* wrongs are righted here,
- *when* justice is had here,
- *when* the laws of man convey the law of God here,
- *when* people are rescued here,
- *when* lives are restored here,
- *when* pain is healed here,
- *when* miracles happen here, and so on.

These are but glimmers of what is coming and will one day be the norm. Until then, we take these glimmers—provided by Christians shining God's light and God extending His common grace—and point to the Savior Jesus and His coming kingdom."[71]

⚘ Kingdom justice in practice.

To the question of what does kingdom justice practically look like for us Christians? Many want specifics regarding justice. What's on limits? What's off-limits? What do we do here? What do we do there? But justice is contextual to the injustice and the person or people involved, sometimes even to the location (e.g., is it in a country where citizens have constitutional rights or not). Sometimes justice may not be had at all. Furthermore, not every Christian will confront injustices the same or always confront the same injustices. Proverbs 26:17 (NIV) warns, *"Like one who grabs a stray dog by the ears is someone who rushes into a quarrel not their own."*

Every claim of injustice is not always an injustice; therefore, discernment is needed. However, discerning an injustice should not be used as an excuse for neglecting justice. Thinking, "I'll wait for the facts to come out before responding," is appropriate reasoning. But when the facts come out and you never move to employ or at minimal become a voice for justice, you have neglected justice. Likewise, suppose we narrow justice for injustices to solely saying something online and protesting a particular way. In that case, we will remain nitpicking and not engage in effective personal practices consistent with kingdom justice. Offline will forever be more impactful than online. You can never say anything online, but you should never *not* be a voice for justice offline in your spheres of inclusion and influence—friends, family, workplaces, church. Yet, if we ignore even those narrow ways, we may be guilty of neglecting our brethren and neighbors by not, at minimum, using our platforms and time for the good of others.

As herald and portraits of the kingdom, if we live out kingdom values, ethics, and civics, *we will* be confronting the injustices in our spheres that are within our power to do so. As herald and portraits of the kingdom, if we live out kingdom values, ethics, and civics, *we will* be more sensitive in our responses to injustices when brought to our attention, whether we can participate in seeking justice for it or not.

Below is a brief list of some indisputable general kingdom justice principles in Scripture applicable for every Christian.[72] While these can be applied to injustices in many different ways, for them to be willingly disregarded by any ambassador of Christ is blatant disobedience to God and misrepresentation of His kingdom.

1. Don't "withhold good from those who need it, when you have the ability to help."

2. Don't "plot evil against your neighbor when he dwells by you unsuspectingly."

3. Don't "accuse anyone without legitimate cause, if he has not treated you wrongly."

4. Don't envy someone who hurts others, and don't choose any of their ways.

5. "Those who oppress the poor insult their Maker, but helping the poor honors him."

6. God detest acquitting the guilty and condemning the just.

7. "It is not right to acquit the guilty or deny justice to the innocent."

8. "It is wrong to show favoritism when passing judgment."

9. "To do what is right and just is more acceptable to the Lord than sacrifice."

10. Don't guarantee another person's loan if you can't repay it.

11. "Don't rejoice when the people you're not fond of fall; don't be happy when they stumble."

12. "Don't accuse anyone who isn't guilty."

13. "Don't ever tell a lie or say to someone, "I'll get even with you!""

14. Don't call evil good and good evil.

15. "Give to Caesar what belongs to Caesar, and give to God what belongs to God."

16. "Love your enemies, and be good to everyone who hates you."

17. "Ask God to bless anyone who curses you, and pray for everyone who is cruel to you."

18. Don't oppose those who mistreat you, be unselfish to them.

19. Don't demand back what was stolen from you.

20. "Treat others just as you want to be treated."

21. "Lend without expecting to be paid back."

22. "Never pay back evil with more evil."

23. "Do things in such a way that everyone can see you are honorable."

24. "Do all that you can to live in peace with everyone."

25. "Never take revenge. Leave that to the righteous anger of God."

26. "Don't let evil conquer you, but conquer evil by doing good."

27. Love your neighbor, for no one who loves others will harm them.

28. Love is not jealous or boastful or proud or rude.

29. Love does not demand its own way.

30. Love is not irritable, and it keeps no record of being wronged.

31. Love does not rejoice about injustice but rejoices whenever the truth wins out.

32. Whenever we have the opportunity, we should do good to everyone—especially believers.

33. "Don't be hateful to people, just because they are hateful to you."

34. "Be good to each other and to everyone else."

35. "Obey the rulers and authorities." Don't be rebellious.

36. "Always be ready to do something helpful."

37. Don't "say cruel things or argue. Be gentle and kind to everyone."

38. "Don't neglect to do what is good and to share."
39. Care for orphans and widows in their distress.
40. Don't let the world corrupt you.

As we can see, kingdom justice is not always in line with the justice the world demands or dismisses. Kingdom justice isn't so much about righting wrongs or correcting the ills of the world. It's more about doing what's right in response to the injustices we see and can counter. Kingdom justice extended to believers and unbeliever is essentially loving-consideration and loving-accountability manifested in the micro to the macro to the nuanced. Therefore, **"so long as these biblical imperatives are being obeyed in a manner in accordance with Scripture and not distracting from the gospel, we should not be criticizing or dismissing fellow believers standing up for justice in social areas or speaking out against social injustices. If anything we should be supporting them because it is biblical to do so, even if it may look different than how we/others may do so."**[73]

For those who still feel the need to critique other believer's levels of involvement in justice, thinking or making statements like: "They're not doing enough." "They're not doing it right." "They're doing too much." "What they're doing won't change anything." And so on. Yet again, Thomas á Kempis offers a great word,

> **"Turn your attention upon yourself, and beware of judging the deeds of other men, for in judging others a man labors vainly, often makes mistakes, and easily sins; whereas, in judging and taking stock of himself he does something that is always profitable."**[74]

Also, Dr. Rick Taylor offers a pivotal point of understanding the believer's involvement in kingdom justice with kingdom vision.

> **"Just as there is diversity within the body of Christ, so too is there variance with issues of moral discernment. Some people are deeply committed to one issue, while others are moved by an entirely different cause. *The beauty of the body of Christ is that***

this diversity assures a wide scope of impact by the people of God."[75]

Later in his book, "The Anatomy of a Disciple," Taylor provides another insight into our hang-ups with kingdom justice.

"Indifference can keep you on the sidelines of the Christian faith. You may never engage, never serve and never show up because you don't care, or you may rationalize that someone else will do it. *How can it be that a person whose heart is submitted to God and whose mind is shaped by His Word remains indifferent?* That is what makes indifference so devasting."[76]

Truthfully, if we simply live like Christians are supposed to, we'll be kingdom justice warriors without thinking and upon request. Shucks, this should be a no-brainer for us. But, instead, we have allowed the lies and lure of the world to divide us from living as kingdom heralds and portraits. Many Christians have become ambassadors of their political parties, social causes, and accommodating narratives, merrily quarreling with other believers to the shame of our King and kingdom.

"As the knowledge of God becomes more wonderful, greater service to our fellow men will become for us imperative. This blessed knowledge is not given to be enjoyed selfishly. The more perfectly we know God the more we will feel the desire to translate the new-found knowledge into deeds of mercy toward suffering humanity. The God who gave all *to* us will continue to give all *through* us as we come to know Him better."[77]

⚑ Purpose in justice.

The buoy for extremism in either direction regarding justice is *kingdom purpose*. When discussing the Christian's involvement in confronting injustices or societal improvement, we must persistently remember that Scripture only teaches redeemed souls are God's aim, not redeemed societies. A.W. Tozer said matter of factly, **"God does** not love populations, He loves people. He loves not masses, but men."[78]

True justice is only ever had *in* Christ, never without (Prov. 29:26). Societies can be gathered, established, dispersed, and forgotten. Kingdoms can be erected and eradicated. Souls are eternal. For a Christian to focus more on what is temporal at the expense of what is eternal is an egregious injustice over any other injustice we can confront in this life—individually, politically, socially, systemically, or institutionally. Temporal success is good, but it fades with the days. That's why unredeemed people must chase it day-to-day. Lasting success is always measured by the purpose of God, never by the purpose of man.

Don't mistake kingdom justice for trying to clean up our world or one's country. If our involvement in social justice is for anything more than the purpose of people seeing life in the King and coming to believe the gospel of His kingdom, then we're merely dressing up corpses to look good but still suffer God's wrath. The salvation of the lost is of utmost importance to their ultimate well-being over everything else. However, this doesn't mean we're careless. Our unsaved neighbors should see us fight for justice with one another and experience our care for them in their present bouts of personal and social injustices. When they don't, they may question the sincerity of our King's care for their eternal predicament. Furthermore, ambassadors of Christ are not to shy away from, be passive-aggressive with, or be combative in having tough and uncomfortable conversations about justice and injustices. We must gracefully engage in these conversations with both believers and unbelievers so people can see life in the King and come to believe the gospel of His kingdom.

At this juncture, let this be heard loud and clear: kingdom justice does not validate sin on any front. It doesn't validate the sin of injustice. It doesn't validate the sin of the person or group who caused the injustice. It doesn't validate any sin of the victim(s) of the injustice. Because kingdom justice is not allegiant to man but to God alone, Christians are free to be gracefully honest (with probable persecution ensuing). We don't have to agree with people's lifestyle and beliefs—

not endorsing or affirming their sin—to advocate justice for them as humans who have experienced injustices. Jesus modeled this for us when He healed people who were not yet born-again and when He associated Himself with prostitutes, tax collectors, sinners, and Pharisees. He never affirmed or endorsed their sin but engaged them with the gospel of the kingdom in person, words, and action.[79]

Accordingly, *whenever we can* meet unbelievers in their injustices with our kingdom justice, our fundamental purpose must be for them to see life in the King and hopefully come to believe the gospel of the kingdom. *When we can* stand alongside other believers with kingdom justice in the injustices they experience or are advocating for, our fundamental purpose must be in walking out love for one another so those around us see life in the King and hopefully come to believe the gospel of the kingdom. *When* we respond to our own injustices with kingdom justice, our fundamental purpose must be for

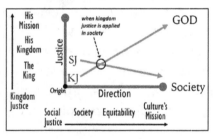

those around us to see life in the King and hopefully come to believe the gospel of the kingdom. No matter whose injustice we are responding to with kingdom justice, the purpose is always for people to see life in the King and come to believe the gospel of His kingdom.

How we live as heralds and portraits of the kingdom in every sphere of life God has strategically placed us should be influencing society for the better, in personal to considerable ways (many times unseen and unknown to the majority). Proverbs 21:15 (NIV) says, *"When justice is done, it brings joy to the righteous but terror to evildoers."* While doing this, we must keep in mind that the betterment of societies *is not* the mission of God. If at any time we think it is, we set ourselves and others up for the grave disappointment of false hope. We are heralds and portraits of life in the King and His kingdom. Our involvement in any society's betterment is a byproduct of employing kingdom justice as we sojourn on earth carrying out God's mission in our particular spheres.[80] Yes, you are to be God's change in the world. But you are not to change the world nor your country nor your state nor your county/city/town; that's God's prerogative to do so. Yes, you are to be God's light in the world. But you are not the Light of the world; that's Jesus' job.

⚓ Checking our hearts.

I feel I must check our hearts here. For some, kingdom justice doesn't sound desirable. For some, kingdom justice sounds too inclusive. For some, kingdom justice sounds unjust. Why is kingdom justice so hard to hear and do? Sin, of course. We know that. But it's more specific than the generality of sin. In light of the fall, our concept of justice toward others has been corrupted and redefined to mean self-serving fairness. Anything we deem fair, or individually beneficial, or mutually beneficial, we label that "just" or "justice." Anything we deem unfair, or individually unbeneficial, or mutually unbeneficial, we label that "unjust" or "injustice." For example, this is why...

- slavery, racism, and segregation was seen as just;
- past talks of building a wall and kicking out millions of illegal immigrants was cheered;
- upholding abortion laws are praised;
- ignoring racial problems and systemic suppression of communities of people is considered "not my problem";
- the senseless killings of people because of hate or racial profiling is dismissible;
- the senseless killings of people because of gangs and drugs is rarely if ever protested or newsworthy;
- disruption and combative protests are seen as freedom of speech and accepted;
- slanderous talk against political parties and their proponents are commonplace;
- walking past those who would be identified as "the least of these" is so easy.

On and on, these examples can go. So, think about it. Why do some deem these examples as fair or just, or at best, not as injustices? Because our concept of justice toward others has been corrupted and redefined to mean self-serving fairness. This should help us understand why God's prescriptives of kingdom justice can sound unfair to us.

Notice how Jesus questions our heart behind kingdom justice.

"32 If you love those who love you, what credit is that to you? Even sinners love those who love them. 33 If you do what is good to those who are good to you, what credit is that to you? Even sinners do that. 34 And if you lend to those from whom you expect to receive, what credit is that to you? Even sinners lend to sinners to be repaid in full." (Luke 6:32-34, CSB)

Jesus points out our default. Our default with others is effortless and self-serving—even the unsaved do this. He draws a distinct line in the sand. Our default is on the opposite side of mercy and grace, which is why it's so hard for us to be merciful and gracious because our fallen nature and world have conditioned us to see mercy and grace as unjust when it's outside of our group. The saying goes, "mercy is not getting what you do deserve," and "grace is getting what you don't deserve." Mercy and grace are unjust to our fallen thinking and in a fallen world, so we more easily withhold this kingdom justice from others. To be merciful and gracious means someone is not getting what they deserve or are getting what they don't deserve, and that's not fair to us. Shucks, some would actually call being merciful and gracious like this an injustice. But kingdom justice is not of this world. Kingdom justice proceeds from the only eternal Just King (Ps. 45:6; 89:14; 97:2). Thus, kingdom justice looks like the King in action in situations of injustice. None other.

⚓ Framing kingdom justice.

In Luke 6:35-36, Jesus gives a four-point frame for kingdom justice: *aim, identity, motive, model.*

"35 But love your enemies, do what is good, and lend, expecting nothing in return. Then your reward will be great, and you will be children of the Most High. For he is gracious to the ungrateful and evil. 36 Be merciful, just as your Father also is merciful." (Luke 6:35-36, CSB)

Our aim: What we're to aim for from kingdom justice is a heavenly reward (v35). We extend kingdom justice not for compensation in this life but for people to come to salvation in Christ and for us to hear from the mouth of God in the next life, "Well done, they good and faithful servant. You represented Me and My kingdom well."

Our identity: Employing kingdom justice identifies us as children of the Most High God (v35). In a world that's in stark contrast to God's kingdom, being merciful and gracious in our loving-consideration and loving-accountability of others will shine like stars burning in the night sky and reveal that we must belong to and be empowered by Almighty God.

Our motive: Our motive for kingdom justice is God's divine injustice toward us (v35). Justice—*getting what we deserve or what is fair*—is what our fallen thinking and fallen world demand. Yet, justice for every human is eternal judgment. Why? Because we are born in sin and defiance to God. Hence, getting what we deserve, getting what is fair, is complete and total separation from God. To receive anything else from God is an "injustice"—*it is grace and mercy*. Paul, in Romans 5:6-10, demonstrates how grace and mercy are the divine injustice from God toward us. Christ took our place to satisfy the justice from God for our sins. Our motive for kingdom justice is what we've received from God.

Our model: Kingdom justice is to model God's character (v36). We are not to base or employ justice on what we or anyone else feels, thinks, determines, or demands; not anyone else's views or policies; not the consensus of a group, or even the letter of the law. In kingdom justice, we are modeling God's example toward us, toward others. What God extends to us, we are to extend to others.

This four-point frame from Jesus can keep us grounded in being kingdom carriers and representations. It can keep us grounded in employing kingdom justice with kingdom vision wherever we are and whenever we can. And, it can keep us grounded in the purpose of people seeing life in the King and coming to believe the gospel of His kingdom. Here's a final word from Kempis,

"Without charity, external work is of no value, but anything done in charity, be it ever so small and trivial, is entirely fruitful inasmuch as God weighs the love with which a man acts, rather than the deed itself. He does much who loves much. He does much who does a thing well. He does well who serves the common good rather than his own interests."[81]

NOW WHAT?

Have you noticed how sometimes the best introductions are made with good first impressions, while poor first impressions often make bad introductions? Have you ever experienced that?

In 2015, after we closed our church plant, I was hired as a pastor some months later by a church in Bakersfield, CA. But before my hiring, upon visiting the church, the first family we met was one of the pastors. Pastor Mark emailed me and invited us over to hang out and watch a UFC fight. When we knocked, his wife opened the door. Right as we were saying "Hi," this pale skin, red-headed, energetic little boy appeared out of nowhere and locked eyes with our youngest son (who was ten at that time). He reached out and grabbed our son's hand, and with genuine excitement, said, "Do you wanna be my car bro?" My family, right on cue, all said, "Aww!" Of course, my son said yes. And it was as if the little boy knew he would because once the word "sure" was heard, the little boy pulled him through the door into their house.

Their family, specifically their son, was our first impression of this potential new church. During our time with them, Pastor Mark was honest about Bakersfield's racial issues and what areas we should stay away from if we moved there. Their honesty and hospitality could not have been any better. But the cherry on top was their son. This little guy put on a clinic of amusement the whole night. After we left and went back to the hotel, my wife and I debriefed about possibly accepting this position if they offered it. We both said we were so glad their family was our introduction to this church. Fasting forward, we became so close to that family that we added them to our power of attorney to care for our children if something ever happened to us. That's the capability of a good first impression.

As ambassadors of Christ, we are the first impressions of Christ. And as with first impressions, we can help or hurt our efforts in introducing people to His reconciliation, to His Person, and to His kingdom. Whatever picture the world paints of Christians or Jesus is partly because of the impression we are giving off.

Fast-forward again, this time six years from that 2015 story. It's 2021 now. Same son, different situation. My son was supposed to be washing the dishes. But my kids know how to delay doing their chores. Ask dad a Bible question. His question was theologically practical. "What's the point of doing anything, working anywhere, pursuing dreams, and so on, if we're only here for the mission of God?" My answer to his question is the point of this chapter: As Christians, in *whatever* we do *wherever* we are, the precedence for why God has sovereignly placed us *wherever* doing *whatever* is to leverage it all for our ambassadorship of Christ. I used his career aspirations as an illustration of this point.

At one point, our son wanted to work for the CIA. Then he realized the number of questionable things he may have to do that would conflict with him being a Christian, so he switched to the FBI. I paralleled being a CIA field agent with being an ambassador. CIA field agents have to blend into their environments. Everything these agents do is intentional. Where they work, where they frequent, whom they befriend, what they learn, so on. They infiltrate their environment and blend in to accomplish their mission. Essentially, the CIA field agents' expertise is at being a double agent. Outside the CIA, they are not what they appear. They become whatever they have to and do whatever they have to in order to fulfill their assignment. I wish you could have seen the lights go on in his eyes! "We're double agents for God!" he replied in an excited whisper. Exactly! He got it.

Christian, as ambassadors of Christ we are God's double agents in this world. This world is no longer our headquarters but the field where we're assigned. We have been redeemed as new creations in Christ, beloved and begotten. We're now citizens of a heavenly homeland and the children of the Most High King. Hence, we are not random ambassadors. We are son and daughter ambassadors. And our Abba, the King, has covertly stationed us all around the world so that in our regular goings and involvements in a myriad of things, we can infiltrate this world as His heralds and portraits of reconciliation, of the Incarnation, and of the kingdom. Our ambassadorship is the royal family business with eternal effects.

As ambassadors we should be aware of what is current and happening in our society. However, we cannot allow ourselves to be influenced by it. We do not make decisions unilaterally or get involved for our own reasons. We receive orders and decisions vertically, which determines our level of involvement in the affairs of the country where we reside. As ambassadors, everything we do and pursue, everywhere we are, every sphere we occupy is *on purpose* by God for the sake of His mission: teacher, salesman, healthcare worker, customer service, student, athlete, scientist, business owner, chaplain, law enforcement, government, education, non-profit, activism, stay-at-home parent, living in a poor neighborhood, a middle-class neighborhood, a wealthy neighborhood, and all others are spaces God has sovereignly situated us to be His ambassadors. Think about all the places we work, all the leadership positions we hold, all the social organizations we're part of, all the spheres of government we occupy, all the communities we live in, all the campuses we're on. Imagine the impact Christians can have for kingdom purpose in those places.

So, you have dreams, great! Pursue them if you can. You want to go to college and pursue some calling? Go for it! Military, missionary, politics, stay-at-home mom? Dive in! No space is off-limits. There is no space where our presence is there by accident. It's all by God's design and assignment. Therefore, as ambassadors, we leverage our locations, positions, dreams, callings, passions, resources, influence, and privileges for our King's agenda, whether covertly or openly. We will never do anything as disciples of Jesus that is not being done from our ambassadorship.

Understanding our identity as ambassadors of Christ—God's double agents in this world—is pivotal to the impression of Christ we give off, because our ambassadorship fully grafts into all of our life. We are never not representing the King and His kingdom. We will never have a more extraordinary work to do in all our life, nor will we ever possess or proclaim a more excellent message or cause than God's reconciliation through Jesus Christ. It is the highest honor and privilege to be Christ's ambassadors in this world.

CHAPTER 5

Missionaries

After six months of observing and evaluating our church in my new senior pastorate, I decided to start 2020 with a teaching series on "mission." The series ended the week before the Covid-19 nation-wide shutdown. The title of my last sermon in that series was *"The Local Church on Mission."* Here is one of the final points I made to our congregation,

> "The Church is the redeemed people of God not the buildings we meet in. The buildings we meet in are resource facilities for the Church to be trained and refreshed to carry out the mission of God together. Therefore, our times of corporate gatherings are to be for coming in to *receive* discipleship and then exiting to *do* discipleship. This is the local church on mission. We gather as the Church *for* the mission to scatter as the Church *on* mission."

This point became reality much faster than people expected. Sadly, over the remainder of that year, I witnessed just how inept and far off so many Christians are regarding the mission.

2020 wasn't the first year Christians and local churches were missionally deficient. As the centuries have gone by, starting when Rome declared Christianity to be the religion of the empire, local churches have moved further and further away from the actual mission of God. They have added other biblical, religious, social, and political tasks and duties into the mission or in place of the mission. Church history is the affidavit to this fact. There are churches today where if you go on their website and see what the mission of their church is, it has absolutely nothing to do with the mission of God. Many American Christians have adopted the idea that the "Christianization of the world" is the mission of God. Then there are other Christians, where if you ask them what their mission is as believers of Jesus, I firmly believe it would have absolutely nothing to do with the mission of God. And I've personally witnessed this. In fact, a Barna study in 2018 showed that fifty-one percent of professing Christians don't know the great commission.[1] All of this is shameful and should not be.

The mission of God is of grave importance, more than what I believe many Christians realize. Therefore, to effectively carry out the correct mission, believers must understand what it actually is, what it isn't, and its direct implications and applications.

WHAT IS "MISSION"?

The term "mission" has several definitions today; mainly due to "mission" being used by everybody—businesses, non-profits, education institutions, churches, the military, so on. These many definitions and usages can cause us to misunderstand the weight of the mission. But thank God for history! History shows the origination of this term had one prime use.

The earliest recorded usage of the term "mission" I could find was in the 13th century with Thomas Aquinas when he penned his "Summa Theologica." In the first part of his summary, his forty-third question is titled, *"The Mission of the Divine Persons."* Aquinas used the term "mission" to describe being sent with an assignment as he explored the activity of the Holy Trinity in how the Father sends the Son and the Father and Son send the Spirit.[2] According to Merriam-Webster and Online Etymology, the next earliest usage of the term "mission" was in the 16th century.[3] It followed Aquinas' usage of being sent as an agent or representative. After the 16th century, the term "mission" was used more and more frequently. With time comes changes, and so the word has evolved to describe several things.

The earliest usage of "mission" meant *to be sent with an assignment*. This doesn't mean mission was created in the 13th century. Mission existed before the term was coined. The word just helps us identify what it is. So to answer the question, what is mission? Originally, *mission is being sent with an assignment to complete*.

The term "mission" is both about the sending and the assignment. It's not an aimless sending. It's not a stagnant, inactive assignment. It's a sending with purpose, an assignment that requires action until it's complete. Mission also implies authority and submissiveness. A mission is given by someone in authority to someone that will submit to the authority. Think of those in the military. They receive missions all the time. Sometimes it's to be carried out at home. Oftentimes, it's for something abroad. Whether they like the mission or not, that does not matter. Those under authority must complete the mission they're assigned. Therefore, mission signifies two subjects and two actions. Subject 1 is the sender with authority, and their action is sending with an assignment. Subject 2 is the sent one under the authority, and their action is completing the assignment.

This is the nature of what mission is and how those with the mission are supposed to be.

WHAT IS GOD'S MISSION?

The explanation of "mission" exhibits how easy it is to see and say that there are many missions God commands. And giving believers and local churches the benefit of the doubt, the impression that there are many missions of God is why I think several have innocently strayed from the actual mission of God. Nevertheless, there are also numerous Christians and churches across history to this very day that have intentionally moved further and further away from the actual mission of God, adding other tasks and duties into the mission or in place of the mission. Whether innocently or arrogantly, both groups have confused the mission of God with other prescriptions for God's people or with whatever they deem important to the day or their cause.

If you could grab a couple of books addressing the mission of God from authors across different denominations and theological positions, guess what you would discover? Diverse definitions of what is the mission of God. I have no doubt some would read them and say, "Oh, that's in the Bible," and then conclude that must be the mission. I could ask you to pick another one, and some would figure, "Oh, that's different from the previous one. But that's in the Bible too, so that must also be the mission of God." This kind of variance is part of the problem. **"If everything is mission, nothing is mission."**[4]

It is too easy for people to conclude that God has different missions when you take what "mission" originally described—*being sent with an assignment to complete*—and read that into the Bible without proper context. Doing this can make the mission of God pretty much any prescriptive God gives His people in Scripture. But that's not the case. God's mission is not subjective nor relativistic; it doesn't change with the person, the local church, the generation, society, or geographic location. The mission of God is singular and indivisible. It's the application of His mission that's manifold. We must not conflate the two. In Kevin DeYoung and Greg Gilbert's book, "What is the Mission of the Church," they assert it this way,

> **"In a world of finite resources and limited time the church cannot do everything. We will not be effective in our mission if everything is mission. Likewise, we will not deliver on our mission if we are not sure what it is. If our mission is discipleship, this will set us on a different trajectory than if our mission is to make earth more like heaven. So definitions matter because focus matters."**[5]

According to Scripture, the "mission" regarding or belonging to God—i.e., God's mission, Jesus' mission, the Church's mission— refers to *the primary assignment that God sends His people to do*. This doesn't discount other assignments God has for His people. But those things would be just that, "assignments," maybe a personal "calling," or biblical convictions, or merely obedience to God's prescriptives for new covenant believers. None of those are the mission. The mission of God is the one dominant assignment that God sends His people to do while they're doing everything else. Other things may be compartmentalized. Conversely, the mission of God fully integrates into all of life for the believer. It's the undercurrent of everything we do in life.

If I asked you what you think this "primary assignment" is, what would your answer be? Hopefully, it would be "the great commission," which is not wrong. However, because so many don't see this as the *only* mission, the *primary* assignment, we must explore the origin story of God's mission.

God's mission was around long before Jesus spoke those words recorded in Matthew 28:18-20 to His 1st century Jewish disciples.[6] From the beginning, God's primary assignment for His covenant people has been multifaceted but one direction. It has been *to disclose His good news of redemption to non-covenant people so they may come to believe in Him, be identified as His family, and teach them to know and obey Him*. This is the mission of God. And what do we see? We see both the subjects and the actions, authority and submissiveness.

The mission of God is the foremost assignment God sends His people to complete. It is the ambassador's diplomatic mission from our King. As we have seen and shall see, any other responsibility from God or for God is an onramp-offramp loop of this mission. Everything we do in life as Christians is to be going in one direction—the mission.

God's plan has always been to unfold His mission in a particular order that gets us to what we know and where we are today. All of this matters for us in understanding our identity in Christ and our purpose in this world.

God Unfolds His Mission: First, He Reveals It

The first step in God unfolding His mission is He reveals His mission *to* His people and *through* His people.

⚘ To His people.

How does God reveal His mission *to* His people? He does so by choosing non-covenanted people to be His first covenanted people.

Before the Jews were covenant people, they were gentiles (Ezek. 16:1-14). It is in this first step that God sets the ethos for His mission. God is about extending His personal love, grace, and power toward His human creation in a covenantal relationship.

"1 Now the Lord said to Abram, "Go from your country and your kindred and your father's house to the land that I will show you. 2 And *I will make of you a great nation* [*a people*], and I will bless you and make your name great, so that you will be a blessing. 3 I will bless those who bless you, and him who dishonors you I will curse, and *in you all the families of the earth shall be blessed*."" (Genesis 12:1-3, ESV; *emphasis* & brackets added)

"1 When Abram was ninety-nine years old, the Lord appeared to him, saying, "I am God Almighty. Live in my presence and be blameless. 2 I will set up my covenant between me and you, and I will multiply you greatly." 3 Then Abram fell facedown and God spoke with him: 4 "As for me, *here is my covenant with you: You will become the father of many nations* [*a group of peoples*]. 5 Your name will no longer be Abram; your name will be Abraham, for I will make you the father of many nations. 6 I will make you extremely fruitful and will make nations [*peoples*] and kings come from you. 7 *I will confirm my covenant that is between me and you and your future offspring throughout their generations. It is a permanent covenant to be your God and the God of your offspring after you*."" (Genesis 17:1-7, CSB; *emphasis* & brackets added)

"32 Indeed, ask about the distant past, starting from the day God created humankind on the earth, and ask from one end of heaven to the other, whether there has ever been such a great thing as this, or even a rumor of it. 33 Have a people ever heard the voice of God speaking from the middle of fire, as you yourselves have, and lived to tell about it? 34 Or has God ever before tried to deliver a nation [*a people*] from the middle of another nation, accompanied by judgments, signs, wonders, war, strength, power, and other very terrifying things like the Lord your God did for you in Egypt before your very eyes? 35 You have been taught that the Lord alone is

God—there is no other besides him. *36 From heaven he spoke to you in order to teach you, and on earth he showed you his great fire from which you also heard his words.* 37 Moreover, *because he loved your ancestors, he chose their descendants who followed them* and personally brought you out of Egypt with his great power 38 to dispossess nations [*other groups of people*] greater and stronger than you and brought you here this day to give you their land as your property." (Deuteronomy 4:32-38, NET; *emphasis* & brackets added)

"6 For you are a holy people belonging to the Lord your God. *The Lord your God has chosen you to be his own possession out of all the peoples on the face of the earth. 7 The Lord had his heart set on you and chose you,* not because you were more numerous than all peoples, for you were the fewest of all peoples. 8 But *because the Lord loved you and kept the oath he swore to your ancestors,* he brought you out with a strong hand and redeemed you from the place of slavery, from the power of Pharaoh king of Egypt." (Deuteronomy 7:6-8 CSB; *emphasis added*)

"14 To the Lord your God belong the heavens, even the highest heavens, the earth and everything in it. *15 Yet the Lord set his affection on your ancestors and loved them, and he chose you, their descendants, above all the nations—as it is today.*" (Deuteronomy 10:14-15, NIV; *emphasis added*)

These verses illustrate how God reveals His mission *to* His people. He first chose them to be His people by extending His love, His grace, and His power toward them. Recall the definition of God's mission. Now notice these details:

- God chose Abraham and his children—Isaac, Jacob, and the people of Israel—for the covenant of redemption. They were once not His people, and then He made them His people from all the other peoples. That's a portrait of redemption.
- God identifies them as His family (His people) through the covenant sign of circumcision (Gen. 17:9-14, 23-27).

- Lastly, God taught them about Himself and how to live for Him by giving them the Law, the prophets, and numerous signs and wonders (cf. book of Deuteronomy).

Thus, establishing a people for Himself was God's first objective in His mission. He reveals His mission *to* His people by carrying it out Himself with them.

⚘ Through His people.

Next, in this first part of God unfolding His mission, He reveals His mission *through* His people. He does this in two ways. One, by illustrating His covenant with His people to the other peoples around them.

"9 The Lord will establish you as his holy people, as he swore to you, if you obey the commands of the Lord your God and walk in his ways. *10 Then all the peoples of the earth will see that you bear the Lord's name, and they will stand in awe of you.* 11 The Lord will make you prosper abundantly with offspring, the offspring of your livestock, and your land's produce in the land the Lord swore to your ancestors to give you. 12 The Lord will open for you his abundant storehouse, the sky, to give your land rain in its season and to bless all the work of your hands. You will lend to many nations [*peoples*], but you will not borrow." (Deuteronomy 28:9-12, CSB; *emphasis* & brackets added)

"*1 May God show us his favor and bless us. May he smile on us.* (Selah) *2 Then those living on earth will know what you are like; all nations* [*peoples*] *will know how you deliver your people.* 3 Let the nations [*peoples*] thank you, O God. Let all the nations [*peoples*] thank you." (Psalm 67:1-3, NET; *emphasis* & brackets added)

"2 The Lord has made his victory known; he has revealed his righteousness in the sight of the nations [*peoples*]. 3 He has remembered his love and faithfulness to the house of Israel; all the ends of the earth have seen our God's victory." (Psalm 98:2-3, CSB; brackets added)

In each of these passages, we see that whatever God was doing to and for His people, a secondary purpose was so He could reveal the ethos of His mission to others through them. Hence, God was known by the other nations as the God of Israel (Josh. 2:1-11; 9:1-10, 1Sam. chs5-6). God blessed His people to be a blessing to others that were not part of the covenant. His people's deliverance showed the other nations that the God of Israel is mightier than all other gods, and if He were their God, He could deliver them too. Ergo, God was illustrating His covenant with His people to the other nations.

That was the first of the two ways. The second way God reveals His mission is by prophesying His mission *through* His people.

"15 And the angel of the Lord called to Abraham a second time from heaven 16 and said, "By myself I have sworn, declares the Lord, because you have done this and have not withheld your son, your only son, 17 *I will surely bless you, and I will surely multiply your offspring as the stars of heaven and as the sand that is on the seashore.* And your offspring shall possess the gate of his enemies, 18 and *in your offspring shall all the nations [peoples] of the earth be blessed,* because you have obeyed my voice."" (Genesis 22:15-18, ESV; *emphasis added*)

"6 Just as Abraham "believed God, and it was counted to him as righteousness"? 7 Know then that it is those of faith who are the sons of Abraham. 8 *And the Scripture, foreseeing that God would justify the Gentiles by faith, preached the gospel beforehand to Abraham, saying, "In you shall all the nations be blessed."* 9 So then, those who are of faith are blessed along with Abraham, the man of faith." (Galatians 3:6-9, ESV; *emphasis added*)

"5 This is what God, the Lord, says—who created the heavens and stretched them out, who spread out the earth and what comes from it, who gives breath to the people on it and spirit to those who walk on it—6 "I am the Lord. I have called you for a righteous purpose, and I will hold you by your hand. I will watch over you, and *I will appoint you to be a covenant for the people and a light to the nations* [*peoples*], 7 in order to open blind eyes, to bring out prisoners from the dungeon, and those sitting in darkness from the prison house. 8 I am the Lord. That is my name, and I will not give my glory to another or my praise to idols. 9 The past events have indeed happened. Now I declare new events; I announce them to you before they occur."" (Isaiah 42:5-9, CSB; *emphasis* & bracket added)

"He says, "It *is not enough* for you to be my servant raising up the tribes of Jacob and restoring the protected ones of Israel. *I will also make you a light for the nations* [*peoples*], *to be my salvation to the ends of the earth*."" (Isaiah 49:6, CSB; *emphasis* & bracket added)

"28 Simeon took him in his arms and praised God, saying: 29 "Sovereign Lord, as you have promised, you may now dismiss your servant in peace. 30 *For my eyes have seen your salvation, 31 which you have prepared in the sight of all nations* [*peoples*]: 32 a *light for revelation to the Gentiles, and the glory of your people Israel*."" (Luke 2:28-32, NIV; *emphasis* & bracket added)

Beginning with Abraham and again during the Israelites captivity, God was clear to and through His people that He would bring non-covenant people into His covenant family. His covenant of redemption was never meant to be secluded only to the Jews because His mission is beyond one people group. The Messiah would come through the Jews and make salvation available for all peoples.

God's first step in unfolding His mission is He reveals it.

God Unfolds His Mission: Second, He Demonstrates It

The second step in God unfolding His mission is He personally demonstrates His mission.

How does God personally demonstrate His mission? I believe we know this answer. Nonetheless, it's still good to contemplate it because it should stir up our awe of God. God personally demonstrates His mission by being both subjects and accomplishing both actions. He is the sender with an assignment and the sent one completing the assignment.

⅄ **First demonstration.**

God's first demonstration of being both subjects and accomplishing both actions is by the Father sending the Son to purchase the eternal salvation of His people and teach them more about God.

"16 "For God so loved the world, that *he gave his only Son,* that whoever believes in him should not perish but have eternal life. 17 For God did not *send* his Son into the world to condemn the world, but in order that the world might be *saved through him.*"" (John 3:16-17, ESV; *emphasis added*)

"31 The one who comes from above is above all. The one who is from the earth is earthly and speaks in earthly terms. The one who comes from heaven is above all. 32 He testifies to what he has seen and heard, and yet no one accepts his testimony. 33 The one who has accepted his testimony has affirmed that God is true. *34 For the one whom God sent speaks God's words, since he gives the Spirit without measure.* 35 The Father loves the Son and has given all things into his hands. 36 The one who believes in the Son has eternal life, but the one who rejects the Son will not see life; instead, the wrath of God remains on him." (John 3:31-36, CSB; *emphasis added*)

"44 Then Jesus cried out, "Whoever believes in me does not believe in me only, but in the one who *sent* me. 45 The one who looks at me is seeing the one who *sent* me. 46 I have come into the world as a light, so that no one who believes in me should stay in darkness. 47 If anyone hears my words but does not keep them, I do not judge that person. For I did not come to judge the world, but to save the world. 48 There is a judge for the one who rejects me and does not accept my words; the very words I have spoken will condemn them at the last day. *49 For I did not speak on my own, but the Father who sent me commanded me to say all that I have spoken.* 50 I know that his command leads to eternal life. So whatever I say is just what the Father has told me to say."" (John 12:44-50, NIV; *emphasis added*)

"6 "*I have revealed you* to those whom you gave me out of the world. They were yours; you gave them to me and they have obeyed your word. 7 Now they know that everything you have given me comes from you. 8 *For I gave them the words you gave me* and they accepted them. They knew with certainty that I came from you, and they believed that you *sent* me."" (John 17:6-8, NIV; *emphasis added*)

Across all four gospel accounts, it is recorded that Jesus said He was *sent* by the Father forty-eight times. Jesus made it abundantly clear: His appearance in the flesh was mission. His work and teachings on earth were mission. His death and resurrection were mission. His work and instructions post-resurrection was mission. His whole life was mission!

❧ Second demonstration.

God's second demonstration of being both subjects and accomplishing both actions is by the Father and the Son sending the Holy Spirit to secure the salvation of His people, baptize them into the family, and continually teach them everything about God and from God.

"And behold, *I am sending* the promise of my Father upon you. But stay in the city until you are clothed with power from on high." (Luke 24:49, ESV; *emphasis added*)

"25 I have spoken these things to you while I remain with you. 26 But the Counselor, the Holy Spirit, whom *the Father will send* in my name, will *teach* you all things *and remind* you of everything I have told you." (John 14:25-26, CSB; *emphasis added*)

"When the Counselor comes, the one *I will send* to you from the Father —the Spirit of truth who proceeds from the Father—he will *testify* about me." (John 15:26 CSB; *emphasis added*)

"13 When the Spirit of truth comes, he will *guide* you into all the truth. For he will not speak on his own, but he will speak whatever he hears. He will also *declare* to you what is to come. 14 He will *glorify* me, because he will take from what is mine and declare it to you. 15 Everything the Father has is mine. This is why I told you that he takes from what is mine and will declare it to you." (John 16:13-15, CSB; *emphasis added*)

"4 But when the kindness and love of God our Savior appeared, 5 he saved us, not because of righteous things we had done, but because of his mercy. *He saved us through the washing of rebirth and renewal by the Holy Spirit, 6 whom he poured out on us generously through Jesus Christ our Savior,* 7 so that, having been justified by his grace, we might become heirs having the hope of eternal life." (Titus 3:4-7, NIV; *emphasis added*)

Without question, the mission of God is trinitarian. The Trinity chose to do a collaborative demonstration of the mission. What the Father sends the Son to do and both send the Spirit to do, Jesus starts and completes in His assignment while the Holy Spirit finishes and solidifies in His assignment. What a magnificent portrait of the holistic, personal demonstration by God of His mission!

☘ The Alpha missionary.

From these first two steps in God unfolding His mission, what should be unmistakable by now is that God Himself is the first missionary. In correlation with His mission, God sought and established a people as His first assignment—a people for Himself who would be submissive to His authority (i.e., bondservants). After establishing a people, He reveals His mission to them and through them. Then, God Himself demonstrates what He revealed.

God's intent was never for the Jews to complete His mission. His purpose for the Jews in His mission was to be a vehicle of revelation. God always planned to demonstrate His mission Himself, giving His redeemed people the example to follow and then the supernatural power to carry it out. Hence, what the third step is in God unfolding His mission.

Also, if you noticed, God didn't ask His people to do something without first showing them how to do it. It's only after God establishes a people, reveals His mission to and through His people, and personally demonstrates His mission Himself, does He then send

His people to do the same. Thus, the Author of the mission is the Alpha of the mission.

God Unfolds His Mission: Third, He Dispatches It

The third step in God unfolding His mission is He dispatches His people to carry out His mission. We discussed this some in chapter 4. One point was, "The Triune God has designated believers in Christ as His official vehicles for His ongoing divine work of reconciling others to Himself." That's all contained in this third step.

⸭ Before the "how".

Particularly here, instead of answering the "how" question, I want to help us grasp the magnitude of God dispatching His people to carry out His mission. This way, our practical application comes from comprehending the significance of what God is doing and not us just checking religious boxes or disregarding it. For if we're only doing the mission as a religious duty or not doing it at all, then there's no reverence and no appreciation of it.

The key passage where God dispatches His people to carry out His mission is Matthew 28:16-20.

> "16 The eleven disciples traveled to Galilee, to the mountain where Jesus had directed them. 17 When they saw him, they worshiped, but some doubted. 18 Jesus came near and said to them, "All authority has been given to me in heaven and on earth. 19 Go, therefore, and make disciples of all nations, baptizing them in the name of the Father and of the Son and of the Holy Spirit, 20 teaching them to observe everything I have commanded you. And remember, I am with you always, to the end of the age."" (CSB)

Every component of mission and God unfolding His mission is present in this passage. The mission is not given to random humans but to Jesus' followers—those He established as His people and submissive to His authority (vv16-17). Jesus identifies that He is subject 1—the sender with authority, and His action is sending them with an assignment (vv18-20). That makes His followers subject 2—the sent ones under His authority, and their action is completing the assignment He gave (vv19-20). This means whether His followers like it or not, want to or not, those under His authority must complete the mission. And Jesus prepared them for this. In John 13:16 (NKJV), He said, "*Most assuredly, I say to you, a servant is not greater than his master; nor is he who is sent greater than he who sent him.*"

Jesus also included God's first step in unfolding His mission in this passage, but He updates it. Instead of God revealing it *through* His people to the nations like before, Jesus now *sends* His people to the nations to do it themselves (v19). Additionally, He includes the second step in God unfolding His mission, but once more with an update. Since God has already personally demonstrated His mission, Jesus declares He will continue to personally demonstrate it by being *with* His people while they do it (v20). Verse 20 is really the anchor of the great commission because Jesus says we're not doing it by ourselves. He's not giving us this mission under the impression that we have to muster up our own strength or ingenuity to complete it. He's carrying out the mission with His people. He's on the front lines with us as the general leading the charge. That's why He sends us the promised Holy Spirit from the Father, so we can accomplish it in His power. Again, every component of mission and God unfolding His mission is present in this passage.

✦ Two significant realities.

Here's where the magnitude of this enters. For Jesus to dispatch His followers to carry out God's mission implies two significant realities.

First, we are saved to be sent. I don't think Christians consider this reality much, if ever. We tend to restrict salvation to just our personal context of being in a reconciled relationship with God. Thus, salvation never extends beyond God and ourselves. Somewhere in the reasoning of our ignorance, selfishness, or fear, we elevate the personal relationship with God at the expense of the mission. As if these two are mutually exclusive. Whenever you think or conclude, "My relationship with Jesus is between God and me; therefore *I can't* _____ (insert whichever applies: talk about Jesus, witness to people, invite people to hear about what I believe, share my testimony, pray with people, etc)," you just sacrificed the mission of God for the gift of God. Jesus rebuked Peter and called him "satan" for thinking similarly (Matt. 16:21-23). That should give us a glimpse of how toxic this kind of thinking is.

God dispatching His redeemed people to carry out His mission implies that salvation involves more than solely the personal reconciliation to God we receive through Jesus. Clearly, it's never anything less. But there is more involved. God's mission implies that salvation is also a shared responsibility. Foremost, between the Father, the Son, and the Spirit; then He also shares this with His redeemed people.

When we reduce salvation to only the gift and detach it from the mission, we undercut the effect of salvation. This minimizes the magnitude of what God has been unfolding throughout human history and our participation with Him. **"The saving work of God is rooted far deeper in the glory of God than in the lost state of a human heart."**[7] God didn't design salvation solely as a gift but also as the goal of His mission (Rom. 10:8-15). Pause and notice what I didn't say. I didn't say it was the sum of the mission, just the goal. Salvation gets one into the kingdom, but discipleship is the earthly tutor for life within the kingdom. Both are contained in the mission of God.

Those whom God saves are born-again into a personal relationship with Him and also a shared responsibility with Him. Therefore, mission is God's divine privilege to His redeemed people to participate in the shared responsibility with the Father, the Son, and the Holy Spirit in redeeming more people. We are saved to be sent because the gift of salvation is the goal of the mission.

Second, mission is in the DNA of the people of God. Christian, we cannot divorce mission from being "in Christ." Mission is not something "they" do. You know, "those Christians"—that group, that gift, that role, that ministry, that church. Mission is in the DNA of every believer in Christ. Let's do some quick doctrinal math:[8]

- How are we redeemed?
  - ✓ By the blood of Jesus shed on our behalf and our belief in what He's done.
- What is the only reason Jesus possessed flesh and blood to give as an atonement for our sins?
  - ✓ Because that was His mission. The Father sent the Son to wrap on flesh and blood to sacrifice His flesh and blood to purchase the eternal salvation of His people. If there were no mission, then there would be no Incarnation.
- What does all this mean?
  - ✓ Mission flowed through the veins of the actual body of Christ, and it continues to flow through the veins of the spiritual body of Christ.

Notice how missional and incarnational Jesus' high priestly prayer is. He intimately links His disciples' mission and oneness to His mission and oneness with the Father.

"18 As you *sent* me into the world, I also have *sent* them into the world. 19 I sanctify myself for them, so that they also may be sanctified by the truth. 20 I pray not only for these, but also for those who believe in me through their word. *21 May they all be one, as you, Father, are in me and I am in you. May they also be in us, so that the world may believe you sent me.* 22 I have given them the glory you have given me, *so that they may be one as we are one. 23 I am in them and you are in me, so that they may be made completely one,* that the world may know you have *sent* me and have loved them as you have loved me. 24 Father, I want those you have given me to be with me where I am, so that they will see my glory, which you have given me because you loved me before the world's foundation. 25 Righteous Father, the world has not known you. However, I have known you, and they have known that you *sent* me. *26 I made your name known to them and will continue to make it known, so that the love you have loved me with may be in them and I may be in them.*" (John 17:18-26, CSB; *emphasis added*)

Jesus told His followers that just as mission flowed through His very veins, it will continue to flow through His veins *by way of us*. We are the extension of Jesus on this earth as He was that of God on this earth. That's ambassadorship. Our identification in Jesus and with Jesus is so that the world may know His mission as Lord and Savior. Our identification in Jesus as His disciples is an apologetic and testimony to the world of God's gift of salvation through Him—hence, the goal of mission. Jesus' mission is in the DNA of His people because it is in His DNA as Savior.

Recall what followed being God's beloved and begotten. There were clear distinguishables because like parent, like child. The same is true here. We cannot claim to be part of Christ's Body—claim to be Christian—and believe or live like we've been omitted or excused from His mission. Similar to not omitting or excusing away any of our other genetic information, we cannot do so with the mission of God.

Mission is part of who we are in Christ. However, the sin in our members wars against God's mission in our redeemed blood. As the battle rages on, in our case, it's for the lives we're on mission to reach. So if you find yourself not caring much about God's mission or not actively participating in carrying out His mission, then my friend, you need to do a serious investigation into why. More than likely, your sin is the culprit. Pray, sniff it out, and repent to God and another Christian to hold you accountable. To not care about God's mission or not actively participate in carrying out His mission is disobedience to God, refusal to revere God, and suppression of your redeemed identity in Christ.

My family and I moved to an apartment building after accepting my current senior pastorate. For the first year and some change, I didn't know any of my neighbors' names. Not a single one. I didn't even ask. Do you know what was most heartbreaking? I was more annoyed with their noise than I was about them being lost. You know what else, that broke my Father's heart too. Instead of praying for their salvation and getting to know them, I prayed more for them to be quiet—shame on me. Not only do I possess this glorious gift because of Jesus, but He's also given me the glorious opportunity to participate with Him and share this gift with the people on the other side of my wall. And I didn't say a single thing to them about Him. Not even an attempt. Not even an invite to the church I pastored. Pitiful. I was guilty of disobedience, irreverence, and suppression of my identity in Christ. I repented to God, my wife, and the church. I became intentional with my face-to-face interactions with my neighbors and in my prayers. The correction reminded me that my obedience to Jesus and their eternity mattered more than my inconvenience.

If you miss the significance of these two realities, then you will continue to reduce mission to a box that you check or an outreach event that you do. The mission of God is nothing like Mormons or Jehovah's Witnesses who go door-to-door as part of their "works." Our mission is so much greater! Mission is the true purpose-driven life for Christians while sojourning on earth as ambassadors. It's not an aimless sending. It's not a works-based assignment nor a stagnant, inactive duty. It's a sending with eternal purpose; an assignment integrated into all of life that requires continual participation until it's complete—which will be when Christ returns and the mission is no longer necessary. In these two realities, we discover the personal relationship God has undeservedly brought us into was purchased with the missional blood of Christ and affixed to a partnership with Him in rescuing His other lost sheep. So, you tell me, what greater purpose in life is there than the mission of God?

JESUS' FOURFOLD APPROACH TO MISSION

Since Jesus knows and demonstrated what it takes to effectively do the mission of God, who better to learn from on how to carry it out. As disciples of Jesus, it is indispensable for us to follow Him as our guide for being on mission.

After surveying the Gospels and the New Testament letters, I discovered that Jesus accomplished the mission of God using a fourfold approach. Everything He did carrying out God's mission all fell under four specific approaches. Recall what the mission of God is: *to disclose God's good news of redemption to non-covenant people so they may come to believe in Him, be identified as His family, and teach them to know and obey God.* As we explore Jesus' approaches, pay close attention to how He accomplishes His mission naturally, not programmatically. This indicates mission can be done with intentionality in the normal rhythms of life.

1st Approach: Incarnational

The first approach Jesus used was incarnational. This is Jesus becoming as we are, entering into our personal world as the sole Agent of change in our life. You can personalize that and say, "Jesus became as I am, entering the world I live in to personally change my life." That's incarnational.

I spent quite some time on incarnational in chapter 4, so I won't belabor this point. Instead, I'll walk through just a couple of passages to exhibit this particular missional approach of Jesus.

"6 Though he was God, *he did not think* of equality with God as something to cling to. 7 Instead, *he gave up* his divine privileges; *he took* the humble position of a slave and was born as a human being. When he appeared in human form, 8 *he humbled* himself in obedience to God and died a criminal's death on a cross." (Philippians 2:6-8, NLT; *emphasis added*)

"4 When the time came to completion, God *sent* his Son, *born of a woman, born under the law,* 5 *to redeem those under the law,* so that we might receive adoption as sons." (Galatians 4:4-5, CSB; *emphasis added*)

"14 Since the children have flesh and blood, *he too shared in their humanity so that by his death he might break the power of him who holds the power of death—that is, the devil—* 15 *and free those who all their lives were held in slavery by their fear of death.* 16 For surely it is not angels he helps, but Abraham's descendants. 17 For this reason *he had to be made like them, fully human in every way,* in order that he might become a merciful and faithful high priest in service to God, and that he might make atonement for the sins of the people. 18 Because he himself suffered when he was tempted, he is able to help those who are being tempted." (Hebrews 2:14-18, NIV; *emphasis added*)

"14 Therefore, since we have a great high priest who has ascended into heaven, Jesus the Son of God, let us hold firmly to the faith we profess. *15 For we do not have a high priest who is unable to empathize with our weaknesses, but we have one who has been tempted in every way, just as we are—yet he did not sin. 16 Let us then approach God's throne of grace with confidence, so that we may receive mercy and find grace to help us in our time of need.*" (Hebrews 4:14-16, NIV; *emphasis added*)

What should we notice about being incarnational in these passages?

First, Jesus set aside His divine privileges to enter into our positional poverty. When the average believer thinks of Jesus sitting aside His divine privileges, usually, we don't really know what that means. Have you ever seen the TV show "Undercover Boss"? I hope so, because that's the closest we're going to get to visualizing what Jesus did. Jesus was the first Undercover Boss. Nobody knew when He came into the world that He was the Creator who runs Creation because He became like an employee of His company. The divine wealth of the Holy One, Jesus sits aside to become just like us— impoverished in comparison. Apart from God, we have no privileges. We are spiritually impoverished. Therefore, Jesus sits aside His divine privileges to enter into our poverty so that we can be spiritually wealthy in Him. As Paul writes in 2Corinthians 8:9 (ESV), "*For you know the grace of our Lord Jesus Christ, that though he was rich, yet for your sake he became poor, so that you by his poverty might become rich.*" That's incarnational.

Second, Jesus became as we are and lived as we are. We are born human, under the law of God, enslaved to sin and death, and separated from God. Jesus became a human. He was born Jewish and under the Law. So, as a Jew, He spoke the same language as them, went to the temple with them, and was in the marketplace with them. He observed the Law with them and was tempted to disobey the Law as they were. He even interacted with the gentiles among them. Jesus lived like any other Jew would've lived during the 1st century. He also experienced death like the history of humanity. Jesus subjected Himself to fully experience life as a human under the law of God, to experiencing temptation, and to experiencing death. He became and lived like this to reconcile Jew and gentile to God, to set us free from the power of sin and fear of death, and to be a present support for us as we suffer in this life as a human. That's incarnational.

Third, Jesus came to sacrifice His life for our death. Yup, you read that right. I'm not sure if we ever consider this. We routinely say Jesus sacrificed His life for our life. Clearly, that's not wrong because the result of His atoning sacrifice is our new life. However, according to Scripture, no one apart from God in Christ is spiritually alive. We're all dead in sins and trespasses (Eph. 2:1-3). Thus, Jesus didn't sacrifice His life for our life, per se. He sacrificed His life for our death so that through His death and resurrection, we can possess new life (Rom. chs 6-7). Apart from God, we are all dead in sins with His eternal judgment rightfully awaiting us. Therefore, Jesus comes as we are to sacrifice His life in place of our spiritual deadness and eternal death. He had to become what we were—dead and separated from God—so we could become as He is—life everlasting. That's incarnational.

From each of these passages, we see Jesus entered into our broken world, into our fallen human experiences, and into our eternal consequence. He entered into this for us. He takes us from where we once were and brings us to where He now is. And once He redeems us, He then sends us back out, but this time to enter into other people's broken worlds with His hope, His grace, and His life that He freely gives us. Accordingly, by being incarnational with others, we get to model to them what Christ has done by being incarnational for us.

If Jesus is our guide to being missional, a few questions for us follow from His incarnational approach:

- What privileges am I willing to set aside to be more effective in reaching those apart from Christ and teaching believers how to follow Jesus biblically?

- What sacrifices am I willing to make to be more effective in reaching those apart from Christ and teaching believers how to follow Jesus biblically?
- Where am I willing to grow and adapt in my life to be more effective in reaching those apart from Christ and teaching other believers how to follow Jesus biblically?

Questions like these are good to examine if we're incarnational in mission as Jesus was incarnational in His mission.

2nd Approach: Intentional

The second missional approach Jesus used was intentional. Jesus was the epitome of missional-minded. Everything He did, He did on purpose for His mission. Notice what Jesus says to different crowds about why He does what He did.

> "16 When he came to the village of Nazareth, his boyhood home, he went as usual to the synagogue on the Sabbath and stood up to read the Scriptures. 17 The scroll of Isaiah the prophet was handed to him. He unrolled the scroll and found the place where this was written: 18 "The Spirit of the Lord is upon me, for he has anointed me to bring Good News to the poor. He has sent me to proclaim that captives will be released, that the blind will see, that the oppressed will be set free, 19 and that the time of the Lord's favor has come." 20 He rolled up the scroll, handed it back to the attendant, and sat down. All eyes in the synagogue looked at him intently. *21 Then he began to speak to them. "The Scripture you've just heard has been fulfilled this very day!"....* 42 Early the next morning Jesus went out to an isolated place. The crowds searched everywhere for him, and when they finally found him, they begged him not to leave them. *43 But he replied, "I must preach the Good News of the Kingdom of God in other towns, too, because that is why I was sent."* 44 So he continued to travel around, preaching in synagogues throughout Judea." (Luke 4:16-21, 42-44, NLT; *emphasis added*)

The macro message Jesus is communicating in these two passages is that everything He said and did while on this earth was on purpose for the sake of the mission. When He read from Isaiah 61 and said, *"this very day"* this scripture has been fulfilled in your hearing. He wasn't stating an "actual day" of the week, month, and year. Jesus was communicating in "this day that I am here upon this earth," this prophecy is fulfilled.[9] And the reason Jesus could guarantee its fulfillment is everything He would say and do was going toward fulfilling, not just this particular prophecy, but all of them (Matt. 5:17). The Promise Maker does not renege on His word. That's why He said He must go to the other towns. He was always on mission.

Jesus wasted nothing. No conversation, no interaction, no opportunity, no relationship. Read the Gospels. He wasted nothing! He didn't even waste meals with His disciples, or resting during storms, or responding to news He received, or being betrayed by a follower. He used pretty much everything in some way for the sake of completing the mission. That's what it means to be intentional, to be missional-minded.

Have you ever played chess? Even if you just put the board up and let your friends beat you, that qualifies as a yes for this example. I'm a chess player. I enjoy chess. Do you know how to win in chess? You have to capture the king first. Clearly, this is easier said than done, especially if your opponent knows how to play. For those who know how to play chess, every move in chess is with a purpose. Every single move. From the first to the last. Every move on the chessboard is with purpose, either for capturing their king or defending your king. There are no wasted moves in the game of chess. It's a game of strategy.

Jesus' intentional approach to mission is like chess. What is the goal of mission? Salvation. Salvation is the dethroning of a false king and enthroning of the true King. Ergo, chess in real life with eternal ramifications. Every move Jesus made—from coming in the womb of Mary to sacrificing Himself and every single thing in between—had one purpose, His mission. To follow our chess Master, being intentional, being missional-minded, is living our life like playing chess. Every move we make in our life is to be on purpose for the mission. This doesn't mean we evangelize non-stop or only ever talk about and do "Christian" things. Jesus didn't do this. He played chess.

You don't win a chess match in one move. A series of strategic moves wins the game. Each piece in chess—the pawns, bishops, rooks, knights, queen, and king—is moved or sacrificed to win the game. The same will be true for us. Our pieces—i.e., our skills, time, energy, intellect, resources, privileges, decisions, opportunities, platforms, authority, and so on—are to be strategically used for the sake of the mission. All we have and what we do is for getting us one step closer to accomplishing the mission of God *within* the spheres of our family, friends, coworkers, neighbors, local churches, schools, communities, state, world, and anywhere else God gives us access. We win in the mission by a series of strategic moves.

For my non-chess players, I hope I didn't lose you with the analogy. And I get it; just like everyone doesn't play chess, not every Christian thinks missionally like this. For some, this may seem overwhelming or frightening. Neither should be the case. Jesus did this in His natural comings and goings. He simply moved about with intentionality. As believers, with mission in our DNA, we have to train ourselves to think the same (Phil. 2:5).

- How do my actions or words move me in position for the mission with this person, group, or opportunity?
- How do my actions or words plant seeds with this person or group for the sake of the mission?

Questions like these are good for challenging ourselves to be more missional-minded. Reflect on these in your prayer to start your day or at the end of your day. Then, as you answer honestly, pray honestly to grow in being intentional in mission as Christ was intentional.

3rd Approach: Contextual

The third missional approach Jesus used was contextual. Whom Jesus went to and how He spoke and taught was appropriate to the time, the audience, and the setting.

We'll see this "contextual" highlighted well in two passages. This first passage highlights Jesus' sending context—the *whom* He went to.

"21 When Jesus left there, he withdrew to the area of Tyre and Sidon. 22 Just then *a Canaanite woman* from that region came and kept crying out, "Have mercy on me, Lord, Son of David! My daughter is severely tormented by a demon." 23 Jesus did not say a word to her. His disciples approached him and urged him, "Send her away because she's crying out after us." 24 He replied, *"I was sent only to the lost sheep of the house of Israel."* 25 But she came, knelt before him, and said, "Lord, help me!" 26 He answered, "It isn't right to take the children's bread and throw it to the dogs." 27 "Yes, Lord," she said, "yet even the dogs eat the crumbs that fall from their masters' table." 28 *Then Jesus replied to her, "Woman, your faith is great. Let it be done for you as you want."* And from that moment her daughter was healed." (Matthew 15:21-28, CSB; *emphasis added*)

What we see here is that while Jesus didn't withhold from those who weren't of Israel, He declared His immediate sending context was to the lost sheep of Israel. Jesus is doing Acts 1:8 before Acts 1:8. Jesus tells the disciples in Acts 1:8 they will be His witnesses in Jerusalem, in Judea, in Samaria, and to the ends of the Earth. Guess what? Jesus models this first.

Jesus' sending context was primarily to the Jews. They were His "Jerusalem" and "Judea." Then it was actual Samaritans (John 4:1-42). They were His "Samaria." Lastly, it was Romans and other gentiles (Matt. 8:5-13, John 12:20). They were His "ends of the Earth." Jesus modeled what He would later command for His disciples. He tells them they will go do what they saw Him doing because they witnessed the context of His command. Jesus' sending context is the example of who is our Jerusalem, who is our Judea, who is our Samaria, and who are the ends of the Earth. He models the context of who we are being sent to.

The second passage highlights "contextual" in *how* Jesus spoke and taught.

"19 The high priest questioned Jesus about his disciples and about his teaching. 20 *"I have spoken openly to the world,"* Jesus answered him. *"I have always taught in the synagogue and in the temple, where all the*

Jews gather, and I haven't spoken anything in secret. 21 Why do you question me? Question those who heard what I told them. Look, they know what I said." 22 When he had said these things, one of the officials standing by slapped Jesus, saying, "Is this the way you answer the high priest?" 23 "If I have spoken wrongly," Jesus answered him, "give evidence about the wrong; but if rightly, why do you hit me?" 24 Then Annas sent him bound to Caiaphas the high priest." (John 18:19-24, CSB; *emphasis added*)

In this passage, Jesus communicates He taught everywhere the Jews congregated and in understandable ways. He said nothing "in secret." That "secret" in the Greek is *kryptō,* as in cryptic.[10] Jesus is testifying that He did not speak cryptically. Everything He said and taught had not been in a way that they couldn't understand, nor had He been communicating in private differently from what He expressed publicly. Jesus didn't speak or teach in code. He didn't speak or teach in what we call today "churchy" or "Christianese." He wasn't tribal. He didn't pander to a base. Jesus spoke and taught the truths of God wherever the people were and in ways they could understand, according to their grouping—followers, crowds, religious leaders, individuals, or small groups.

Reading through the Gospels, you can't miss Jesus' contextualization in how He spoke and taught. For example, you'd find that...

✓ *He spoke and taught from the Old Testament.* Dr. Harold Willmington wrote, **"It has been estimated that over one-tenth of Jesus' recorded New Testament words were taken from the Old Testament. In the four Gospels, 180 of the 1,800 verses that report His discourses are either Old Testament quotes or Old Testament allusions."[11]**

✓ *He spoke and taught in parables.* Now some may question, "Aren't parables kind of cryptic?" Only to the people who didn't get it. When Jesus would share a parable, He'd often provide commentary to His disciples. There are some accounts where the Pharisees would come to Him and ask was He talking about them. He'd respond, "yup."

✓ *He spoke and taught according to their culture.* They were an agrarian people. Thus, He used wheat, chaff, seeds, trees, fruit, wineskins, bread, sheep, wolves, etc. Obviously, they were Jewish. So He participated in and addressed their customs, feasts, the temple, and so on.

✓ *He spoke and taught according to their vocations.* In light of tax collection, He talked about Caesar and taxes, and looking for a lost coin. In light of fishing, He called His disciples fishers of men, engaged them on fishing boats and while they were fishing. In light of shepherding, He talked about sheep, shepherds, and hirelings. In light of ministry, He reasoned with priests, scribes, Pharisees, etc.

In carrying out the mission of God, Jesus spoke and taught contextually to where the people of His day were. Taking these cues from Jesus, contextualization is then about how to best address one's immediate audience for the sake of the mission, usually by utilizing the context of the audience. Jesus contextualized how He spoke and taught whoever was before Him so that His words and actions would be in a way they could understand.

We, too, need to be thinking about contextualization when we speak to unbelievers about the gospel or other truths of God. We have to use language and examples they can understand so that our message may make more sense to them in realizing their need for Jesus. Therefore, as discerned, refrain from using biblical and religious jargon when talking to an unbeliever. They don't read the Bible. They don't understand our Christianese or doctrine. Nowadays, who knows how certain Christian terms, phrases, and teachings they are familiar with have been distorted by the culture, politics, and false or inadequate teachers. Meet them with language and examples suitable to their context to help them better understand the good news we want them to believe.

Additionally, we have to use contextualization with other believers. Christians aren't monolithic. We have different learning styles, different communication styles, different cultural backgrounds, different education levels, and so on. Contextualization in discipleship is necessary for individual growth in understanding and applying the truths and instructions in God's Word.

Some good measuring questions for us would be:

- Do I know my sending context—who is my Jerusalem, my Judea, and my Samaria?
- Do I know the gospel well enough to make it plain to someone who does not know it?
- Do I know the truths of God according to Scripture well enough to explain it in a way a third-grader could understand?

Questions like these are good for us to gauge the extent of our contextualization. We must become well-versed in our sending context *and* in what we believe so we can carry out the mission of God contextually as Jesus did.

4th Approach: Reproducible

The fourth approach Jesus used was reproducible. This approach is essential in discipleship—*follow Me, then go and do likewise*. Reproducible is the post-salvation missional approach. It's the evolution of an unbeliever into a believer into a disciple-maker.

The great commission is truly the quintessence of reproducibility. However, there was a process that led to the point of this great commissioning. In one verse, Jesus encapsulates the whole process.

> "A disciple is not above his teacher, but *everyone who is fully trained will be like his teacher.*" (Luke 6:40, CSB; *emphasis added*)

This is the patent verse for discipleship. Jesus is communicating here that if you follow Me as My disciple, I will train you to become like Me. That's discipleship: *following your teacher to become like your teacher*. This was nothing new for His disciples then. Discipleship was part of their culture. Jesus being incarnational, intentional, and contextual, used rabbinical discipleship to train up followers whom He would send to carry out His mission in like manner.[12]

It has been said, the way this looked during their time was that a young Jewish guy would request to follow a rabbi. If the rabbi thought the person could become like he was, he would invite the person to come "follow him"—i.e., come learn to be like him. Then there would be a long period of formal and informal mentoring and training between the rabbi and the disciple. Finally, once the rabbi knew the disciple was ready, he would send out his disciple to go do what they had been taught—do with others what he did with them. This was rabbinical discipleship.

Jesus did this also. As the greatest Rabbi ever, He trained His disciples similarly to the other 1st century rabbis, but better. Every one of His twelve disciples, He called them first to follow Him—to come and learn to be like Him (Luke 6:12-16). Then He spent the next three years with them, teaching them, building relationships with them, eating with them, serving with them, and in every way training them to be like Him. Lastly, right before Jesus ascends, He commissions His disciples as disciple-makers and entrusts them with one final task—His mission. Jesus sends them out to go *be as He was* (His type of character), to go *do as He did* (His type of actions), to go *do what He taught* (His type of obedience), and to go *do with others what He did with them* (His type of discipling).

Jesus didn't deviate from the reproducible model of disciple-making. He used it to reproduce mini-mes of Himself that can continue to reproduce more mini-me's of Himself and carry out His mission until He returns. Even though today, we are Christians scattered world-wide and don't follow rabbis, this model of discipleship is how Jesus instituted His mission to be fulfilled. Yes, it looks a little different be-cause of contextualization, but it fits the same model. In fact, Jesus makes this reproducible model of disciple-making better because He guarantees the outcome and sends the Holy Spirit to empower and sustain us so we can do it.

Jesus carried out the mission of God reproducibly, leaving us a model to follow. So here's a provoking question for us to reflect on.

- How am I in this approach of being reproducible?
  - What unbelievers am I discipling to become believers?
  - What believers am I discipling into disciple-makers?

This question brings us back to the classic struggle for many Christians: salvation only being about our personal relationship with Jesus. Hence, the reason many don't venture outside of themselves and God. Possibly unknowingly, they've turned the gift into an idol which obstructs them from being missional. If we're sincerely following Jesus, not only should we possess a desire for being reproducible, but in some way, we should be attempting to do so as well—even if we're failing along the way. This is part of our discipleship in Christ. Jesus calls people to follow Him, trains them up, and sends them to go and do likewise, guaranteeing the end result.

Is there a better way to carry out the mission of God than by knowing and following how the Master Himself did it? There is no better way. Jesus showed us how to get the job done and with 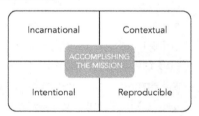 the desired results! His fourfold approach is adjustable for the organic and the planned, for the flexible and the structured. It's the perfect approach to mission because it's how the Master approached mission. Therefore, our accomplishing the mission of God will require us to utilize this fourfold approach to mission like Jesus. They work together as a unit. They can all be done within one another, and they reinforce the effectiveness of each other in carrying out the mission.

Remember, in God's mission, salvation is the goal that gets one into the kingdom, but discipleship is the earthly tutor for life within the kingdom. Thus, my fellow Christian, determine to go forth carrying out the mission of God incarnationally, intentionally, contextually, and reproducibly just as Jesus did.

LIVING THE MISSION

The great commission and its application are the product of the sequence of God unfolding His mission. Let's recall the mission of God again: *to disclose God's good news of redemption to non-covenant people so they may come to believe in Him, be identified as His family, and teach them to know and obey God.* What God starts in the beginning, He sees it through until the end. But He does not do this without showing and telling us how we can do so with Him.

If you're anything like I am, you probably think you stink at being missional. Something's missing, right? Maybe you figure you need to do more or that you need to discover what to do altogether. Perhaps you reason that you're not qualified enough, or extroverted enough, or not well-spoken enough, or don't have enough time. Personally, there was a period where being missional felt more burdensome than natural. Then around the fall of 2009, my wife and I got plugged into an urban discipleship church in Los Angeles. It was there that I saw the mission lived out organically and joyfully. For the next decade in California, God shaped my understanding of the mission being lived out like this—organically and joyfully. No doubt, I still struggle and fail. But mission is no longer a burden. It's simply me living out my discipleship everywhere, all the time; no different than I live out being a husband everywhere and all the time. Hence, when the Spirit convicted me for my lack of engagement with my former neighbors, I didn't feel condemned. Rather, I felt reminded not to hide my light and love of God.

When we understand what the great commission means and how to apply it realistically, it isn't terrifying, unachievable, or reserved for the "skilled." On the contrary, we'll find that it's designed to be clothed in our natural living. Its simplicity is both liberating and empowering.

> "18 Jesus came near and said to them, "All authority has been given to me in heaven and on earth. 19 Go, therefore, and make disciples of all nations, baptizing them in the name of the Father and of the Son and of the Holy Spirit, 20 teaching them to observe everything

I have commanded you. And remember, I am with you always, to the end of the age."" (Matthew 28:18-20, CSB)

Living the Mission: "Go..."

In Matthew 28:19, when Jesus said *"Go, therefore..."*, that "go" is the clearest declaration that every disciple of Jesus is a missionary. Yup, we're all missionaries, not just the apostles, or those who move overseas, or those who are missionaries by vocation. All of us.

Our God is the first missionary. He saved us to send us. His mission is in our DNA as His people. We share this responsibility with the Trinity. To be a believer in Jesus means that as His follower you are His missionary. Our salvation is our qualification for mission, our call to mission, and our ordination as a missionary.

Since every Christian is a missionary, we must know how missionaries go and engage a people group because we don't commonly think like missionaries. This way, we can employ the same strategies wherever we are.

⚡ Four essential missionary strategies.

Here are four essential strategies long-term missionaries use to reach those where they're sent:

1. *Missionaries determine to love the people where they're sent,* regardless of how they are received or treated.

Love is why Jesus was sent, and for love is why they go. Thus, as missionaries, we too must determine to love the people where we are sent. Sounds cliché-ish, right? Especially when Christians regularly throw out that we "love everyone." But love is a moving influence manifested in action. Therefore, we must determine to make a willful decision, a conscious choice, to love with the love of Christ the people we are sent to, regardless of how they treat us or receive us.

A pastor I read said he had to admit to himself that the reason he hadn't given a **"single thought to a neighbor or colleague"** was that he didn't **"truly love the lost."**[13] I can echo the same sentiment with my former neighbors. I didn't love them enough for that year to talk to them about their life, or my story, or invite them to church, or plant seeds about Jesus. As missionaries, we must determine to love the people where we are sent.

2. *Missionaries learn the people where they're sent*—their language, their culture, their region, and so on.

Learning is indispensable to leading. You can't lead a person to Jesus if you haven't first learned where they are in life and how to address them. Thus, as missionaries, we must also learn the people where we are sent—their worldviews, culture, stories, hurts, hopes, etc. And just as learning is indispensable to leading, listening is indispensable to learning. Listen to people to learn how to pray for them, how you can possibly care for them, how to answer their questions or misunderstandings about our God or Christianity, and ultimately how to point them to Jesus. Again, we have to learn the people where we are sent.

3. *Missionaries adapt to the people where they're sent.*

Adaptation is not conforming. Adapting is simply adjusting to new or different conditions. Conformity is complying to be molded after something else. Adapting is saying I'm going to remain as the original product I am, but I'm going to learn and, to some degree, mirror the conditions around me. Conformity is saying I'm no longer going to remain the original product I was; I'm going to become something else, whether good or bad. Paul tells us in Romans 12:2 to *"not be conformed to this world"* but be transformed by the truth of God renewing our mind. Thus, for us as missionaries, we must adapt by adjusting to reach the people where we are sent, not conforming to reach them.

4. Through loving, learning, and adapting, *missionaries discover the most effective way to reach the people where they're sent.*

The fourth strategy is the culmination of the first three. Discovery is Jesus' contextual approach. Discovery is the sum of being incarnational and intentional. Thus, through loving, learning, and adapting, we discover the most effective way to reach the people where we are sent.

I need you to hear this, Christian, especially for my saints over forty. When you were a teen and a young adult, what worked for you may not work for the current teens and twenty-somethings. Shucks, it may not work for people your age anymore. The cultural landscape appears to be changing quicker than a new generation can arise. So what does this mean? It means you, fueled with the love of Christ for the lost, have to learn and adapt. You have to discover what it takes to reach those of today. If you keep trying to reach people today using the ways that worked for your generation in the past, you probably won't connect with the people of today. Think about it, many of them speak a different cultural language. Many of them may not have been raised with your worldview. As stated, because of the changing landscape and whoever influences them, they may have completely different worldviews. If we don't love, learn, and adapt to discover how to reach them, we will miss them.

⚡ Is this truly real to us?

I have a close friend named Cecil. I love this guy and his family. I believe he is the first Christian brother I met that exceeded my passion and loudness. I look tame next to him. But I love it!

Cecil is a Hispanic American brother from the east side of Bakersfield. He was a hothead before Christ who got radically saved and said he knew God called him to be a missionary. After he got married, he and his wife, Tracy, received some training from their denomination. Then they sent them to Canada and told them (my paraphrase), "If you want to be a missionary, you have to know how to adapt to wherever you are and reach the people where you are. Stay here. Survive. Make friends. Plant seeds. See how close you can get to some people and help them better understand who God is."

After Canada, they made another short-term trip to Thailand. And that was it. He would later tell me they knew that's where they were supposed to go because they fell in love with the Thai people.

Not their culture, but the people. Their heart was moved for the people, so much so that they prayed about moving there for ten years. This was their first long-term assignment.

I remember having a conversation with Cecil where he told me, "I really did at that moment feel like Jesus, Chris. I'm interacting with these Thai people and I realize they are like sheep without a shepherd. My heart was moved with compassion for them. So we decided to go."

Cecil is Hispanic and Tracy is Anglo. Even though their kids are multiethnic, they look Anglo. None of that deterred them. They immersed themselves among the Thai people. They learned the people and their customs. They learned their language. They taught their kids the language. They dress similarly. They follow certain traditions. In a nutshell, they adapted. And in their adapting, they discovered how to reach the Thai people.

I had the privilege of going to spend some time with them. I met the people they've helped lead to Christ. I participated in a Thai worship service with a local church they helped established. I witnessed the impact they're having at being a gospel presence and community. As a friend and a believer, I see what they're doing, and my heart says I need to do the same where I am. So I begin to self-reflect: Do I really love the lost around me? Am I willing to learn the lost around me? Am I willing to adapt and discover the best way to reach them? And who is the one person I can begin with?

Apostle Paul said, *"though I am free from all men, I have made myself a servant to all, that I might win the more.... I have become all things to all men, that I might by all means save some."*[14] This is the mantra for the missionary. This is what thinking like a missionary is all about. Wherever we are and whatever lost people are around us, we love, learn, adapt, and discover to become all things to all people so that we, by all means, might save some.

⸙ *How* are we to "go"?

Jesus gives us quite a lot in this little two-letter word. "Go," in the context of Matthew 28:19 in the Greek, is conveying *as you are already going.*[15] Jesus is communicating that we are to be on mission in the normal rhythms of our life, in the things we are already doing. Think of the things you usually do in a day or a week. Where do you go? How many people are you around? How often do you bump into your neighbors? It's in those places, among those people—from strangers to family—that we are to be missional-minded. Our life already provides natural springboards into mission. It's there if we're looking. Our mission field is everywhere we already are.

Jesus knew all of this and modeled it first. He was on mission during the normal ebb and flow of life (e.g., John 1:35-51; 4:1-43). And He's communicating this to His followers: be on mission in your goings how I was on mission in My goings. Jesus is shattering the concept that the mission is something we have to add to our schedules. He's instructing how mission is what we do *while* we're doing everything and going everywhere. How perfect is this for 21st century believers? Think about it. How often do you feel like, "How can I possibly fit the "mission" into my schedule when it's already so full with family, work, activities, church, and so on?" Guess what? You don't have to add it in; just be on mission *while* you're already doing things and going where you're going. "Go" is the command for us to wear the mission like we wear clothes everywhere we go.

Ben Connelly is the pastor I mentioned earlier. I love what he wrote about everyday mission. It's convicting and spot-on.

> "Let's never miss the things of *eternal* importance for the sake of *momentary* urgency. We must consider how to move from that which *seems* urgent to that which *is* important: mission in the cracks of daily life, mission on the clock as part of our job, and mission-minded caution with our calendars."[16]

This "go" Jesus is commanding for His disciples, He displayed it when He was on mission in His approach of being incarnational. We are to "go" incarnationally as Jesus was incarnational.

⚜ *Where* are we going?

The "where" we are going is unmissable—Jerusalem, Judea, Samaria, and to the ends of the Earth. But, since our locales are different from our 1st century brethren, what does this look like for us?

- *Jerusalem* can be seen as those closest to us relationally, geographically, and vocationally—e.g., immediate family, friends, associates, neighbors, people where we frequent, coworkers, etc.
- *Judea* can be seen as those nearby but not too far away from us geographically, vocationally, and relationally—e.g., extended family, friends of friends, people who live anywhere within our city-county limits.
- *Samaria* can be seen as those anywhere within our state and nationwide—e.g., people outside our city and county but within our state and country.
- *Ends of the Earth* is everybody everywhere else outside our country.

Don't reduce this to some rigid formula and miss missional opportunities. The fluidity of where we're going is based on wherever we are. What is Jerusalem for you may be Samaria for me. What the ends of the Earth are for you now could become your Jerusalem if the Lord called you to move. For my boy Cecil, Thailand was once the ends of the Earth and then became his Jerusalem for the next ten years. For myself, Bakersfield was my Jerusalem and Maryland was Samaria. That all flipped when the Lord called me to pastor a church in Reisterstown, MD. We "go" where God assigns us, and wherever we are, we are to carry out His mission there and unto the ends of the Earth.

Josh Reeves, the teaching pastor at Redeemer Round Rock in Texas, said this,

> "Although the word "missional" has become quite a buzzword recently, it really just means that we live every day as missionaries. Jesus said that "As the Father has sent me, so I send you" (John 20:21). That word "sent" is where we get the word "mis-

sional." It simply means that we live as Jesus lived – as sent people who live everyday life with gospel intentionality."[17]

This essentially is what Jesus was communicating when He commanded us to "go, therefore." He's saying we are His missionaries. Therefore in all our comings, goings, and while we're doing whatever we're doing, think like missionaries—love, learn, adapt, discover— and live our everyday life incarnationally with gospel intentionality.

Living the Mission: "make disciples..."

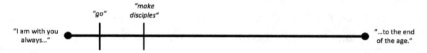

In the biblical-Jewish context, a disciple is one who faithfully follows their teacher to become like their teacher. The term "disciple" in both Hebrew (*talmidim*) and Greek (*mathētēs*) has a consistent meaning and portrayal. Disciple means *a learned one, a committed follower*. However, in the context of Matthew 28:19 in the Greek, "disciples" is not a noun, so it's not referring to a person.[18] It's a verb. It's about the action of discipling. (Hence, why the English translations add the word "make" in front of it).

"Make disciples" is about the action of teaching and being taught to become a learned one, a committed follower. In this phrase "make disciples," Jesus essentially says go do with all the nations what He did with His disciples. And we saw Jesus made disciples through His words (explanation), His works (demonstration), and how He lived (lifestyle). Therefore we, in our goings, are to be explaining, demonstrating, and modeling to unbelievers *why* they should follow Jesus and *how* to follow Jesus.

⚓ Explain. Demonstrate. Model.

Explain (i.e., the verbal), demonstrate (i.e., the good works), and model (i.e., the lifestyle) is simply what we know as *evangelism* and *witnessing* fleshed out in Jesus' approach.

"Explain" is about sharing *what you know* regarding the gospel, the testimony of your relationship with Jesus, the teachings in the Bible, God's character, and so on. This includes answering people's questions about Jesus and whatever else Christians believe (or don't believe) according to the Bible (1Pet. 3:15). Explaining can be done with anybody, anywhere, at any time—in person, online, over the phone, and in text. However, this doesn't mean you have to talk about these things all the time; rather, you're ready to do so when opportunities present themselves. And when you don't have an answer for people's questions or comments, be honest and say that. Then go research to be ready to give an answer the next time.

Explaining is not about how much you know but what you know confidently (e.g., John 15:26-27). Remember, you're talking about spiritual things to someone without the Holy Spirit and your intent is for them at some point to come to believe in Jesus for salvation. Therefore, wowing them with knowledge is of little value apart from salvation. Sincerity, on the other hand, is a more potent seed to plant. So be honest. Stick with explaining what you confidently know. If that's just the basics of the gospel and your testimony, then be honest about it and stay there (Rom. 1:16-17). As you mature in the faith, your knowledge of God's truth will follow. In fact, the more you talk to others about what you know, the more exposed you'll become to your own holes, and the more you'll want to grow in your knowledge of what we—Christians—believe.

No matter how much or little we know, remember this,

> "24 The Lord's servant *must not* quarrel, *but must be* gentle to everyone, able to teach, and patient, 25 instructing his opponents with gentleness. Perhaps God will grant them repentance leading them to the knowledge of the truth. 26 Then they may come to their senses and escape the trap of the devil, who has taken them captive to do his will." (2Timothy 2:24-26, CSB; *emphasis added*)

"Demonstrate" is about being Christlike and bearing the fruit of the Spirit so that the people around you may see something different and then be pointed to God. Unfortunately, in our day today, the Christian message is often discredited by the actions of Christians that don't line up with what we preach.

Martin Luther, the great reformer, is noted with saying, *"God does not need our good works, but our neighbor does."*[19] Apostle Paul said in Galatians 6:9-10,

> "9 Let us not become weary in doing good, for at the proper time we will reap a harvest if we do not give up. 10 Therefore, *as we have opportunity, let us do good to all people*, especially to those who belong to the family of believers." (NIV; *emphasis added*)

Demonstration is doing good to everyone in every opportunity. However, there is a caveat to this being missional. Whenever asked or there's an opportunity to share, we must always credit the good we're doing to Jesus (and why). If they don't know it's Jesus behind our good works, then it's not missional. It's humanitarianism. It's just doing good for goodness sake, not good for the sake of the mission. Demonstration is with anyone and anywhere when the opportunity arises or is needed. Sometimes opportunities are provided, and sometimes they need to be created to do good. Something else worth pointing out, this prescriptive in Galatians 6:10 means we don't get to use busyness, or idleness, or tribalism, or political differences, or any other thing as an excuse to not demonstrate when we have the opportunity or when there is the need to do so.

Demonstration is also an opportunity for the Holy Spirit. We have no idea how God may work through our good works or what kind of gospel seeds may be planted by us choosing to be missionally-demonstrative.

"Model" is about living out our authentic beautiful-messy faith and relationship with Jesus. Yup, the beautiful-mess is missional. It's messy because of us. It's beautiful because of Jesus.

> "4 Remain in me, and I will remain in you. A branch can't produce fruit by itself, but must remain in the vine. Likewise, *you can't produce fruit unless you remain in me.* 5 I am the vine; you are the branches. If you remain in me and I in you, then you will produce

much fruit. *Without me, you can't do anything.*" (John 15:4-5, CEB; *emphasis added*)

Our life is a constant presence of victories and falls, successes and failures, and freedom from hurts and habits while still battling our present shortcomings. That's the messy part: *us*. But Jesus adds the beauty. His constant grace. His eternal forgiveness. His unrelenting mercy. His inexhaustible love. His personal presence. His hopeful promises. His transforming power. This kind of authentic beautiful-messy faith and relationship with Jesus shows unbelievers that Jesus isn't some mythical figure we believe in, but a real personal God we need and depend on. We have a real love relationship with God through Jesus—real highs, real lows, real struggles, and real growth.

Our lifestyle is to reveal Jesus' good and faithful character in light of our redeemed but still messy lives (2Cor. 12:8-10). This is not a license for hypocrisy or comprising with sin, rather an emphasis on authenticity. Think about it, our authentic beautiful-messy faith and relationship with Jesus is an immediate common ground we have with the unbelieving world. Their lives are broken and messy too. They need the wholeness we have in Christ. Therefore, we can share how in our relationship with Jesus a transformation has happened and is continuing to happen in the mess they see. Hence, what they need, as we did, only Jesus has.

Modeling is to be done for those **"we're able to establish time or relationships with like relatives, friends, neighbors, coworkers, fellow students... etc."**[20] Not everyone will be able to see our lives lived like this. Nevertheless, this doesn't mean we keep our relationship with Jesus so private that no unbeliever or very few can see it or hear about it. If you aren't afraid to be public with any other relationship, don't be afraid to be public with Jesus. And public doesn't mean flaunting; it simply means not hidden. Moreover, for those on social media, the blogosphere, podcasting, the gaming world, and so on, this is where your online presence can serve as another mission field. Who knows how living out your authentic beautiful-messy faith and relationship with Jesus publicly and online can reach people in your Jerusalem, Judea, Samaria, and to the ends of the Earth.

Explain, demonstrate, and model is all contained in "make disciples." Jesus displayed this when He was on mission in His intentional approach—He did everything on purpose for the mission. Thus, we are to make disciples intentionally as Jesus made disciples intentionally.

✦ Overcoming the hang-up.

Knowing what it means to "make disciples" is one thing, actually doing it is another. Truth be told, for many Christians, it's the doing that's the bigger hang-up. Ask any Christian. The most challenging part of making disciples is the application of making disciples.

The Christian organization, CRU, put out an evangelism resource in 2010 that shares some thoughts on why this is most difficult for us. I think this is a perfect portrayal of why most of us aren't as missional as we should be.

> "Sometimes Christians cocoon into spiritual safety and security *rather than* take risks to build relationships with the lost. We fill our evenings with Bible studies, fill our lives with Christian friends and end up isolating ourselves from the very culture to which we were called to be salt and light. The Christian community *should* be a place from which we can confidently *go out* into battle building common-ground relationships with the lost. It *should not* be our fortress where we hide from the world separating ourselves from those we are seeking to reach."[21]

Dr. Alvin Reid addresses evangelism extensively in his prior works. However, in one sentence I believe he hit the nail of our missional hang-up on the head. He wrote, **"In our mastery of fellowship with the saints, we've lost a burden for a friendship with sinners."**[22]

Since the application of being missional is the most difficult, I want to offer a simplistic and more natural way of making disciples in our goings like Jesus is commanding. I taught an acrostic to our church to simplify how to be on mission in their goings. This "LEAD" acrostic captures and summarizes what has been explained thus far in "go" and "make disciples."

> **L - Listen** (Matt. 9:10-13)
> - o   Listen to people to learn how to pray for them, to learn how you can possibly care for them, and to learn how to point them to Jesus.
>
> **E - Express** (Col. 4:5-6)
> - o   Express sincere thoughts about what you hear from people as you listen to them. Express their needs in praying *for* them *with* them (and include the gospel in your prayers with them because that's their greatest need, and you have their captive attention). Express God's care for them. Express how your relationship is with Jesus, how there's hope in Jesus, and how they can have a personal relationship with Jesus.
>
> **A - Ask** (Matt. 22:1-10)
> - o   Ask people to come with you to church, to a small group, to a ministry event, to hang out with you, and so on. Invite them to something that will bring them in the presence of other believers and/or under the clear proclamation of the gospel.
>
> **D - Do** (Matt. 5:1-16, Luke 6:27-36)
> - o   Do what's right *according to* Jesus when around people and toward people. You can never go wrong acting like Christ.

People are more receptive to our message if they see and know we care about them and that they aren't simply a project for us—which is why being incarnational matters. As Dr. Reid articulated, **"think of evangelism as making friends instead of [making] contacts."**[23] Thus, these are four simple, organic ways to plant and water gospel seeds to help lead people to Jesus. No matter our age or maturity level, we all can do this with whomever and wherever we are in the comings and goings of our life. This does, however, require intentionality because you can't accidentally lead people to Jesus. You do have to be conscientious of where you're pointing them.

Being missional is not about having all the answers or being eloquent with your words. It's not even about their response to us. As missionaries for Jesus, our responsibility is about guiding spiritually blind people to the path of Jesus so that Jesus can open their eyes to see Him and be saved. Hence, missionaries are tour guides for life in Christ—our words, actions, and lifestyle are to always point to life in Jesus. And be encouraged,

> *"Our confidence is not in ourselves, but in the gospel and in who God made us to be. The only "failure" in witnessing is the failure to witness, and even when that happens God still loves you."*[24]

Living the Mission: "of all nations..."

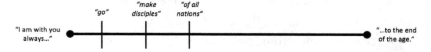

The term "nations" in Matthew 28:19 in the Greek is *ethnē*, which means *people groups,* not merely recognized countries with govern-ments.[25] *Ethnē* is a cognate of *ethnos*, and *ethnos* is where we get the term ethnicity, which means *the people group one is born from.* Hence, everyone has an ethnicity. For example, Israel was a "nation" (*ethnos*) long before they were officially recognized as a nation in the 20th century. Similarly, the U.S. as a nation is also an *ethnos* (ethnicity), which is why every person born in the U.S. has "American" after their ethnicity of descent—e.g., Native American, African American, Asian American, Hispanic American, Anglo-American (those of European descent).

This Greek term *ethnē/ethnos* used for "nations" is trans-lated more often in the New Testament as "gentiles" to distinguish the people groups as non-covenant people.[26] But when Jesus says "all nations" here, He's using *ethnē/ethnos* to mean *all the different eth-nicities and cultures of people everywhere*—every people group and sub-group within a people group—*that are non-new covenant people*. Ergo, gentiles and Jews. This is why Acts 1:8 is part of the great commission mandate because Jesus was telling His disciples where the nations are—they're in Jerusalem, in Judea, in Samaria, and to the ends of the Earth. Jesus takes how God first unfolded His mission by revealing it through His Jewish people to the nations, and now He updates it and sends His born-again people to the nations as the mission. Do you know how significant this is? The nations are all around us, Christian! Non-new covenant people from numerous ethnicities and cultures are everywhere in our Jerusalems, our Judeas, our Samarias, and all over the Earth.

⚡ How to live this out.

So what does it look like to live out this phrase, "of all nations"? It looks like not staying secluded in your ethnicity or culture. That's what Jesus' Jewish disciples would have heard in Acts 1:8:

- Jerusalem = same ethnicity, same culture
- Judea = same ethnicity, same or different culture
- Samaria = different ethnicity, different culture
- the ends of the Earth = different ethnicities, different cultures

To Jesus' Jewish disciples this phrase meant "expand out." And the meaning hasn't changed. As God sends us into environments with different ethnicities and cultures than our own, be on mission. As God brings people from different ethnicities and cultures than our own across our path, be on mission. It may be scary. It may be awkward. It may be uncomfortable. But none of this is by accident. It's all by God's design. To *only* be missional within our ethnicity or culture is disobedient to the mission of God and a distortion of the vision of His kingdom.

This "of all nations" is the command from Jesus to be missional outside our ethnic and cultural comfort zones. Think about it, can you reach the nations if you are secluded in your own ethnicity or culture? Nope. But don't mistake me here. I'm not saying Jesus' command is to move somewhere or force integration. Yet, with that said, His command does imply not deferring the mission to the nations because of comfort or dislike. Forced or willful segregation and tribalism are tactics used by the enemy to keep Christians from being missional to the nations around them. Do you know what God does when Christians settle in segregation from the nations? He sends persecution to cause the Church to scatter into the nations.

"1 Saul was one of the witnesses, and he agreed completely with the killing of Stephen. *A great wave of persecution began that day, sweeping over the church in Jerusalem; and all the believers except the apostles were scattered through the regions of Judea and Samaria. 2* (Some devout men came and buried Stephen with great mourning.) 3 But Saul was going everywhere to destroy the church. He went from house to house, dragging out both men and women to throw them into prison. *4 But the believers who were scattered preached the Good News about Jesus wherever they went.*" (Acts 8:1-4, NLT; *emphasis added*)

Please do not defer this aspect of the mission because of comfort or dislike unless you prefer God using persecution to bring about your obedience. And I am not using persecution as a scare tactic but as a reality check. In his book "Unparalleled," Jared Wilson points this out also.

"Many religions, like Islam for example, seem to thrive on conquest and power. Christianity grows best under hardship.... I sometimes wonder if God has set the growth of Christianity to work this way to keep in the forefront of our minds the treasure and glory of heaven over and above the treasure and glory of earth."[27]

For my brethren living in a monoethnic or homogeneous environment that are thinking, "So, what does this look like for me?" To start, it does not look like you bypassing the nations in your Jerusalem, Judea, and Samaria to go to the nations in another country. At a 2015 conference, I heard Dr. Ray Bakke make two superb statements about this during his presentation. First, he said, **"Don't go around the zip codes you don't like to do missions at zip codes further away."** Then he added, **"The frontier of missions is right across the street, not**

across the ocean." The nations for you would obviously be any ethnicity different from your own, but also the different cultures among you—e.g., someone from another religion, with a dissimilar upbringing, unalike in political and/or social views, and so on.

Monoethnic doesn't always equate to monocultural and vice-versa. Homogeneous, on the other hand, could be monoethnic but multicultural (e.g., Anglo but diverse socio-economically), or monocultural but multiethnic (e.g., both Anglo and African Americans but all socially conservative), or both—monoethnic and monocultural. Furthermore, culture is not always the same as ethnicity, although it is included in Jesus' use of *ethnē/ethnos*. Culture simply means *the traditions, customs, and ways of a particular group of people*. Therefore, whatever your environment is, be aware of those ethnically and culturally different among you and be on mission to them. They are your "of all nations."

Remember, we engage the nations as missionaries: determined to love them, learn them—their worldviews, their culture, their hurts, their hopes, so on—while adjusting and discovering the most effective way of reaching them. Likewise, we must also consider, mission success always requires death (2Cor. 4:1-15). In order to effectively engage the nations, it will cost us and cause us to die to ourselves: die to our known and unknown stereotypes and prejudices of other ethnicities and cultures, die to our political barriers, die to our echo chambers—the environments and groups that only reinforce our views—and die to our preferences and privileges (i.e., following Jesus' incarnational approach). Notice what Jesus says,

> "24 Truly I tell you, unless a grain of wheat falls to the ground and dies, it remains by itself. *But if it dies, it produces much fruit.* 25 The one who loves his life will lose it, and the one who hates his life in this world will keep it for eternal life. 26 *If anyone serves me, he must follow me.* Where I am, there my servant also will be. If anyone serves me, the Father will honor him." (John 12:24-26, CSB; *emphasis added*)

It will cost some of you to die to yourselves to be missional outside of your ethnic and cultural comfort zones. But it will cost all of us to die to ourselves to be missionally effective in our Jerusalem, Judea, Samaria, and to the ends of the Earth, just as it did our Savior. Jesus' sacrifice tore down the dividing wall of separation between Jew and gentile, and now all who are part of the covenant family of God are one Body of Christ. We cannot resist the sacrifices we must make following after our Savior for the success of the mission.

♭ A global mission.

Not sure if you knew this, but "the nations"—the non-new covenant people from every ethnicity and culture—are the primary subject of Jesus' command in the great commission. Jesus informs everyone that the nations were always to be the primary recipients of God's mission, which is why we must "expand out."

Dr. Vince Bantu opens his book, "A Multitude of All Peoples," plainly stating, **"Christianity is and always has been a global religion. For this reason, it is important never to think of Christianity as *becoming* global."**[28] And, providentially, we get a heavenly glimpse of what the culmination of the mission of God will look like in Revelation 5:9-10 and 7:9-10. People of every ethnicity and culture from every neighborhood, village, city, and country worldwide will be reached because of every believer's obedience to Jesus' command to go make disciples of all the nations.

> **"With so many other religions being almost inextricably tied to specific tribal or national cultures, Christianity stands apart as especially nimble in the global age. You will find vibrant Christian communities among a wide variety of people groups all over the world, and while their expressions and cultural characteristics will be all over the map, their essential beliefs will be on the same page. Christianity is amazingly adaptable."**[29]

This "of all nations" Jesus is commanding, He displayed it when He was on mission in His approach of being contextual—whom He went to and how He spoke and discipled. Thus, we're to go make disciples of all the nations contextually as Jesus was contextual.

Living the Mission: "baptizing them...and teaching them..."

As encompassing and weighty as going and discipling all nations already is, and as tough as that would've been to hear for Jesus' Jewish disciples, He doesn't end His commission here. To make sure His disciples clearly understood this radical mission He was telling them to do, Jesus continued.

↳ Baptism.

Jesus said when these non-new covenant people from every ethnicity and culture come to believe in Him, He wants us to then publicly identify them as part of the new covenant family, as part of the new covenant community (e.g., Acts 3:38; 10:44-48; 19:1-6). In this command to baptize them, Jesus is establishing a new sign for the new covenant. His Jewish disciples would've heard and understood this water baptism command to be like a Jew circumcising a gentile proselyte of Judaism—marking them with the sign of the old covenant. Hence, why Jesus says baptize these new disciples from all nations in the name of Father, the Son, and the Holy Spirit. Being baptized in the name of the Holy Trinity identifies the new covenant: believers are reconciled to *the* Father through our belief in the death and resurrection of *the* Son, and eternally sealed by *the* Spirit (Eph. 1:3-14).

I must quickly say to eliminate any ambiguity: baptism does not save (Eph. 2:8-9).[30] Baptism is not *for* salvation, nor does it *affect* your salvation. For believers in Jesus, baptism in the name of the Father, the Son, and the Spirit is an outward sign declaring what we've believed to be saved. Water baptism is the most meaningful event that represents us having entered into the new covenant of God in Christ. Additionally, it signifies being part of God's redeemed family, part of

His new covenant community. Picture a football or basketball game. Have you ever seen them run out of the tunnel while being introduced as part of the team? Baptism is similar to this, spiritually speaking. After professing Christ for salvation—putting on the same blood-bought family jersey—baptism is the public pronouncement of your spot on the same team with all the other believers in Jesus across history from every ethnicity and culture.

As for how this fits with being on mission, it's disciples who baptize disciples (Acts 8:26-39). Baptizing believers is both a responsibility and an honor of disciples going and making more disciples of Jesus. Thus, be baptized if you haven't since being born-again. And, if you can, participate in baptizing someone you discipled or helped come to faith in Jesus. That's a part and reward of the mission!

This "baptizing them" Jesus is commanding, He displayed it when He was on mission in His approach of being reproducible—do as I did and taught. Jesus baptizes all of His disciples with the Holy Spirit in regeneration from death to life and then commands His disciples to water baptize other disciples to signify that they've gone from death to life and are part of the new covenant community. Go do as Jesus did.

⚑ Teaching them.

If you haven't noticed, there has been a shift in the great commission. Starting with baptism, we're at the part of the mission where the focus has shifted from unbeliever to believer. We've been told by Jesus to disciple unbelievers into believers ("make disciples"), and now we're told to disciple believers into disciple-makers ("teaching them to observe"). This is every single believer's responsibility as disciples of Jesus—young, old, male, female, single, married, leader, non-leader, trained, untrained, ordained, non-ordained, local churches, parachurch ministries, and Christian institutions. No one born-again is exempt from this. To be a beloved and begotten believer in Jesus is to be a missionary. And now we see to be a missionary is also to be disciple-maker, because making disciples who can go make more disciple-makers is the whole mission. We tend to miss closing the circle in mission when we think the mission is over after someone becomes born-again. The mission is complete with a person once they become a disciple-maker. Until then, we are still on mission with whomever we are discipling.

So what did Jesus mean by this "teaching them"? Was He referring to formalized preaching and instruction or something else? The context of "teaching" in Matthew 28:19 pretty much encompasses *sharing (in any capacity) with someone your knowledge of what Jesus taught in a way for them to come to know it.*[31] The sharing of this knowledge in any capacity can be from the simple form of regular conversation to encouraging, advising, explaining, instructing, or preaching. Jesus used the Greek term for teaching in a context so that it wouldn't require any qualification to do it. He simplified it for every disciple. No matter their level of maturity or education, any disciple can do it. However, there is a point of caution. Just because we're commanded to share what we know with each other, that doesn't mean everything someone shares is right. It is your responsibility to be always learning what is biblically accurate so you can discern biblical truth from what is false (Phil. 4:8-9, 2Tim. 1:13).

When Jesus said teach one another "everything I have commanded you," the context of "command" in the Greek implies the what, why, and how of whatever is commanded.[32] In other words, this phrase means *whatever I've told you to do, why I told you to do it, and how to do it.*

To put this into perspective, we have twenty-three more books making up the New Testament fleshing out what Jesus taught and told His followers to do. Furthermore, Jesus said Himself in Luke 24:44 that He practically referred to the whole Old Testament while He was with His disciples. Therefore, wherever the Old and New Testament are revealing to us what we need to know about God and obey to become more like Jesus, that's what we are to learn, observe, and teach other believers in a way that they can come to know and obey it too. Again, this does not mean you have to be a Bible scholar. If you know little, teach that little; if you know more, teach the little and the more. Also, this "teaching" is not from the position of know and do what you don't know or don't do. Instead, it's know and do as you too are learning and doing. Part of your obedience to this command is to continue learning to observe all Jesus taught and then to share with other believers what you're learning and applying yourself.

Another point of simplification from Jesus in this command is that He hasn't broken away from His starting position of the great commission. This "teaching them" is still attached to "go, therefore." Jesus is saying we are to teach other believers the same way we discipled unbelievers into believers, in our goings and whatever we're doing. Does this mean Christians can't do this from formal preaching and instruction? Not at all. Jesus' context is intended to not limit it only to those more formal forms because that's not the only way He taught His disciples. Jesus' model of discipleship is life-on-life, which incorporates the formal, the informal, the spontaneous, and the scheduled. Thus, whenever other believers are around us—and every occasion fits—that's always an opportunity to share what we're learning and applying from the Word in a way they can receive and observe it too.

As for how this would practically look, that would be in the natural ways we exchange or express with other believers: in a *word of encouragement*, a *brief testimony*, an *explanation of Scripture*, a *personal reflection*, an *instruction from Scripture*, in *accountability*, *reconciling* with another believer, *repenting* to another believer, in *correction* of another believer, *comforting* another believer, and so on. These examples are merely following the natural model of how Jesus taught His disciples. He taught them through discourses, at the dinner table, in conversations while they were walking or fishing or feeding thousands of people, through parables and debates with religious leaders, through questions and answers with the people, in the temple, etc. We see that Jesus' "teaching them" was in many capacities, and His disciples are to imitate Him. Therefore, He meant "teaching them" like they saw and experienced with Him.

What Jesus is commanding in this "teaching them" He displayed it in all four of His approaches when He was on mission—

incarnational, intentional, contextual, and reproducible. Hence, we are to follow suit in our discipling of others.

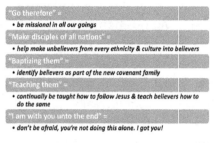

"Go therefore" =
• be missional in all our goings
"Make disciples of all nations" =
• help make unbelievers from every ethnicity & culture into believers
"Baptizing them" =
• identify believers as part of the new covenant family
"Teaching them" =
• continually be taught how to follow Jesus & teach believers how to do the same
"I am with you unto the end" =
• don't be afraid, you're not doing this alone. I got you!

Our discipleship with Jesus is following our Master to become like our Master. Therefore, carrying out the mission of God is our discipleship in action. Living on mission is simply living as a disciple of Jesus. The mission is not unachievable. It is very much doable and can become normal if we see it as a component of our relationship with Jesus lived out with and among others. Remember, the mission is in our DNA. Being a missionary is more natural than we realize. We have to stop being afraid and letting other things or voices psyche us out.

Moreover, the mission is far more organic than programmatic. Unfortunately, too many Christians have become dependent on programs and a select few people in the Church to carry out the mission for the rest of us. Are these programs and people needed? Yes! Are they helpful in accomplishing the mission? Certainly! However, leaning on programs and the spiritually gifted or ministry professionals in the Church has caused the common Christian to lose the art of simply being a disciple on mission. Suppose we shifted our perspective and understood there are things we already do and can be doing that are naturally missional. In doing this, we can reclaim the art of being everyday missionaries—taking our discipleship on the go with us everywhere and in everything.

NOW WHAT?

I hope as you read through this chapter, your mind was at work thinking about how you have treated and responded to God's mission in your own life. I hope you were encouraged to see ways you are being missional and were convicted about why at times you are not missional. Also, along the way, I hope it was made clear that the mission of God is not about us. Not even a little bit. The mission is not about our needs, our wants, our preferences, our ideals, our life plans and goals, our politics, our causes, our countries, our comfort, our convenience, etc.

The temporal things of this world have their place. But they are not the mission. The mission always takes priority over the "ours." Thus, whatever we put above the priority of the mission of Christ is an idol. We need to be reminded of this often because we all do it, and do so easily. Are good things out there to be done? Of course. Yet, the moment you place more emphasis on whatever "___" is over the mission of Christ, you have made that good thing an idol. It is no longer a good thing so long as it's above the mission. It has become a stumbling block to why you were saved to be sent. And please don't brush over that fact; it's a slippery slope into missional stagnation or disobedience if you do.

I feel this must be stated explicitly to my fellow American Christians: Don't forfeit the biblical worldview in pursuit and expectation of social and political change. No prophet, no apostle, nor Jesus ever did this. Their greatest priority, along with ours, was and is always to be the mission of God. So don't abandon biblio-missiology for any socio-political movement. We were redeemed to be Christ's mission-aries everywhere in everything, not redeemed to sit, nor to build or defend other kingdoms. Whatever we put above the priority of the mission of Christ is an idol.

God would not have gone through what He did for a mission that did not gravely matter to Him. Hence, we should never think He is okay with His people being flippant in carrying out His mission or placing other less important things above it. Think about what we've explored. God's mission mattered so much that He established a people just to reveal it, personally demonstrated it in the coming of Jesus and the Holy Spirit, then redeemed a people with the Son's missional blood so we can partner with the Trinity. In light of this, how much should the mission of God matter to us? How much does it matter to you?

Every believer in Jesus is to carry out the mission of God. Every single one of us. There is no such thing as "I'm not qualified." There is no exception for introverts, or the uneducated, or those not well-spoken, or based on age. There is no sitting on the sideline. There is no retirement. Every single person who professes Jesus Christ as their Lord and Savior is called and spiritual-genetically modified to carry out the mission of God as long as they're alive. Now how we carry out this mission can look different from person to person, church to church, and situation to situation. We're not robots, and being missional is not cookie-cutter. But there is absolutely nothing that negates any believer in Jesus from carrying out God's mission.

Are you familiar with the children's story of the tortoise and the hare? I hope so, because being missional is more like the tortoise than the hare. Some Christians may lead people to Jesus with ease or in a far greater quantity than the average believer. Praise God for them and those saved souls! However, those Christians are the exceptions, not the standard. Yet, even as the standard, each of us will still have to give an account to God for what we did for His mission with our time, our provisions (i.e., abilities, resources, platforms, so on), and our opportunities. If you're the average believer, your missional sphere will probably have you laboring over one to a handful of people for an extended period of time before something changes. That's not a bad thing. That's the tortoise. That's common.

My wife and I spent two years laboring missionally at a local gym—countless conversations and even more missed ones. Then one week, an opportunity and right timing finally connected. One of the former gym employees I used to speak with returned to work there. During his time away, his dad had passed, his relationship with his girlfriend ended, he was living more reckless, and he was about to drop out of college. I shared some of my story with him. I prayed *for* him *with* him there in the gym. Then I invited him to hear me share more of my story that coming Sunday at our church. And he actually came. He listened to my testimony and how Jesus rescued a sinner like me. He responded and requested salvation. Later, he told me that "God" and "church" had kept being mentioned to him or around him for that past week, and my personal invitation he received as a sign. That was his first time in church and his first time hearing the gospel. Two years of missional labor yielded one soul saved and several seeds planted. That's the tortoise. That's what's common.

You may never personally lead an unbeliever to salvation in Jesus. You will, however, play a part in many people coming to salvation. Some you may find out about, many you probably won't ever know. Nevertheless, this counts as an assist on your part. And that's a missional win! Maybe your gifts and opportunities fall more on the side of helping a believer become a disciple-maker; that's a missional win too! You closed a missional circle. You finished what another believer started. Hence, another joy of understanding God's mission, it's a team assignment. Every single believer plays a part. Every single local church plays a part. This is the reason each of us being on mission in our individual lives matters so greatly. We have no idea how our obedience as missionaries assists in someone's story of redemption or their story of going and making more disciple-makers.

Hallelujah to Jesus for addressing our natural fears to His mission! He includes His promise that He is with us to the end of the age. Therefore, accomplishing the mission of God is possible because our Savior not only showed us how, He guaranteed it, and then empowers us with the Holy Spirit to do it. Oh, what thankfulness, boldness, and eagerness this should produce in us all!

"19 Go, therefore, and make disciples of all nations, baptizing them in the name of the Father and of the Son and of the Holy Spirit, 20 teaching them to observe everything I have commanded you. And remember, I am with you always, to the end of the age.'" (Matthew 28:19-20, CSB)

Going Forward

I began the book sharing about the kinds of experiences and conversations I had been having since 2014. This led me to realize the predominant theme in them was explaining to Christians *who* they are and *how* to think and be Christian. The idea was to centralize and continue that conversation with you the reader. Thus, by the time you reached this conclusion you would know *who* you are and *how* you can be effectively living in our current days facing the way the world is now and its ever-changing complexion. We are not merely Christian, or believers, or disciples in title are we? By no means! We are beloved and begotten bondservants of God, sojourning on this earth as official ambassadors on mission for Christ. What a holy position and a holy calling we possess from our Most Holy God! This is *who* we are and *how* we are to think and be. This is our identity in Christ. And this identity prevails no matter the time or issues of the day.

Have you seen or do you know of the movie "Wonder Woman 1984"? It's okay if you haven't seen it or don't know what it is. According to the critics it wasn't that good of a movie anyway. I remember telling my wife after we saw it in the movie theaters, "I think the movie was alright. Not as good as the first Wonder Woman. But what I do know is that movie will preach. I'm definitely going to find a way to use this in a sermon or the book." She laughed and said, "Of course you are."

In "Wonder Woman 1984," Wonder Woman fought two villains: Barbara Minerva (Cheetah) and Maxwell Lord. Of the two villains,

Maxwell Lord was the dominant threat. He wasn't as strong, fast, or brave as Wonder Woman, or even as much as Barbara. What made Maxwell more lethal was him weaponizing and personifying an idea: *the desires of the heart*. Scripture calls this the lust of the eyes, the lust of the flesh, and the pride of life (1Jn. 2:15-17). Maxwell stole some ancient magical stone and used it to grant his wish of becoming the stone so he could grant the wishes of others while in turn receiving more wishes for himself. Consequently, he became more and more powerful as the world became more and more chaotic with everyone receiving the desires of their hearts. Sounds a lot like the day we live in to me. By the end of the movie, Maxwell Lord became what Apostle John describes in 1John 5:19 (CSB), *"the whole world is under the sway of the evil one."* Wonder Woman's superhuman physical abilities weren't enough to defeat him. She had to rely on her lasso of truth. Literally, the truth set all the people free. Wonder Woman came this to conclusion upon remembering who she was and what her role was in this world. Her identity brought about how she would become victorious.

Although this is a fiction movie, the parallels are scary accurate for us as Christians. Our most formidable foe is any idea contrary to God (2Cor. 10:3-5). We see this in the garden of Eden. The Serpent whispered a God-contrary idea to Eve. Eve passed that on to Adam. They both believed it and acted on it, which then produced the fall of mankind. The formidability of this threat hasn't changed. If anything, as Christians we tend to overlook its lethality at the expense of what we want, or what we think is best, or doing what we feel, or believing what we want to believe, etc. Whenever we entertain these God-contrary ideas that promise us the desires of our heart, we forget or suppress who we are and our role in this world. And in a way, we place ourselves back under the sway of the evil one. We return to idolatry. It is only the truth that will set us and others free. The truth in this case is our identity in Christ. John, in the first part of 1John 5:19, actually says the reason believers are not under the sway of the evil one is *"we know that we are of God."* In other words, we know our identity—*who* we are (or Whose we are) and *how* we are to think and be. Our identity in Christ is what brings about our victorious and effective living in a world that remains under the sway of the evil one. Living from our identity in Christ is how we fight against every God-contrary idea that plays the tune of the desires of our hearts—flaunting ungodly things as good and turning good things into idols. Identity and idolatry are the antithesis of one another.

> "18 We know [with confidence] that anyone born of God does not habitually sin; but He (Jesus) who was born of God [carefully] keeps and protects him, and the evil one does not touch him. *19 We know [for a fact] that we are of God, and the whole world [around us] lies in the power of the evil one [opposing God and His precepts].* 20 And we [have seen and] know [by personal experience] that the Son of God has [actually] come [to this world], and has given us understanding and insight so that we may [progressively and personally] know Him who is true; and we are in Him who is true—in His Son Jesus Christ. This is the true God and eternal life. *21 Little children (believers, dear ones), guard yourselves from idols—[false teachings, moral compromises, and anything that would take God's place in your heart].*" (1John 5:18-21, AMP; *emphasis added*)

The remaining question from knowing now about your particular identity in Christ is what does it produce *in you*? Remember, this book is not merely about what you know. It's about what you do with what you know. It's about the influence of what you know in your life, for knowledge without transformation is wasteful, and there can be no transformation without a renewing of our mind. We either live from our identity in Christ or we are living from our identity in something else. So what does going forward with the knowledge of your identity in Christ look like *for you*?

My heart and hope is that you've reclaimed *who* you are as a Christian and *how* you are to live as a Christian in this world. My heart and hope is that you're repenting with me for where you can agree you've been guilty of not living how we are to in this world. And my heart and hope is that you are resolved on moving forward determined to live from your identity of being *beloved and begotten* of God, *bondservants* of the Lord, *sojourners* on earth, *ambassadors* of Christ, and *missionaries* for Jesus.

> "*The gospel not only furnishes transforming power to remold the human heart; it provides also a model after which the new life is to be fashioned, and that model is Christ Himself.* Christ is God acting like God in the lowly raiments of human flesh. Yet He is also man; so He becomes the perfect model after which redeemed human nature is to be fashioned. The beginnings of that transformation, which is to change the believing man's nature from the image of sin to the image of God, are found in conversion when the man is made a partaker of the divine nature. By regeneration and sanctification, by faith and prayer, by suffering and discipline, by the Word and the Spirit, the work goes on till the dream of God has been realized in the Christian heart. *Everything that God does in His ransomed children has as its long-range purpose the final restoration of the divine image in human nature. Everything looks forward to the consummation.* In the meantime the Christian himself can work along with God in bringing about the great change. Paul tells us how: "But we all, with open face beholding as in a glass the glory of the Lord, are changed into the same image from glory to glory, even as by the Spirit of the Lord" (2 Corinthians 3:18)."[1]

Study Guide

Sometimes simple questions can allow for greater discussion. If you are interested in using this book for a group study, here are a few general questions that could assist in the chapter discussion.

1. How has this chapter helped refresh or reform your understanding of our identity in Christ? Explain how so.

2. Did this chapter challenge, expand, or reinforce *any* of your views? If so, explain.

3. Was there anything else you learned in this chapter that you didn't know before? Did you gain any new insight? If so, explain.

4. Discuss your personal takeaways and anything else that stood out to you from this chapter.

5. If you haven't discussed it yet, share what you can apply to your life from this chapter.

Don't hold back. Engage with one another's answers and ask each other follow up questions. Press into the "whys" and "hows." Hold each other accountable to however you hear the Spirit is working in your lives. Be sure to start and end your group time in prayer.

Notes

Chapter 1

1. "Beloved" as an adjective in the Greek is: ἀγαπητός (*agapétos*), ἀγαπητοὶ (*agapētoi*), ἀγαπητόν (*agapēton*), ἀγαπητοῖς (*agapētois*), ἀγαπητήν (*agapētēn*), ἀγαπητὰ (*agapēta*), ἀγαπητοῦ (*agapētou*), ἀγαπητῷ (*agapētō*), ἀγαπητέ (*agapēte*). BibleHub, retrieved in 2013, https://biblehub.com/greek/strongs_27.htm.
2. In the Greek, "love" in 1John 3:1 is ἀγάπην (*agapēn*, a noun). Grammatical context can be found here: BibleHub, https://biblehub.com/interlinear/1_john/3-1.htm, (retrieved in 2013).
3. A.W. Tozer, *The Knowledge of the Holy* (New York, NY: HarperCollins, 1961), 100-101. Emphasis added.
4. Acts 10:34, Romans 2:11, Galatians 2:6, Ephesians 6:9, 1Peter 1:17
5. Ecclesiastes 5:18-20; 7:15; 8:14-15; 9:1-3, Matthew 5:45
6. Quote is attributed to Jonathan Edwards. Rick Holland, *Uneclipsing the Son* (The Woodlands, TX: Kress Biblical Resources, 2011), 17.
7. 1John 3:2, ESV; *emphasis added*
8. In the Greek it's ἁγνίζει (*hagnizei*, a verb). Grammatical context can be found here: BibleHub, https://biblehub.com/interlinear/1_john/3-3.htm, (retrieved in 2013).
9. R.C. Sproul (ed.), *The Reformation Study Bible* (Sanford, FL: Reformation Trust Publishing, 2015), 2271.
10. Tim Clinton and Joshua Straub, *GOD Attachment* (New York, NY: Howard Books, 2010), 39.
11. In the Greek, "believes" in 1John 5:1 is πιστεύων (*pisteuōn*, a verb). Grammatical context can be found here: BibleHub, https://biblehub.com/interlinear/1_john/5-1.htm, (retrieved in 2013).
12. In the Greek it's ὁμολογήσῃ (*homologēsē*, a verb). Grammatical context can be found here: BibleHub, https://biblehub.com/interlinear/1_john/4-15.htm, (retrieved in 2013).
13. Tozer, *The Knowledge of the Holy*, 115.
14. A.W. Tozer, *The Pursuit of God* (Camp Hill, PA: Christian Publications, Inc., 1982, 1993), 14.
15. T. Rees, "Begotten," *International Standard Bible Encyclopedia*, retrieved in 2013, https://www.internationalstandardbible.com/B/begotten.html.
16. Bruce B. Barton, Dave Veerman, and Linda K. Taylor, *Life Application Bible Commentary: Luke* (Wheaton, IL: Tyndale House Publishers, Inc.,

1997), 78. Robert L. Thomas and Stanley N. Gundry, *A Harmony of the Gospels* (New York, NY: HarperCollins Publishers, 1978), 317.

17. Thomas and Gundry, *Harmony of the Gospels*, 316-318. Not all scholars agree on Luke presenting the genealogy of Jesus' physical claim to the throne of David from Mary's side. However, context clues favor this view over the others. One, Luke spent more time than any other gospel writer talking about Mary and her divine pregnancy with Jesus. Thus, when we get to his genealogy, it would make sense he would show her lineage and not Joseph's. Two, Matthew had already traced Joseph's lineage in his gospel. Three, Luke's account was not intended for the same primary audience as Matthew's. And fourth, Joseph is only mentioned after Jesus because women weren't included as heads of the family in genealogies—which is why Luke inserts "*as was supposed* son of Joseph" (Luke 3:23b). Again, makes sense for Luke sharing Mary's line for Jesus.

18. Shelbi Austin and U.S. News Staff, "Countries With Monarchies," *U.S. News*, April 25, 2019, https://www.usnews.com/news/best-countries/slideshows/countries-with-current-monarchies, retrieved in 2020. The World staff, "There are 28 other monarchies in the world," *The World*, May 18, 2018, https://www.pri.org/stories/2018-05-18/there-are-28-other-monarchies-world, retrieved in 2020.

19. Psalm 10:16; 22:27-28; 29:10; 45:6; 93:1-2; 103:19; 145:13, Daniel 7:13-14, 27, Matthew 13:41-43, 1Corinthians 15:24-26, 1Timothy 1:17, Hebrews 12:28, 2Peter 1:11, Revelation 11:15; 19:11-16

20. Tozer, *The Knowledge of the Holy*, 99. Brackets added.

21. Tozer, *The Knowledge of the Holy*, 102. Emphasis added.

22. In the Greek it's ποιῶν τὴν δικαιοσύνην (*poiōn* [verb] *tēn dikaiosynēn* [noun]). Grammatical context can be found here: BibleHub, https://biblehub.com/interlinear/1_john/3-7.htm, (retrieved in 2013).

23. Aaron Clay Denlinger and Burk Parson (eds.), John Calvin, *A Little Book on the Christian Life* (Sanford, FL: Reformation Trust Publishing, 2017), 3.

24. Calvin, *A Little Book on the Christian Life*, 8.

25. Calvin, *A Little Book on the Christian Life*, 9.

26. Calvin, *A Little Book on the Christian Life*, 16.

27. 1John 3:7, ESV; *emphasis added*

28. In the Greek it's ἀγαπῶν (*agapōn*, a verb). Grammatical context can be found here: BibleHub, https://biblehub.com/interlinear/1_john/3-10.htm, (retrieved in 2013).

29. 1John 2:6, NIV; *emphasis added*

30. Tozer, *The Knowledge of the Holy*, 102. Emphasis added.

31. Thomas á Kempis, *The Imitation of Christ* (Peabody, MA: Hendrickson Publishers Marketing, LLC, 2004), 15.

32. Holland, *Uneclipsing the Son*, 50.
33. Credited to Dr. Tim Clinton. Retrieved from unknown source.
34. I wrote a blog-article answering the question "Aren't all religions the same? Don't all religions point to the same God?" You can read that here: https://www.biblicallyshaped.com/blogs/are-all-religions-the-same.
35. Ronald Nash, *Is Jesus the Only Savior?* (Grand Rapids, MI: Zondervan Publishing House, 1994), 22.
36. Barbranda Lumpkins Walls, "Spirituality According to Oprah," *AARP Bulletin*, October/November 2015, https://www.aarp.org/entertainment/style-trends/info-2015/oprah-winfrey-belief-series.html, retrieved in 2020.
37. Nash, *Is Jesus the Only Savior*, 24.
38. Walter A. Elwell (ed.), *Evangelical Dictionary of Theology,* 2nd Edition, (Grand Rapids, MI: Baker Academic, 1984, 2001), 1232.
39. "Agnosticism," retrieved in 2021, Encyclopedia Britannica (https://www.britannica.com/topic/agnosticism) and Dictionary.com (https://www.dictionary.com/browse/agnosticism).
40. Holland, *Uneclipsing the Son*, 61. Emphasis added.
41. Kempis, *The Imitation of Christ*, 61. Bracketed word added.
42. Tozer, *The Knowledge of the Holy*, 100.

Chapter 2

1. In Hebrew it's עֶבֶד (*ebed*, a noun); BibleHub, retrieved in 2020, https://biblehub.com/hebrew/5650.htm. In the Greek it's δοῦλος (*doulos*, a noun or an adjective); BibleHub, retrieved in 2020, https://biblehub.com/greek/1401.htm. William Edward Raffety, "Slave; Slavery," *International Standard Bible Encyclopedia*, retrieved in 2020, https://www.internationalstandardbible.com/S/slave-slavery.html.
2. F. L. Cross and E. A. Livingston (eds.), *The Oxford Dictionary of the Christian Church* (New York: Oxford University Press, Inc., 1997), 1508-1509. Justo L. Gonzales, *The Story of Christianity,* Volume I (New York, NY: HarperCollins Publishers, 2010), 449-485. Michael O. Emerson and Christian Smith, *Divided By Faith: Evangelical Religion and the Problems of Race*, (New York, NY: Oxford University Press Inc., 2000), 21-37. Katharine Reid Gerbner, "Christian Slavery: Protestant Missions and Slave Conversion in the Atlantic World, 1660-1760," Doctoral dissertation, *Harvard University*, 2013.
3. M. G. Easton, "Slave," *Easton's Bible Dictionary*, retrieved in 2020, https://eastonsbibledictionary.org/3458-Slave.php. Emphasis added.

4. Raffety, "Slave; Slavery," *International Standard Bible Encyclopedia*, retrieved in 2020, https://www.internationalstandardbible.com/S/slave-slavery.html. Emphasis added.
5. John MacArthur, *Slave* (Nashville, TN: Thomas Nelson, 2010), 27-28.
6. MacArthur, *Slave*, 35. Emphasis added.
7. Matthew 1:19, NIV; *emphasis added*
8. Luke 1:34, CSB; *emphasis added*
9. Luke 1:38, ESV; *emphasis added*
10. MacArthur, *Slave*, 25.
11. Ben Gutierrez, *Living out the Mind of Christ* (Thomas Road Baptist Church, 2008), 85.
12. In the Greek it's δοῦλος (*doulos*, an adjective and a noun). *Doulos* is a cognate of the different Greek stems of this term that's used depending on its grammatical context. BibleHub, retrieved in 2020, https://biblehub.com/greek/strongs_1401.htm.
13. In the Greek it's σωτηρία (*sótéria*, a noun) and σώζω (*sózó*, a verb). *Sótéria* and *sózó* are the cores of the words "salvation" and "saved" used in both Romans 10:9-10 and Ephesians 2:8-9. BibleHub, retrieved in 2020, https://biblehub.com/greek/strongs_4991.htm and https://biblehub.com/greek/strongs_4982.htm.
14. Jerry Bridges, *The Practice of Godliness* (Colorado Springs, CO: NavPress, 1983, 1996), 17.
15. Galatians 5:1, CSB; *emphasis added*
16. MacArthur, *Slave*, 160.
17. MacArthur, *Slave*, 154-157.
18. Thomas Watson, *The Godly Man's Picture* (Carlisle, PA: The Banner of Truth Trust, 1666, 1992), 13. Emphasis added.
19. 1Corinthians 1:4-9, Philippians 1:6, 1Thessalonians 3:11-13; 5:23-24, Jude 1:24-25
20. John 14:16-17, 26; 16:13-15, 1John 2:24-27, Ephesians 1:13-14
21. Aaron Clay Denlinger and Burk Parson (eds.), John Calvin, *A Little Book on the Christian Life* (Sanford, FL: Reformation Trust Publishing, 2017), 66. Emphasis added.
22. Watson, *The Godly Man's Picture*, 14.
23. Watson, *The Godly Man's Picture*, 14.
24. W. M. Christie, "Nazirite," *International Standard Bible Encyclopedia*, retrieved in 2020, https://www.internationalstandardbible.com/N/nazirite.html. Emphasis added.
25. Watchman Nee, *The Normal Christian Life* (Carol Stream, IL: Tyndale House Publishers, 1957, 1977), 99.
26. Nee, *The Normal Christian Life*, 100. Emphasis from the author.

27. Thomas á Kempis, *The Imitation of Christ* (Peabody, MA: Hendrickson Publishers Marketing, LLC, 2004), 31. Bracketed word added.
28. Bridges, *The Practice of Godliness*, 28.
29. Dictionary.com, "preeminent," retrieved in 2021, https://www.dictionary.com/browse/preeminent.
30. Kempis, *The Imitation of Christ*, 93.
31. Psalm 34:1-22, 1Peter 2:1-10, Hebrews 6:4-20; 10:26-39
32. Tim Clinton and Joshua Straub, *GOD Attachment* (New York, NY: Howard Books, 2010), 147.
33. Clinton and Straub, *GOD Attachment*, 148.
34. In the Greek, "worthy" in Matthew 10:37-38 is ἄξιος (*axios*, an adjective). Grammatical context can be found here: BibleHub, https://biblehub.com/interlinear/matthew/10-37.htm, https://biblehub.com/interlinear/matthew/10-38.htm, (retrieved in 2020).
35. Watson, *The Godly Man's Picture*, 50-51. Emphasis added.
36. A.W. Tozer, *The Pursuit of God* (Camp Hill, PA: Christian Publications, Inc., 1982, 1993), 27. Emphasis added.
37. Calvin, *A Little Book on the Christian Life*, 67-68. Emphasis added.
38. Tozer, *The Pursuit of God*, 19. Emphasis added.
39. Exodus 6:6-7; 19:5-6, Deuteronomy 4:20; 7:6-9; 14:1-2; 26:18-19, Romans 9:21-26, Ephesians 2:10-22, Titus 2:14, 1Peter 2:9-10, Revelation 5:8-10; 21:3
40. Nee, *The Normal Christian Life*, 102. Emphasis added.
41. Nee, *The Normal Christian Life*, 103-104. Emphasis added.
42. Military.com, "Be Ready To Raise Your Right Hand," retrieved in 2021, https://www.military.com/join-armed-forces/swearing-in-for-military-service.html.
43. Calvin, *A Little Book on the Christian Life*, 80. Emphasis added.
44. Kempis, *The Imitation of Christ*, 32. Emphasis added.

CHAPTER 3

1. Ecclesiastes 3:1, CEV; *emphasis added*
2. The three Hebrews terms for "sojourner" are גֵּר (*ger*, a noun), גּוּר (*guwr*, a verb), and תּוֹשָׁב (*toshab*, a noun). BibleHub, retrieved in 2020, https://biblehub.com/hebrew/strongs_1616.htm, https://biblehub.com/hebrew/strongs_1481.htm and https://biblehub.com/hebrew/strongs_8453.htm.
3. The two Greek terms for "sojourner" are παρεπίδημος (*parepidémos*, an adjective) and πάροικος (*paroikos*, an adjective). BibleHub, retrieved in 2020, https://biblehub.com/greek/3927.htm and https://biblehub.com/greek/3941.htm.

4. John J. Davis, *Paradise to Prison* (Salem, WI: Sheffield Publishing Company, 1975, 1998), 182.
5. Howard F. Vos, *An Introduction to Church History,* Revised (Chicago: Moody Press, 1984), 27.
6. Philip Schaff (ed.), Augustine of Hippo, *St. Augustin's City of God and Christian Doctrine*, (Grand Rapids, MI: Christian Classics Ethereal Library), 296. Retrieved PDF version from http://www.holybooks.com/augustins-city-god-christian-doctrine/.
7. Augustine, *St. Augustin's City of God and Christian Doctrine*, 425. Bracketed word added.
8. John F. Walvoord, *The Holy Spirit* (Findlay, OH: Dunham Publishing Company, 1958), 150.
9. Augustine, *St. Augustin's City of God and Christian Doctrine*, 296.
10. Michael O. Emerson and Christian Smith, *Divided By Faith: Evangelical Religion and the Problems of Race*, (New York, NY: Oxford University Press Inc., 2000), 2-3. Emphasis added.
11. Emerson and Smith, *Divided By Faith: Evangelical Religion and the Problems of Race*, 5-49. Justo L. Gonazales, *The Story of Christianity,* Volume II (New York, NY: HarperCollins Publishers, 2010), 275-347.
12. George Thomas Kurian, *A Quick Look at Christian History* (Eugene, OR: Harvest House Publishers, 2015), 19, 26.
13. Kurian, *A Quick Look at Christian History*, 19.
14. Robert A. Baker and John M. Landers, *A Summary of Christian History,* 3rd Edition (Nashville, TN: Broadman & Holman Publishers, 2005), 43-44.
15. Vince L. Bantu, *A Multitude of All Peoples: Engaging Ancient Christianity's Global Identity* (Downers Grove, Illinois: InterVarsity Press, 2020), 16. Emphasis from the author.
16. Baker and Landers, *A Summary of Christian History*, 67.
17. Kurian, *A Quick Look at Christian History*, 31.
18. Kurian, *A Quick Look at Christian History*, 24.
19. Justo L. Gonzales, *The Story of Christianity,* Volume I (New York, NY: HarperCollins Publishers, 2010), 147.
20. Francis A. Schaeffer, *How Should We Live Then?* (Wheaton, IL: Crossway Books, 1976, 2005), 39.
21. Standing for Freedom Center, "Falkirk Podcast 31: Church Is Essential w/Pastor John MacArthur," *YouTube*, August 12, 2020, https://youtu.be/IK26ZXi2K3g, retrieved in 2020.
22. John Fea, "This interview tells us a lot about John MacArthur and the movement he represents," August 22, 2020, *Current*, https://thewayofimprovement.com/2020/08/22/this-interview-tells-us-a-lot-about-john-macarthur-and-the-movement-he-represents/,

retrieved in 2020. I do not endorse, promote, nor claim to agree with all of the points made by the writer.

23. In Ephesians 2:19, the Greek term is συμπολῖται (*sympolitai*, a noun) and in context it's conveying part of the citizenship of the saints of God (natives of the same country). BibleHub, retrieved in 2020, https://biblehub.com/greek/4847.htm. In Philippians 3:20, the Greek term is πολίτευμα (*politeuma*, a noun) and in context it's conveying a community of people under a [heavenly] government. BibleHub, retrieved in 2020, https://biblehub.com/greek/4175.htm. In Philippians 1:27, the Greek term is πολιτεύομαι (*politeuomai*, a verb) and in context it's conveying to recognize and live under the authority of a set of laws [i.e., "the gospel of Christ"]. BibleHub, retrieved in 2020, https://biblehub.com/greek/4176.htm.
24. Rick Holland, *Uneclipsing the Son* (The Woodlands, TX: Kress Biblical Resources, 2011), 36. Emphasis added.
25. Romans 9:1–10:13, Ephesians 2:11-22, Galatians 3:7-29, Revelation 7:9-17
26. Isaiah 9:6-7, Ephesians 1:22-23, 1Corinthians 15:24-28
27. Tweeted by R.C. Sproul Jr. (@rcsprouljr) on 7/16/20.
28. Aaron Clay Denlinger and Burk Parson (eds.), John Calvin, *A Little Book on the Christian Life* (Sanford, FL: Reformation Trust Publishing, 2017), 92.
29. Augustine, *St. Augustin's City of God and Christian Doctrine*, 577. Emphasis added.
30. Holland, *Uneclipsing the Son*, 88.
31. Baker and Landers, *A Summary of Christian History*, 12-22. Vos, *An Introduction to Church History,* Revised, 23-28. Kurian, *A Quick Look at Christian History*, 7-12. Gonzales, *The Story of Christianity,* Volume I, 41-48.
32. Schaeffer, *How Should We Live Then?*, 24-26. Baker and Landers, *A Summary of Christian History*, 12-13. Vos, *An Introduction to Church History*, 24. Gonzales, *The Story of Christianity,* Volume I, 105-107.
33. Augustine, *St. Augustin's City of God and Christian Doctrine*, 591. Emphasis added.
34. Augustine, *St. Augustin's City of God and Christian Doctrine*, 394.
35. Augustine, *St. Augustin's City of God and Christian Doctrine*, 13.
36. Ephesians 2:4-5, CSB; *emphasis added*
37. Calvin, *A Little Book on the Christian Life*, 31-33.
38. Matthew 4:8-9, CSB
39. Holland, *Uneclipsing the Son*, 88-89. Emphasis from the author.
40. Thomas á Kempis, *The Imitation of Christ* (Peabody, MA: Hendrickson Publishers Marketing, LLC, 2004), 105. Emphasis added.
41. Schaeffer, *How Should We Live Then?*, 23. Emphasis added.
42. Calvin, *A Little Book on the Christian Life*, 24-25. Emphasis added.
43. Hebrews 12:28, NLT; *emphasis added*

44. Augustine, *St. Augustin's City of God and Christian Doctrine*, 393-394. Emphasis added.
45. I believe both the presence and power of the Holy Spirit and possessing an attainable target to obey will help in keeping you consistent in your obedience. But rather than calling you to obey without equipping you or providing an attainable target, allow me to do so here. A simple, attainable obedience target is: *Every day, pray for the Spirit's help to focus on doing what you already know is pleasing to God according to the Bible*. That's it. Don't try to take on more. Little things become bigger things over time. When you make a mistake in your day, repent, make any amends you may have to and get back to focusing on what you already know is pleasing to God. A simple way of how you can learn more to obey is: 1. As you read Scripture (in your devo time or Bible study) and listen to sermons or do group studies, write down anything you can apply to your life. See with your eyes what it is you can be working on. 2. Hold yourself accountable to do something from what you wrote down that day/week/month, and then ask another believer to hold you accountable to what you're working on applying to your life. Repetition breeds retention. The more you do this, the more it becomes a habit of applying what you're learning to obey. Start from what you already know to do, then slowly build up from there with whatever else you're learning to obey. The more you learn from God's Word, the more your desire will grow to obey God's Word, and grace covers your mistakes while you work to get it right.
46. 1Peter 1:17-19, NIV; *emphasis added*
47. Mark 9:23-24, NKJV
48. Tweeted by Troy Dixon (@dixontroy) on 8/30/20. Brackets added.

CHAPTER 4

1. "Ambassador," retrieved in 2020, Dictionary.com (https://www.dictionary.com/browse/ambassador) and Encyclopedia Britannica (https://www.britannica.com/topic/ambassador).
2. Career Explorer, "What does an ambassador do?," retrieved in 2020, https://www.careerexplorer.com/careers/ambassador/.
3. The National Museum of American Diplomacy, "What are the roles of a diplomat?," retrieved in 2020, https://diplomacy.state.gov/diplomacy/what-are-the-roles-of-a-diplomat/.
4. The Hebrew terms and stems used for "ambassador" are מַלְאָךְ (*malak*, a noun = messenger), צִיר (*tsiyr*, a noun = envoy), צָיַר (*tsayar*, a verb = to act as envoy), and לִיץ (*luts*, a verb = to speak for or speak as). BibleHub, retrieved in 2020, https://biblehub.com/hebrew/4397.htm,

https://biblehub.com/hebrew/6735.html, https://biblehub.com/hebrew/6737.htm, and https://biblehub.com/hebrew/3887.htm.

5. In Hebrew it's וַיִּצְטַיָּרוּ (*way·yiṣ·ṭay·yā·rū*, a verb = can be translated as ambassador). Grammatical context can be found here: BibleHub, https://biblehub.com/interlinear/joshua/9-4.htm, (retrieved in 2021).

6. In Hebrew it's מַלְאָכִים (*mal·'ā·ḵîm*, a noun = can be translated as ambassador). Grammatical context can be found here: BibleHub, https://biblehub.com/interlinear/isaiah/18-2.htm, (retrieved in 2021).

7. In Hebrew it's מַלְאָךְ (*mal·'āḵ*, a noun = can be translated as ambassador). Grammatical context can be found here: BibleHub, https://biblehub.com/interlinear/proverbs/13-17.htm, (retrieved in 2021).

8. In Hebrew it's וְצִיר (*wə·ṣîr*, a noun = can be translated as ambassador). Grammatical context can be found here: BibleHub, https://biblehub.com/interlinear/proverbs/13-17.htm, (retrieved in 2021).

9. In the Greek, "ambassador" is πρεσβεύω (*presbeuó*, a verb). This term is from the same Greek root for the translation of "elder." BibleHub, retrieved in 2021, https://biblehub.com/greek/strongs_4243.htm.

10. Credited to Dr. Elmer Towns. Retrieved from unknown source.

11. The Greek term Paul uses for "reconciliation" is καταλλαγῆς (*katallagēs*, a noun). This comes from another Greek term καταλλάσσω (*katallassó*, a verb), which comes from two other Greek terms, κατά (*kata*, is a preposition) and ἀλλάσσω (*allassó*, a verb). Grammatical context can be found here: BibleHub, https://biblehub.com/interlinear/2_corinthians/5-18.htm, (retrieved in 2021).

12. D.A. Horton, *Intensional: Kingdom Ethnicity in a Divided World* (Colorado Springs, CO: NavPress, 2019), 69-70, 78.

13. Matthew 12:36-37, CSB

14. Alvin L. Reid, *Sharing Jesus Without Freaking Out* (Nashville, TN: B&H Academic, 2017), 57.

15. Philippians 2:5, NKJV; *emphasis added*

16. John J. Davis, *Paradise to Prison* (Salem, WI: Sheffield Publishing Company, 1975, 1998), 199. Emphasis added.

17. In the Greek it's παρακαλοῦντος (*parakalountos*, a verb). This comes from two other Greek words, παρά (*para*) and καλέω (*kaleó*). Grammatical context can be found here: BibleHub, https://biblehub.com/interlinear/2_corinthians/5-20.htm, (retrieved in 2021).

18. Matthew 5:14-16, John 8:12, Romans 13:12-13, 2Corinthians 6:14, 1Thessalonians 5:5-8

19. In the Greek it's ζωὴ, (*zōē*, a noun). Grammatical context can be found here: BibleHub, https://biblehub.com/interlinear/john/1-4.htm, (retrieved in 2020).

20. In the Greek it's φῶς (*phos*, a noun). Grammatical context can be found here: BibleHub, https://biblehub.com/interlinear/john/1-5.htm, (retrieved in 2020).

21. Psalm 36:9; 119:105, Proverbs 6:23, Isaiah 8:19-20, Romans 2:17-20; 7:7, 12-13

22. In the Greek it's σκοτία (*skotia*, a noun). From the Greek root word σκότος (*skotos*). Grammatical context can be found here: BibleHub, https://biblehub.com/interlinear/john/1-5.htm, (retrieved in 2020).

23. In Greek κατέλαβεν (*katelaben*, a verb). Grammatical context can be found here: BibleHub, https://biblehub.com/interlinear/john/1-5.htm, (retrieved in 2020).

24. Davis, *Paradise to Prison*, 247. Bracketed word added in replace of Davis' phrase "Jacob's bigamy."

25. Propaganda, "Precious Puritans," *Excellent* (Humble Beast, 2012).

26. Davis, *Paradise to Prison*, 178.

27. New Oxford American Dictionary, "empathy," retrieved in 2016, https://www.lexico.com/definition/empathy.

28. New Oxford American Dictionary, "sympathy," retrieved in 2016, https://www.lexico.com/definition/sympathy.

29. Aaron Clay Denlinger and Burk Parson (eds.), John Calvin, *A Little Book on the Christian Life* (Sanford, FL: Reformation Trust Publishing, 2017), 43-44.

30. Horton, *Intensional: Kingdom Ethnicity in a Divided World*, 81-82. Emphasis added.

31. Isaiah 9:6-7, Micah 5:5, John 14:27; 16:33, Acts 10:36, Romans 5:1, Ephesians 2:14-17, Colossians 1:17-20, 2Thessalonians 3:16, Hebrews 7:1-2; 13:20-21

32. Rick Taylor, *The Anatomy of a Disciple* (The Well Community Church, 2013), 225.

33. Taylor, *The Anatomy of a Disciple*, 180.

34. A perfect example of this is in Matthew chapters 5-7.

35. John 8:31-32; 16:13-15; 17:17-21, Matthew 28:19-20

36. 2Timothy 3:16-17, 2Peter 1:12-15; 3:1-2, 16-18, 1John 4:6, 2John 1:7-9

37. In the Greek, "abide" is μείνητε (*meinēte*, a verb). Grammatical context can be found here: BibleHub, https://biblehub.com/interlinear/john/8-31.htm, (retrieved in 2021). In Hebrew, "be joined" in Genesis 2:24 is וְדָבַק (*wǝḏāḇaq*, a verb). Grammatical context can be found here: BibleHub, https://biblehub.com/interlinear/genesis/2-24.htm, (retrieved in 2021).

38. 2Timothy 1:13-14; 2:15; 3:14-17; 4:1-2

39. The proper principles of sound biblical hermeneutics (interpretation) naturally follow the way the text was originally written according to the author's intent and context. Why? Because the Bible is written by

real people, about real people, across a real time, going through real events, using real languages, with objective, absolute, divine truth being revealed to them by their Covenant God who they really believe in, are being led by, and live for. Thus, these principles are all based on that context: (i)the historical context (i.e., *of* the time and setting, *of* the book, and *of* the point of the text), (ii)the literary context (i.e., the genre [narrative, prophetic, etc] and type [literal, figurative, etc]), (iii)the grammatical context (i.e., words have intended meanings, and context determines meaning), (iv)the divinely inspired and inerrant context (i.e., the Holy Spirit is the divine Author and Superintendent of Scripture), and (v)the timeless theological context (i.e., the instructions, wisdom, and truths not confined to a particular time or culture or covenant but applicable across time, cultures, and into the new covenant)—(some references: Ps. 19:7-11; 119, John 5:39-47; 7:14-17; 8:31-47; 16:13-15; 17:17, 2Tim. 2:15; 3:16-17, Heb. 4:12). To disconnect Scripture from its immediate context is to sever the veins through which its life-blood flows. No matter what we go to Scripture for or attempt to take away from it, the context of the text must not be violated or we'll disconnect it from its historic and divine life-blood and may come away with a Frankenstein because of our subjective interpretations.

These above principles are not the same as methods of interpretation, but rather they are the boundaries that rightly determine however we enter Scripture we do so in-bounds and not out of bounds. Methods, on the other hand, are the useful mechanisms to assist in rightly reading and studying Scripture to understand it and apply it. Proper principles and methods work hand in glove for sound biblical hermeneutics. Some good books for proper biblical hermeneutics and methods of study would be *"Knowing Scripture"* by R.C. Sproul, *"Grasping God's Word"* (2nd Edition) by Duvall & Hayes, and *"Living by the Book"* by Hendricks & Hendricks.

40. Brian Davies and G.R. Evans (eds.), Anselm of Canterbury, *The Major Works* (New York, NY: Oxford University Press Inc., 1998, 2008), 87. Emphasis added.
41. Anselm, *The Major Works*, 235-236. Emphasis added.
42. Thomas á Kempis, *The Imitation of Christ* (Peabody, MA: Hendrickson Publishers Marketing, LLC, 2004), 5. Emphasis added.
43. 1Timothy 4:6-10, 16; 6:3-5, 20, 2Timothy 2:14–3:9; 4:1-4, 2Peter 2:1-22, Jude 1:3-4, 16-21
44. "Tribalism," retrieved December 21, 2020, Merriam-Webster (https://www.merriam-webster.com/dictionary/tribalism), Dictionary.com (https://www.dictionary.com/browse/tribalism),

Cambridge Dictionary (https://dictionary.cambridge.org/us/dictionary/english/tribalism), and Encyclopedia.com (https://www.encyclopedia.com/humanities/dictionaries-thesauruses-pictures-and-press-releases/tribalism).

45. Kamal Misra, "Tribalism," *Encyclopedia.com*, May 11, 2018, https://www.encyclopedia.com/social-sciences-and-law/sociology-and-social-reform/sociology-general-terms-and-concepts/tribalism, retrieved December 21, 2020.

46. Dan M. Kahan, Donald Braman, John Gastil, Paul Slovic, C.K. Mertz, "Culture and Identity-Protective Cognition: Explaining the White Male Effect in Risk Perception," Journal of Empirical Legal Studies, Volume 4, Issue 3, 465–505, November 2007, *Yale Law School*, Public Law Working Paper No. 152. Retrieved PDF version from https://ssrn.com/abstract=995634. Kahan et al. explain, "Individuals tend to adopt the beliefs common to members of salient "in-groups." They also resist revision of those beliefs in the face of contrary factual information, particularly when that information originates from "out group" sources, who are likely to be perceived as less knowledgeable and less trustworthy than "in group" ones (Mackie & Quellar, 2000; Clark & Maas, 1988; Mackie, Gastardoconaco & Skelly, 1992).... The motivational effect of group membership on information processing is most easily explained by the inference that individuals do have a profound emotional and psychic investment in seeing their groups beliefs confirmed (Giner-Sorolla & Chaiken, 1997; Chen, Duckworth & Chaiken, 1999)."

47. Ezra Klein, *Why We're Polarized* (New York, NY: Avid Reader Press, 2020), 49-102. Dan M. Kahan, "Misinformation and Identity-protective Cognition," John M. Olin Center for Studies in Law, Economics, and Public Policy Research Paper No. 587, *Yale University*, October 2017. Retrieved PDF version from https://ssrn.com/abstract=3046603. In this paper, Kahan writes, "Identity-protective cognition (IPC) is a species of motivated reasoning. Motivated reasoning refers to the unconscious tendency of people to selectively credit and dismiss factual information in patterns that promote some goal or interest independent of the truth of the asserted facts."

48. Kempis, *The Imitation of Christ*, 104. Emphasis added.

49. 1Corinthians 15:33, CJB

50. Davis, *Paradise to Prison*, 207.

51. Kempis, *The Imitation of Christ*, 5.

52. John MacArthur (ed.), *Fool's Gold?* (Wheaton, IL: Crossway Books, 2005), 31-32. Emphasis from the author.

53. Colossians 1:15, 19; 2:9, 2Corinthians 4:3-6, Hebrews 1:1-3

54. Anselm, *The Major Works*, 236.

55. Howard G. Hendricks, *Teaching to Change Lives: Seven Proven Ways to Make Your Teaching Come Alive* (Colorado Springs, CO: Multnomah, 2003), 59.

56. Kempis, *The Imitation of Christ*, 3. Emphasis added.

57. In the Greek it's κτίσις (*ktisis*, a noun), from the Greek word κτίζω (*ktizó*, a verb). Grammatical context can be found here: BibleHub, https://biblehub.com/interlinear/2_corinthians/5-17.htm, (retrieved in 2021).

58. John 14:15-23, 1Corinthians 6:19, 2Corinthians 6:16

59. Matthew 6:9-13

60. Grammatical context can be found here: BibleHub, https://biblehub.com/interlinear/matthew/6-10.htm, (retrieved in 2021).

61. Allen Mitsuo Wakabayashi, *Kingdom Come: How Jesus Wants to Change the World* (Downers Grove, IL: InterVarsity Press, 2003), 141. Emphasis added.

62. Philip Schaff (ed.), Augustine of Hippo, *St. Augustin's City of God and Christian Doctrine*, (Grand Rapids, MI: Christian Classics Ethereal Library), 592. Emphasis added. Retrieved PDF version from http://www.holybooks.com/augustins-city-god-christian-doctrine/.

63. Kingdom values, ethics, and civics are all the biblical principles and instructions for born-again sojourning bondservants of Jesus living under the new covenant rule and domain of God.

64. Wakabayashi, *Kingdom Come: How Jesus Wants to Change the World*, 150.

65. Matthew 28:19, Mark 16:15, Acts 1:8, Revelation 5:9; 7:9

66. Job 15:14-16, Psalm 51:5, Isaiah 64:6-7, Romans 3:9-20, 23; 5:12, Ephesians 2:1-3

67. Credited to Matt Chandler. Retrieved from unknown source.

68. Acts 6:1-7; 10:24-28; 14:19-21; 15:1-29, Romans 2:1-29, Galatians 2:1-21; 6:11-15, Colossians 2:16-23, James 2:1-13

69. Christopher Davis, "A Biblical Response: Social Justice & the Christian," *Biblically Shaped Ministries*, September 14, 2017, https://www.biblicallyshaped.com/blogs/2017/9/biblical-response-social-justice-christian, retrieved January 14, 2021.

70. Augustine, *St. Augustin's City of God and Christian Doctrine*, 63. Emphasis added.

71. Christopher Davis, "My Heart Decompressed with the Reminder of What Matters Most," *Biblically Shaped Ministries*, May 28, 2020, https://www.biblicallyshaped.com/blogs/the-reminder-that-decompressed-my-heart, retrieved January 14, 2021.

72. #1-3 is from Proverbs 3:27-30 (NET). #4 Is from Proverbs 3:31-32 (NLV). #5 is from Proverbs 14:20-21, 31; 22:22-23 (NLT). #6 is from Proverbs 17:15 (CSB). #7-8 is from Proverbs 18:5; 24:23-25 (NLT). #9 is

from Proverbs 21:3 (NIV). #10 is from Proverbs 22:26-27 (CEB). #11 is from Proverbs 24:17-18 (NLT). #12-13 is from Proverbs 24:28-29 (CEV). #14 is from Isaiah 5:20 (NIV). #15 is from Matthew 22:15-22 (NLT). #16-21 is from Luke 6:26-36 (CEV). #22-26 is from Romans 12:17-21 (NLT). #27 is from Romans 13:8-10 (CEV). #28-31 is from 1Corinthians 13:4-7 (NLT). #32 is from Galatians 6:10 (NLT). #33-34 is from 1Thesselonians 5:15 (CEV). #35-37 is from Titus 3:1-3 (CEV). #38 is from Hebrews 13:16 (CSB). #39-40 is from James 1:27 (NLT).

For the believers who may be wondering why I didn't cite more direct justice passages from the Old Testament, allow me to explain. Not every verse and passage that commands justice is to be done by Christians. The majority of the Old Testament laws and prescriptives for justice cannot be divorced from the distinct people of Israel and their context. That's bad exegesis to do so. It opens the door to other misinterpretations. And, unfortunately, this is something many American Christians have already done. In turn, this has led them to demand that Christians in the U.S. uphold certain civil laws specifically for Israel when certain injustices arise, and/or they seek to hold the U.S. accountable to uphold certain civil laws specifically for Israel when certain injustices occur. That's incorrect and unnecessary. As seen here, there are some verses and passages that are perpetual kingdom justice commands for God's kingdom people across the old and new covenant.

73. Davis, "A Biblical Response: Social Justice & the Christian," retrieved January 14, 2021.
74. Kempis, *The Imitation of Christ*, 14.
75. Taylor, *Anatomy of a Disciple*, 144. Emphasis added.
76. Taylor, *Anatomy of a Disciple*, 296. Emphasis added.
77. A.W. Tower, *The Knowledge of the Holy* (New York, NY: HarperCollins, 1961), 116. Emphasis from the author.
78. Tozer, *The Knowledge of the Holy*, 102.
79. Matthew 4:23-24; 8:1-13; 9:10-13, 35-38; 21:28-32, Mark 2:13-17, Luke 7:34-50; 11:37-54; 14:1-25; 15:1-7, John 4:1-30
80. As a point of clarity, this "by-product" is not a uniform promise. I think American Christians forget the things we argue for and fight for here in our country may not be a fight in other countries because not all Christians have the same constitutional rights. Does that mean our brethren in countries outside the U.S. are exempt from kingdom justice as ambassadors? Absolutely not. One's residency does not dictate obedience to Scripture. Their application may look different in their contexts compared to ours in the U.S., which also means we cannot place any expectations or pressure on them to respond to their

injustices based upon how we respond in the U.S. The commands of kingdom justice are universal. The application is contextual.

81. Kempis, *The Imitation of Christ*, 15.

CHAPTER 5

1. Barna Group, "51% of Churchgoers Don't Know of the Great Commission," *Barna Group*, March 27, 2018, https://www.barna.com/research/half-churchgoers-not-heard-great-commission/, retrieved April 5, 2021.
2. Thomas Aquinas, *Summa Theologica* (1265-1274), 489-490. Retrieved PDF version from Christian Classics Ethereal Library, https://www.ccel.org/a/aquinas/summa/cache/summa.pdf.
3. "Mission," retrieved in January 2020, Merriam-Webster (https://www.merriam-webster.com/dictionary/mission) and Online Etymology Dictionary (www.etymonline.com/word/mission).
4. Stephen Neill, *Creative Tension: The Duff Lectures*, 1958 (London: Edinburgh House Press, 1959), 81.
5. Kevin DeYoung and Greg Gilbert, *What Is the Mission of the Church? Making Sense of Social Justice, Shalom and the Great Commission* (Wheaton, IL: Crossway Books, 2011), 241-242.
6. Matthew 28:18-20 cf. Mark 16:14-20, Luke 24:44-49, John 20:21-23, Acts 1:4-8
7. Bill Clem, *Disciple: Getting Your Identity from Jesus* (Wheaton, IL: Crossway Books, 2011), 155.
8. John 3:16-18, Romans 5:6-11, Ephesians 1:7, Philippians 2:6-8, Colossians 1:13-23
9. Bruce B. Barton, Dave Veerman, and Linda K. Taylor, *Life Application Bible Commentary: Luke* (Wheaton, IL: Tyndale House Publishers, Inc., 1997), 94-95. R.C. Sproul (ed.), *The Reformation Study Bible* (Sanford, FL: Reformation Trust Publishing, 2015), 1791.
10. In the Greek it's κρυπτῷ (*kryptō*, an adjective). Grammatical context can be found here: BibleHub, https://biblehub.com/interlinear/john/18-20.htm, (retrieved in 2020).
11. Harold Willmington, "Old Testament Passages Quoted by Jesus Christ" (2017). *The Second Person File*. 71. Retrieved April 4, 2021, https://digitalcommons.liberty.edu/second_person/71.
12. Michael J. Wilkins, *Following the Master* (Grand Rapids, MI: Zondervan Publishing House, 1992), 75-121.
13. Ben Connelly, *A Pastor's Guide to Everyday Mission* (Austin, TX: GCD Books, 2016), 14.
14. 1Corinthians 9:19-23, ESV

15. In the Greek it's πορευθέντες (*poreuthentes*, a verb). Grammatical context can be found here: BibleHub, https://biblehub.com/interlinear/matthew/28-19.htm, (retrieved in 2020).
16. Connelly, *A Pastor's Guide to Everyday Mission*, 60. Emphasis added.
17. Credited to Pastor Josh Reeves. Retrieved in 2020 from unknown source.
18. In the Greek it's μαθητεύσατε (*mathēteusate*, a verb). Grammatical context can be found here: BibleHub, https://biblehub.com/interlinear/matthew/28-19.htm, (retrieved in 2020).
19. Quote taken from Alvin L. Reid's, *Sharing Jesus Without Freaking Out* (Nashville, TN: B&H Academic, 2017), 16.
20. Christopher Davis, *Discipleship State of Mind Workbook* (Relevant Books, 2018), 116.
21. CRU, "Relational Evangelism," *CRU Press* (2010), crupress.com. Emphasis added.
22. Reid, *Sharing Jesus Without Freaking Out*, 10
23. Reid, *Sharing Jesus Without Freaking Out*, 84. Brackets added.
24. Reid, *Sharing Jesus Without Freaking Out*, 17. Emphasis added.
25. In the Greek it's ἔθνη (*ethnē*, a noun). Grammatical context can be found here: BibleHub, https://biblehub.com/interlinear/matthew/28-19.htm, (retrieved in 2020).
26. BibleHub, retrieved in 2020, https://biblehub.com/greek/ethne__1484.htm and https://biblehub.com/greek/strongs_1484.htm.
27. Jared C. Wilson, *Unparalleled* (Grand Rapids, MI: Baker Books, 2016), 197.
28. Vince L. Bantu, *A Multitude of All Peoples: Engaging Ancient Christianity's Global Identity* (Downers Grove, Illinois: InterVarsity Press, 2020), 1. Emphasis from the author.
29. Wilson, *Unparalleled*, 206.
30. I wrote a blog-article addressing this topic, "Salvation: Does Baptism Save?" You can find that here: https://www.biblicallyshaped.com/blogs/2011/1/salvation-does-baptism-save.
31. In the Greek it's διδάσκοντες (*didaskontes*, a verb). Grammatical context can be found here: BibleHub, https://biblehub.com/interlinear/matthew/28-20.htm, (retrieved in 2020).
32. In the Greek it's ἐνετειλάμην (*eneteilamēn*, a verb). Grammatical context can be found here: BibleHub, https://biblehub.com/interlinear/matthew/28-20.htm, (retrieved in 2020).

Conclusion

1. A.W. Tozer, *The Root of the Righteous* (Chicago, IL: Moody Publishers, 2015), 71-72. Emphasis added.

Other Works

Discipleship State of Mind Workbook:
A Handbook for Developing Biblical Disciples (2018)

The *"Discipleship State of Mind Workbook"* is the perfect companion for discipleship development. It is truly a one-of-a-kind discipleship workbook. It covers *our Basis (the Bible), our Purpose, our Motive, our Witness, our Lifestyle, our Foundation, Foundational Principles, and Spiritual Disciplines*. You will not find this collection of content in any other workbook!

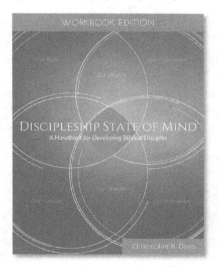

Find it here: www.biblicallyshaped.com/relevantbooks

CPSIA information can be obtained
at www.ICGtesting.com
Printed in the USA
BVHW091212021121
620551BV00001B/186